DEBATING
for GOD

DEBATING for GOD

ALEXANDER CAMPBELL'S CHALLENGE TO SKEPTICISM IN ANTEBELLUM AMERICA

RICHARD J. CHEROK

Abilene Christian University Press

Abilene, Texas

DEBATING FOR GOD
Alexander Campbell's Challenge to Skepticism in Antebellum America

Copyright 2008 by Richard J. Cherok

ISBN 978-0-89112-530-3 cloth
ISBN 978-0-89112-531-0 paperback

Library of Congress Control Number: 2007942402

Printed in the United States of America

Cover design by Rick Gibson
Interior text design by Sandy Armstrong

For information contact:
Abilene Christian University Press
1648 Campus Court
Abilene, Texas 79601

1-877-816-4455 toll free
www.abilenechristianuniversitypress.com

DEDICATION

With grateful appreciation for their love and encouragement,
both in this project and in every other aspect of life,
I dedicate this book to my parents, John and Mary Cherok.

CONTENTS

ILLUSTRATIONS

PREFACE

As an undergraduate student in a survey course on the history of the Stone-Campbell Movement, I first heard the fascinating story of Alexander Campbell's debate with Robert Owen on the evidences of Christianity. This incredible event, I thought to myself, must be the topic of numerous books and journal essays. So, with a desire to learn more about this encounter, I began to search for all the available information I could find on the topic. Much to my dismay, there simply was not much information to be found. How, I wondered, could this spectacular encounter between two incredible men of America's antebellum era be overlooked?

My interest in the Campbell-Owen debate grew steadily stronger as I continued my education at the graduate level. In fact, I wrote a few research papers and at least one seminar paper exploring the debate and the activities that prompted it. Through my research, I soon realized that Alexander Campbell's defense of the Christian religion went well beyond this singular meeting with Owen. The *Millennial Harbinger*, I discovered, contained numerous accounts of debates and challenges to investigate the veracity of the Christian faith. Furthermore, it appeared as though Campbell was always ready to contend for the faith and to provide an answer to those who questioned the reliability of the gospel message. As a result of his enthusiasm for championing the cause of Christ, Campbell contended with some of the most notable skeptics of his era. His persistent encounters with the proponents of unbelief and the apparent success he enjoyed in these efforts to sustain the reasonableness of Christianity and revelation, identify Campbell as the most significant Christian apologist of America's antebellum period.

In this investigation of Campbell's apologetic endeavors, my intent is to recover a part of the Campbell lore that has been sadly neglected and overlooked. Many historians have recognized Campbell as an advocate of

Christian unity, a Christian reformer, a preacher, the leading figure in an important American religious movement, a debater, and an educator, and he certainly left his mark on antebellum Christianity in each of these areas. The significance of his role as an apologist, however, has been forgotten. After all, it was in the role of apologist, in his debate with Robert Owen, that Campbell was first catapulted into a position of national and international notoriety. Throughout the remainder of his life, in his many travels and speaking engagements, Campbell was repeatedly recognized as the defender of the faith. Even in death, the monument erected over Campbell's grave would identify him as the "Defender of the faith once delivered to the saints." So, it is with this volume that I hope Campbell's reputation as the greatest apologist of his era will to some degree be restored.

Because the production of a volume such as this is never the task of only one person, I would like to express my gratitude to a few of the many who assisted me with this project. First, I want to thank Dr. Robert P. Swierenga, my Ph.D. advisor, who directed me through my dissertation and the completion of my degree. Dr. Swierenga is truly a scholar and a gentleman. I'm also thankful that Dr. C. Leonard Allen, the editor and director of ACU Press, has deemed this study worthy of broader readership and agreed to take it on as a publication project. Dr. Allen's editorial suggestions have been most helpful and his assistance is greatly appreciated. Additionally, I want to thank Robyn Smith, Robert Brown, and Steven Reeves, three of my graduate assistants who were exceptionally helpful in the completion of this project.

An additional note of appreciation must be extended to the numerous libraries, and the staffs of these libraries, at which I have studied in preparation of this volume. Among them are the Disciples of Christ Historical Society, Historic Bethany and the Bethany College Archives, the Western Reserve Historical Society, the Massillon Public Library, the Stark County Historical Society, the Tennessee Historical Society, the Filson Club, the Cincinnati Historical Society Library, and the library of the Kent State University. A special word of appreciation must also be extended to the staff of the George Mark Elliot Library on the campus of Cincinnati Christian University. James Lloyd, the director of the George Mark Elliot Library, and Scott Lloyd, the library's Information Services Specialist, went above and beyond the call of duty in their efforts to acquire the materials I needed to complete this research.

Space requirements limit me from adding many additional pages of recognition for each and every contributor to this work, so I hope a closing note of appreciation to all who have added to the work in any way will be sufficient. So I say, "Thank You," to each person who has encouraged, assisted, or added to this study. I owe a great deal to a great many people.

In reading this book, I hope that some might be inspired to rise up, as Campbell did, and "contend earnestly for the faith which was once for all delivered to the saints" (Jude 3).

1

INTRODUCTION: ALEXANDER CAMPBELL AND THE MASS RELIGIOUS CULTURE OF ANTEBELLUM AMERICA

The development of the European Enlightenment in the mid-seventeenth century carried with it a shift in the paradigm of how Europeans, and later Americans, viewed their universe, themselves, and the relationship between the two. In the medieval era, prior to the Enlightenment, mysticism and superstition were invoked as a means for explaining the phenomena of the surrounding universe. With the advent of the Enlightenment, however, reason and science became the standards by which universal truths were ascertained and understood.

To many Christians, most notably the Protestants of Northern Europe, enlightened rationalism was acknowledged as a tool by which the myths and traditions that had been hoisted upon Christianity in an earlier era could be further peeled away. "Just as the Lutheran Reformation had purged the Medieval church of its corruptions, so, they argued, the age of reason would complete the process." By thus paring Christianity down to its most basic beliefs and practices, the rational Christians believed they could offer a purified religion that was commensurate with both science and reason.[1]

On another level, however, the age of reason was a substantial intellectual threat to Christianity. Rather than accept the traditional Christian views of revelation, miracles, and the fallen state of humanity, some philosophers of the Enlightenment emphasized universal natural laws to explain the world's operations and environmentalism to account for individual makeup.[2] As a substitute for traditional Christianity, these advocates of rationalism embraced deism, which recognized God as the first mover and creator of natural law.

In Great Britain's early-eighteenth century, John Toland (1670-1722), Anthony Collins (1676-1729), and Matthew Tindal (1656-1733), among others, created a rising tide in the deist population through their books, pamphlets, and public lectures in support of the "religion of nature." By the 1740s, however, the deist movement began to subside in England as the spiritual awakening spearheaded by John Wesley (1703-1791) and George Whitefield (1714-1770) advanced. At the time of its demise in England, deism began a migration to France where Voltaire (1694-1778), Montesquieu (1690-1755), and Jean-Jacques Rousseau (1712-1778) became its leading spokesmen. The writings of these and other French deists, along with those of their British counterparts, eventually made their way across the Atlantic Ocean and prompted the further growth of deism in the English colonies of North America.

By the latter half of the eighteenth century, deism had gained a wide hearing in America and made considerable inroads into the nation's religious landscape. Among the more notable American deists were Benjamin Franklin (1706-1790), Thomas Jefferson (1743-1826), Ethan Allen (1728-1789), and Elihu Palmer (1764-1806). Thomas Paine (1737-1809), though British rather than American, also influenced American deism with his publication of *The Age of Reason* in 1794. The popularity of Paine's book, which went through seventeen American editions and sold tens of thousands of copies in the mid-1790s, made it the "Bible" of American deism and anointed its author the patron saint of American skepticism.[3]

The beginning of the nineteenth century, however, brought a dramatic reversal for evangelical Christianity.[4] Deism lost much of its appeal when the Second Great Awakening, which began around 1800, led to a spectacular period of Christian revival. A renewed Protestant fervor spread across the young country like a fire through dry kindling and made an impact upon every aspect of society. Antebellum America was truly an evangelical nation, explains Mark Noll, "not only because every feature of life in every region of the United States was thoroughly dominated by evangelical Protestants, but because so many dynamic organizations were products of evangelical conviction."[5] As the impact of deism upon the American religious mind dissipated through the early years of the nineteenth century, the effects of traditional Christianity became more readily observed.

Amid the revitalization and expansion of American Christianity during the Second Great Awakening, the objections to religion continued to resound from the mouths and pens of unbelieving rationalists. Though severely weakened by the revivals, enlightened skeptics continued their attack against the claims of revealed religion. By the mid 1820s, Albert Post argues, a resurgence of freethought developed as a "reaction against excessive evangelical emotionalism."[6] Through publications, lectures, and "rational education," American unbelievers, whether skeptics, infidels, atheists, materialists, deists, freethinkers,[7] Unitarians, or Universalists,[8] attempted to thwart the efforts of evangelical Christianity.

This study explores one aspect of the interaction between evangelical Christianity and skepticism by examining Alexander Campbell's confrontations with some of his era's leading spokesmen for rationalistic unbelief. As a prominent evangelical and the principal leader of the emerging Restoration Movement,[9] Campbell differed from many of his contemporaries in his decision to confront the claims of skepticism. With a determination to eradicate unbelief from the American intellectual landscape, Campbell boldly challenged its adherents to discuss the issues of revealed religion, the truths of the Bible, the nature of humanity, and the claims of Christianity. In Campbell's mind, skepticism was untenable as a belief system. "I have never read, nor heard a philosophic, rational, logical argument against Christianity," Campbell wrote, "nor have I ever seen or heard a rational, philosophic, or logical argument in favor of any form of skepticism or infidelity."[10] Guided by such absolute convictions, Campbell addressed the problems he found in skepticism through public discourses, debates with the opponents of Christianity, and numerous published objections to the claims of "unbelievers."

CAMPBELL AS AN ORATOR

As an orator, Campbell was highly acclaimed by his contemporaries. His initial experience with public speaking came in 1810 when his father urged him to address a small crowd that had gathered at the home of a family acquaintance. According to Robert Richardson, Campbell's long-time associate, "this was really Alexander's first attempt at [public] speaking." The positive response to Campbell's lecture encouraged him to prepare and deliver his first sermon on July 15, 1810, before his father's

Brush Run Church in Washington County, Pennsylvania. Inspired by the congregation's unanimous approval of his message and speaking abilities, the twenty-two-year-old Campbell sought additional preaching opportunities. Before the close of 1810, he preached 106 sermons.[11] Throughout the remainder of his life, Campbell's reputation as a preacher grew and his services were constantly in demand.[12]

Though most eminently known for his expositions of Scripture, Campbell did not confine his oratorical skills to sermons. As a popular speaker on numerous subjects, Campbell traveled the country speaking at lyceums, courthouses, churches, and any other location where he could gain a hearing. The lecture circuit, as a tool for social education and the propagation of ideas, "became one of the most socially acceptable forms of recreation" during this period.[13] "The organization, length, and style of the lyceum lecture closely resembled that of the religious homily," Carl Bode explains, making it a medium of communication to which most Americans were already accustomed.[14] Because the lyceum discourse resembled the sermon, Campbell had no difficulty making the transition from preacher to public speaker.

The substance of Campbell's addresses covered a broad spectrum of topics. He often spoke on religious themes, but also considered non-religious issues that provided his audiences with scholarly insight into various subjects.[15] Among Campbell's favorite topics was his plea for the "reformation" of Christianity by making a return to the principles of the New Testament. The theme of Christian primitivism resounded in Campbell's many speaking tours in America and abroad. A second priority to Campbell was challenging the claims of skepticism. Campbell's frequent travels into areas where freethinkers had developed a following gave him many opportunities to refute the claims of skepticism while defending the assertions of Christianity.

CAMPBELL AS DEBATER

In addition to his addresses against "unbelief," Campbell engaged those who were skeptical of Christianity in written and oral debates. To nineteenth-century Americans, debate was a prevalent method for investigating and communicating issues of political, social, and religious disagreement. During America's antebellum period, debating societies developed rapidly throughout the nation.[16] Functioning as institutions of education, entertainment, and mass communication, these societies gained a wide popularity. Alexis de Tocqueville reported that Americans were so attracted to these "clubs" that they often "take the place of theaters." Furthermore, Tocqueville said that Americans were not only observers of debate but practitioners. "An American does not know how to converse," he wrote, "but he argues."[17]

The extent of debate's appeal can be seen not only in the plentitude of antebellum debates, but also in the vast spectator turnout for these events. By presenting opposing arguments on an issue for the acceptance or rejection of the populace, debate had an egalitarian attractiveness that captivated the attention of Americans. The Lincoln-Douglas debates of 1858 illustrate the immense popularity of public debate in pre-Civil War America. As Abraham Lincoln and Stephen A. Douglas campaigned for an Illinois seat in the United States Senate, they participated in a series of seven debates within the state. Crowd estimates for these debates range from 1,200 in Jonesboro to 20,000 in Galesburg.[18] The political significance of the campaign enlarged these attendance figures, but these forums illustrate the interest that public dispute could generate in nineteenth-century America. Religious debates frequently attracted audiences in excess of one thousand people, and the published transcripts of these contests reached additional thousands.[19]

Though an opponent of public debate as a young man, Campbell eventually became an accomplished disputant.[20] His initial aversion to debate originated in his father's dislike for controversy. "We ... humbly advise our friends ... to avoid this evil practice," Thomas Campbell wrote in 1809. "We shall thankfully receive, and seriously consider" any written objections to our views, he went on to explain, but "verbal controversy we absolutely refuse."[21] In Thomas' thought, public debate hindered the promotion of Christian union and inspired contestants to pursue victory as opposed to truth. Thus when John Walker, a Presbyterian minister from Mt. Pleasant, Ohio, challenged Alexander to a debate on the subject of baptism in the spring of 1820, he resolutely declined. "Public debates," he said, are not "the proper method of proceeding in contending for the faith once delivered to the saints." This opinion, Campbell's biographer noted, was adopted "more from deference to his father's feelings on the subject, than from his own matured convictions of expediency or from his natural temperament."[22]

In the months following Campbell's rejection of a proposed debate with Walker, a number of his colleagues urged him to reconsider his decision. Though he needed little encouragement to animate his desire to enter the fray with Walker, Campbell had to secure his father's approval before he would proceed. Following a consultation with his father about the value of publicly defending the gospel, the elder Campbell granted his blessings and Alexander agreed to a June 19-20, 1820, debate in Mt. Pleasant, Ohio. Campbell's overwhelming success in this contest significantly altered his opinion of the merit of public discussion. Though he entered this debate reluctantly, Campbell concluded it with an invitation for "any Pedo-baptist minister [i.e., minister who practices infant baptism] of any denomination" to engage him in a future debate on the topic of baptism.[23]

For nearly three years Campbell's challenge went unanswered. In May of 1823, however, William L. Maccalla, a Presbyterian minister from Augusta, Kentucky, accepted Campbell's solicitation. The Campbell-Maccalla debate convened in Washington, Kentucky, on October 15-22, 1823. As in the contest with Walker, Campbell proved himself too formidable an opponent for Maccalla. Decisive victories in his initial forays completely changed Campbell's evaluation of public discussion. Following the Maccalla debate, Campbell stated that he was "convinced" that public debate "is ... one of the best means of propagating the truth and of exposing error in doctrine or practice." Moreover, he explained, "we are fully persuaded that a week's debating is worth a year's preaching ... for the purpose of disseminating truth and putting error out of countenance."[24]

THE VALUE OF RELIGIOUS CONTROVERSY

Campbell's reputation as a debater was well known after his 1829 debate with Robert Owen. Though he defended Christianity against Owen's objections to revealed religion, Campbell received criticism from some who considered religious dispute of any kind to be "a great and manifold evil to the combatants and to society." To these people Campbell felt it necessary to compose a defense of religious debates in 1830. "Whenever society, religious or political, falls into error," Campbell informed his readers, " ... it is the duty of all who have any talent or ability to oppose error, ... to lift up a standard against it, and to panoply themselves for combat." After all, he continued, "controversy ... is only another name for opposition to error," and "there can be no improvement without controversy."[25]

Furthermore, Campbell claimed that religious controversy cultivated the ground from which democracy and scientific enlightenment grew. "It was the tongue and pen of controversy," Campbell suggested, "which developed the true solar system—laid the foundation for the American Revolution—abolished the slave trade—and which has so far disenthralled the human mind from the shackles of superstition." "Truth and liberty, both religious and political, are the first fruits of well directed controversy," he wrote, but "peace and eternal bliss will be the 'harvest home.'"[26]

Campbell was well aware that controversy played an integral part in the history of Christian apologetics. During the developing years of the Christian religion, the New Testament authors and early Christians argued for the validity of Jesus' claims to be the Messiah described in the Jewish Scriptures. Early Christian apologists such as Irenaeus and Augustine contended with paganism and sought to explain God's workings within human affairs. Anselm, Aquinas, and the scholastic theologians of the later Middle Ages debated the relationship between faith and philosophic reasoning. And, in the period from the Protestant Reformation to the end of the Enlightenment, the growth of modern thought, with its emphasis on scientific observation and natural law, brought contentions about the relationship between science and Christianity.[27] Reflecting this tradition of Christian apologetics, Campbell maintained his belief in the necessity of religious controversy. In 1857 he professed that "the true church is a church militant." "Every useful citizen in Christ's kingdom is a citizen soldier," he surmised, because "there can be no real and enduring termination of controversy so long as there are two rival kingdoms on this earth."[28]

CAMPBELL AS EDITOR

In addition to his oral forays, Campbell successfully used the printing press as a tool for confronting the claims of his adversaries and communicating his ideas to the general public. His first encounter with journalism came in 1810 when William Sample, the editor of the *Washington Reporter*, a weekly newspaper in Washington, Pennsylvania, asked Campbell to write a series of essays for the paper. Under the pseudonym "Clarinda," Campbell submitted ten essays that addressed the moral lapses of his community. He went on to anonymously publish additional essays and poems that received a wide readership in the *Reporter*.[29]

Not until 1823, however, after the successful distribution of both a first and second printing of his debate with John Walker, did Campbell recognize the press as a valuable tool for the mass communication of his ideas. Armed with this new-found realization, Campbell purchased a printing press and began publishing a monthly periodical that he called the *Christian Baptist*. Campbell's *Christian Baptist* reached only a small audience at its inception in 1823, but by the time of the magazine's conclusion in 1830 the Campbell press had issued no less than forty-six thousand volumes of his writings.[30] In 1830, Campbell replaced the *Christian Baptist* with the *Millennial Harbinger*, a periodical that he published until his death in 1866 (though he surrendered his position as editor after the final edition of 1864). Campbell's magazines, along with a number of books that he authored, did more than any of his other ventures to place his ideas squarely in the public eye.

In the pages of both the *Christian Baptist* and the *Millennial Harbinger*, Campbell confronted the challenges of those who scorned the Christian religion. Desiring that his magazines might be viewed as a level ground upon which a war of opposing ideologies might be waged, Campbell freely opened the pages of his periodicals to the writings of his skeptical adversaries. "We have uniformly and without a single exception," he wrote, "given to our readers both sides of every question upon religion, morality or expediency, that has appeared upon our pages."[31] In so doing, Campbell explained, his purpose has always been to "hear both sides, and then judge."[32] He was convinced that the democratic, open exchange of ideas, even amid the editorial duties of his periodicals, would ultimately bring truth to the forefront.

Along with the essays of his opponents, Campbell invariably published his personal reactions to their claims. As his adversaries composed additional articles in reply to his remarks, Campbell included further editorial comments about the newly received pieces. These exchanges, which often occurred over a lengthy period of time, resulted in written debates between Campbell and his competitors. Through the medium of written debate Campbell was convinced that the truths he perceived in Christianity could never be subdued by the challenges of its foes. Nevertheless, as Robert Frederick West asserts, Campbell's determination to note his opponent's views as well as his own resulted in the publication of "many of the most effective criticisms of Alexander Campbell's ideas . . . in his own magazines."[33]

CAMPBELL'S PUBLIC LIFE

Campbell's mastery of the communication mediums of his day made him one of the most widely recognized religious leaders of the nineteenth century. "No man of the present age," an unidentified editor wrote in the introduction to Campbell's *Popular Lectures and Addresses*, "has been more frequently before the public, both in his addresses, debates, and writings, than Alexander Campbell." Furthermore, this editor opined, "the impress of his mind he has left on the age, and will leave to future generations."[34] Through his travels, lectures, disputations, and publications, Campbell placed himself, his ideas, and his beliefs before both a national and an international audience.

The coupling of Campbell's emerging reputation as a Christian scholar with his eagerness to discuss controversial issues brought him face-to-face with the advocates of America's resurgent skeptical movement of the mid-1820s. What began as a series of essays in response to a letter from an unknown deist identified only as "D.," led to a series of conflicts with some of Antebellum America's most distinguished critics of Christianity. Campbell made it his lifelong duty to both respond to the anti-Christian rhetoric of Antebellum America's unbelievers and to sustain the assertions of Christianity and the Bible. Through his debates, writings, and lectures, Campbell seldom missed an opportunity to challenge the beliefs of skepticism and contend for the veracity of his Christian faith.

Campbell's confrontations with the proponents of unbelief, beginning with the readers of the *New Harmony Gazette* and continuing with such notable skeptics as Robert Owen, Humphrey Marshall, Dr. Samuel Underhill, Charles Cassedy, Jonathan Kidwell, Dolphus Skinner, and Jesse B. Ferguson, furnish a glimpse into the struggles between the proponents of natural religion and revealed religion. By examining Campbell's antagonists and their claims, one can observe the roots of a far more secular society that developed in the latter-nineteenth and twentieth centuries. Furthermore, Campbell's frequent encounters with freethinkers and his cogent arguments to sustain Christianity demonstrate that he was the most significant Christian apologist of America's antebellum period.

2

ALEXANDER CAMPBELL AND NINETEEN-CENTURY CHRISTIAN RATIONALISM

At the youthful age of twenty-one, Alexander Campbell arranged for his mother and siblings to join him on an ocean voyage that would carry them from Londonderry, Ireland, to Philadelphia in the United States. The goal of the Campbell family's journey was a reunion with the patriarch of their family, Thomas, who had embarked upon a trans-Atlantic voyage nearly one-and-one-half years earlier. Prompted by his physician's orders as therapy for his failing health, Thomas set sail for the shores of North America. Finding the United States much to his liking, Thomas soon invited his family to join him in this new land and set about procuring lodging for his family's eventual arrival. Though Alexander expected nothing beyond a safe voyage and a secure landing in the New World, the events that transpired as a result of his short-lived expedition made a far-reaching impact upon the course of his life.

On the autumn evening of October 7, 1808, just one week into their voyage, their ship, the *Hibernia*, was swept into some rocks along the coast of Scotland by a fierce and sudden gale. The anguish of this ordeal induced Alexander to offer his life in service to God in exchange for God's protection in the immediate situation. When he and his family were safely removed from the wreckage, Campbell resolved to uphold his end of the deal by spending his life as a minister of the Christian gospel.[1] Little did he know his pact with God would lead him to become a prominent American religious leader, a reformer of Christianity, and an able defender of a rational Christian faith and its biblical moorings.

GLASGOW UNIVERSITY

Impressed upon Alexander Campbell's mind from his earliest years were the ideas of the Enlightenment and a rational Christian faith. His father, Thomas Campbell (1763-1854), studied at the University of Glasgow and was profoundly influenced by the Enlightenment philosophies of Francis Bacon (1561-1626), Isaac Newton (1642-1727), and John Locke (1632-1704). Unlike in England and the European continent, however, the adoption of the "scientific method" at Glasgow did not stimulate the development of natural theology and a deistic worldview. Rather, the Glasgow faculty insisted that science was the tool for understanding nature, while revelation was the method for correctly perceiving religion.[2] This Glasgow interpretation of science that so dramatically shaped Thomas' thought would later be passed on to Alexander, who spent much of his early life under the tutelage of his father.

The shipwreck that prompted Alexander's decision to embark upon a ministerial career also afforded him the opportunity to add to the education he had gleaned from his father's instruction. Due to the lateness of the season, the Campbell family was forced to spend the winter of 1808-1809 in Scotland before completing their voyage to the United States. Taking up residency in the city of Glasgow, Alexander enrolled for classes at the University of Glasgow in December, 1808, and concluded his studies with the end of the academic year in June, 1809. Alexander's experiences at the University of Glasgow not only augmented his earlier instruction in Enlightenment ideology, but they firmly entrenched these ideas within his mind and thereby made a significant impact upon the development of his philosophical thought and makeup.

From both his father's instruction and from the University of Glasgow's classrooms, Alexander learned to rely upon the Enlightenment principles of Baconian reasoning as filtered through the lens of Scottish Common Sense Realism.[3] Like Francis Bacon, he was convinced that inductive inquiry was the only reliable source for acquiring knowledge and understanding. "The principles of investigation on which the inductive philosophy of Lord Bacon are founded, and those adopted by the christian philosopher, Sir Isaac Newton," he stated in his debate with Robert Owen, "are those which should govern us on this occasion."[4] To further clarify his position to Owen, Alexander borrowed a quote from Newton (who he referred to as the "great teacher"): "Everything is to be submitted to the most minute observation. No conclusions are to be drawn from guesses or conjectures. We are to keep within the certain limits of experimental truth. We first ascertain the facts, then group them together, and after the classification and comparison of them, draw the conclusions. There are generic heads or chapters in every department of physical or moral science. We are never to shrink from the test of those principles."[5]

Campbell's insistence that he and his opponents rely on the Baconian "principles of investigation" was the typical approach by which an early-nineteenth-century scholar would probe for truth. "Baconianism,"

(Courtesy of Disciples of Christ Historical Society, Nashville, Tennessee)

Figure 1 – Thomas Campbell (c.1834)

As Alexander Campbell's father and adolescent instructor, Thomas Campbell (1763-1854) equipped his son with a thorough knowledge of both the Bible and the principles of Enlightenment rationalism. Throughout the remainder of his life, Alexander would rely on the knowledge he gained from his father to contend with the advocates of skepticism.

according to Theodore Dwight Bozeman, "became a conspicuous and generally lauded factor in American (and British) intellectual life in the antebellum period," and remained the "single most powerful current in general intellectual and academic circles until after the Civil War."[6] Where Campbell was unique, however, was in his application of Bacon's "inductive (or scientific) approach" to the study of Scripture. Campbell's use of Baconian principles in his biblical research, Leroy Garrett contends, was "something as new in his day in regard to Scripture as it was in Bacon's time in reference to general knowledge." "Bacon thus helped Campbell to develop an inductive approach to the Bible," according to Garrett, "in which one draws conclusions only in terms of what is observably evident, rather than the traditional deductive approach of having one's conclusions already in hand and using the Bible to support them."[7]

Even more significant to Campbell's development was the philosophical influence of John Locke. Inspired by Locke's reverence for the Bible, Campbell developed a deep admiration for both the man and his philosophy. Locke "spent the last fourteen or fifteen years of his great and useful life," Campbell wrote, "in reading scarcely any other book except the sacred Scriptures." Moreover, when asked about "the shortest and surest way for a young gentleman to attain the true knowledge of the Christian religion," Locke responded, "Let him study the Holy Scriptures, especially the New Testament." So venerated was Locke in the eyes of Campbell that he continually referred to Locke as the "Christian philosopher" and described him as "the ornament of his country and of humanity itself."[8] In his abundant praise and frequent quotation of Locke, as well as his rigid adherence to the principles of Lockean empiricism, Campbell viewed himself as a descendant of the Christian rationalism that Locke advocated.

Under his father's tutorship, Campbell "learned greatly to admire the character and the works of Locke, whose *Letters on Toleration* seem to have made a lasting impression upon him, and to have fixed his ideas of religious and of civil liberty." Furthermore, Richardson wrote, "he appears to have thoroughly studied" Locke's *Essay Concerning Human Understanding* previous to his entry into the University of Glasgow.[9] Nevertheless, Campbell's continued exposure to Locke while a student at Glasgow undoubtedly shaped the development of his thought and theology.

Campbell's epistemological views came directly from Locke's ideas as expressed in his *Essay Concerning Human Understanding*. Just as Locke claimed that a child's mind at birth is a "white paper ... without any ideas," and that the origin of human knowledge is the perception of "external, sensible objects" and "the internal operation of our minds" upon these objects,[10] so Campbell told the readers of his *Christian Baptist* that "all our simple ideas" are "the result of sensation and reflection!"[11] "Locke, Hume, and all the mental philosophers," he stated in his debate with Robert Owen, "agree that all our original ideas are the result of sensation and reflection; that is, that the five senses inform us of the properties of bodies, that our five senses are the only avenues through which ideas of material objects can be derived to us; that we have an intellectual power of comparing these impressions thus derived to us through the media of senses: and this they call reflection."[12]

Campbell's rejection of innate ideas was also the rejection of an inborn or "natural" knowledge of God. By thus dismissing "natural religion," Campbell affirmed that the only valid source of religious knowledge is what God has revealed about himself in the Bible. "I contend that no man, by all the senses, and powers of reason which he possesses, with all the data before him which the material universe affords," he explained, "can originate or beget in his own mind the idea of a God, in the true sense of that word." Nature, he believed, may confirm what God has revealed about himself, but it is not in itself a means of knowing God. Thus, "so soon as the idea of Deity is suggested to the mind," he continued, "every thing within us and without us, attests, bears testimony to, and demonstrates the existence and attributes of such a being."[13] This, Garrett contends, was a "revolutionary point of view" that reflected the new thinking of the Enlightenment. "Theologians and philosophers from Anselm to Thomas Aquinas to Descartes had contended that God could be known through reason and that his existence could be proved by logic, which was the essence of 'natural religion,' summarily rejected by both Locke and Campbell."[14]

Campbell also embraced Lockean definitions of the words "revelation," "faith," and "reason." To both Locke and Campbell, "the term revelation ... means nothing more or less than a Divine communication concerning spiritual and eternal things."[15] "To constitute a divine revelation," Campbell wrote, ". . . it is not only necessary that God be the author of it, but that the things exhibited be supernatural, and beyond the reach of our five senses."[16] Faith, on the other hand, "is the simple belief of testimony, or of the truth, and never can be more nor less than that."[17] "The value of faith," Campbell explained, "is the importance of the facts which the testimony presents, and the assurance afforded that

the testimony is true."[18] Campbell further described faith as "the enno-
bling faculty of man" because it "encompasses the area of universal experience, and appropriates to its possession the acquisitions of all men in all
ages of time."[19] Lastly, Campbell understood reason to refer to human
intellect or the faculty by which a person acts and reflects upon the knowledge attained through revelation, tradition, and the senses.

Rebuking the "speculative" philosophers who exalt reason above revelation and contend "that man is more liable to be deceived by *faith*
than *reason*," Campbell recognized that humankind "is by an insuper-
able necessity compelled to make the first step in physical, intellectual and
moral life by faith in tradition." An infant, he asserted, does not "experiment with the asp, the adder, the basilisk, the fire, the flood, [or] the
innumerable dangers around it." Rather, it learns to walk by faith in the
traditions of its nurse.[20] Furthermore, he stated,

> some philosophers have almost deified reason, and given to it
> a creative and originating power. They have so eulogized the
> light of reason and the light of nature, that one would imagine
> reason to be a *sun*, rather than an eye; a revelation, rather than
> the power of apprehending and enjoying it. But when accu-
> rately defined, it is only a power bestowed on man, of compar-
> ing things, and propositions concerning things, and of deducing
> propositions for them. . . . It is not, then, a creative power. It
> cannot make something out of nothing. It is to the soul what
> the eye is to the body. It is not light, but the power of perceiv-
> ing and using it. And as the eye without light, so reason without
> tradition or revelation would be useless to man.[21]

Campbell's intention was not to dismiss the value of reason, but to put it
in proper perspective. "Intellect and reason," in his estimation, "are . . . as
necessary to faith as they are to moral excellence; for a creature destitute
of reason is alike incapable of faith, morality and religion." "Reason" he
continued, ". . . examines the tradition and the testimony, whether it be
that of our five senses, our memory, our consciousness, or that of other
persons; faith receives that testimony, and common sense walks by it."[22]

SCOTTISH COMMON SENSE REALISM

Another important influence that shaped the thought of Campbell
during his brief stay in Glasgow was his reliance upon Common Sense

Realism as a tool for understanding both Scripture and the world in which he lived. Common Sense Realism developed as a reaction against the excesses of Scottish philosopher David Hume's (1711-1776) radical empiricism. Like Campbell, Hume had developed his assumptions upon the philosophical ideas of John Locke. Unlike Campbell, however, Hume had used Locke's ideas to question the existence of matter as anything beyond sensory impressions. Even an individual's very existence, he suggested, is nothing more than a result of sensory impression and can only be recognized as an unverifiable inference. Additionally, Hume argued, the existence of God is beyond the realm of proof or disproof, thus questioning the validity of all human religion. The skepticism evoked by Hume's extreme empiricism gave rise to an opposing school of thought that became known as the Common Sense Philosophy of Scotland or Common Sense Realism.

Scottish Common Sense Philosophy was the creation of Thomas Reid (1710-1796), a minister and professor at Glasgow University. Reid's Common Sense Realism was a balanced view that "rejected metaphysical speculation, as did Locke and Hume, and yet appealed to 'common sense' in interpreting the world, lest doubt lead one to the point of being ridiculous." In his *Inquiry into the Human Mind on the Principles of Common Sense* (1764), Reid attempted "to justify the ordinary man in believing in what his five senses tell him about the world."[23] According to Reid's philosophy, "all knowledge is built upon principles that are self-evident, and every man with common sense is aware of such principles."[24] Among the self-evident principles espoused by the Common Sense philosophers were existence outside of perception, the natural functioning of the universe, and a belief that whatever exists—including this world—must have a cause which produced it (i.e., God).

From the Common Sense philosophers Campbell gleaned a common sense view of Scripture for the ordinary person. Convinced that the Bible "contains a full and perfect revelation of God and his will,"[25] Campbell frequently expressed his dislike for the commentators, teachers, and "sermonizers" who caused confusion among the populace by promoting their doctrinal beliefs rather than a genuine understanding of Scripture.

> If any other book in the English language had as many commentaries written upon it, had as many systems based upon it, or upon particular construction of it; if any other book were exhibited in the same dislocated and distracted light, had as many

debates about its meaning, and as many different senses attributed to its words; if any other book were read as the scriptures
are commonly read, in the same broken, disconnected and care-
less manner; with the same stock of prejudices and preconceived
opinions, there is every reason to believe that it would be as unin-
telligible and as little understood as the bible appears to be.[26]

Though widely misunderstood, Campbell contended, "the Bible was
made to be understood." Furthermore, "it was addressed to all classes
of people," and is not beyond the grasp of any class of society.[27] "To
understand the meaning of what is commanded, promised, taught,
etc.," Campbell wrote, "*the same philological principles, deduced from the
nature of language, or the same laws of interpretation which are applied to
the language of other books, are to be applied to the language of the Bible*"
(Campbell's italics).[28] People would be better off in their effort to understand God's Word, he concluded, if "they acknowledged no other guide,
overseer, or ruler, than plain, honest common sense."[29]

AMERICA AND PRIMITIVISM

With the close of the school year, the Campbells prepared to continue their journey to America. On August 4, 1809, the Campbell family
boarded the *Latonia* for what proved to be a grueling fifty-five-day journey across the Atlantic Ocean. Surviving a severe storm and a leak that
required the passengers to pump water out of the ship's hull each day, the
Latonia finally anchored in New York harbor on September 29, 1809.
The Campbells remained in New York City for a week before under-
taking a 350-mile overland journey to their new home in Washington,
Pennsylvania. Upon learning of his family's arrival, Thomas Campbell
set out to meet them. Some three days from their destination, Thomas
and his family were reunited after a separation of nearly two-and-one-
half years.

The Campbell reunion was a joyous occasion, and for Alexander
and his father a time of unanticipated disclosure. Much to the surprise of
Alexander, Thomas told his family how he had been drummed out of the
Presbyterian Church for taking a more ecumenical approach to his dealings
with Christians outside of the Presbyterian camp. Alexander then revealed
to his father how he too could no longer wear the Presbyterian moniker
because of his conscientious objection to denominational control over

the belief and practices of individual Christians. With an ocean between them and no knowledge about the other's activities, Alexander and his father both came to the conclusion that Christianity must divorce itself of human-developed creeds and the restraints of denominational sectarianism. In so doing, they believed, those who claim allegiance to Christ can then unite around the biblical essentials of the Christian faith (while allowing freedom in the area of non-essentials to the faith), and get about the central task of evangelizing the world with the saving knowledge of Jesus Christ.

In the transitional years that followed Alexander's arrival in America, he grew from being an obscure frontier immigrant owning little more than a small personal library and the essentials for life, into a wealthy entrepreneur and controversial leader of an effort to restore Christianity to its pristine form. He initially worked for his father in America while he continued his study of Scripture and the liberal arts. In the performance of an errand for his father, Alexander met Margaret Brown, the daughter of a wealthy carpenter, in Buffalo, Virginia.[30] Campbell's introduction to Margaret proved fortunate in that he gained both a wife and an estate by marrying her on March 12, 1811. When John Brown, Campbell's father-in-law, learned that his new son-in-law was considering a move that would take his daughter west into Ohio, he kept him in the area by deeding over to Alexander his large two-story home and the extensive land area that surrounded it. This gift made Campbell a wealthy man, though he used these holdings wisely to gain greater wealth through his farming and sheep-herding enterprises.[31]

Less than two months after his marriage, Alexander and his father organized the Brush Run Church as a nondenominational Christian congregation that met in a small wooden structure in southwestern Pennsylvania. With Alexander as their preacher and Thomas as their only elder, the small church of "about thirty regular members"[32] sought to establish "a distinct religious community based solely upon the Bible."[33] The Campbells' insistence on recapturing the primitive practices of the New Testament church and their reliance upon a Baconian approach to biblical interpretation induced the members of the tiny Brush Run congregation to abandon denominational authority and to question the doctrines and practices they had learned from the confessional groups to which they had previously belonged.

Within a few months of the Brush Run Church's inauguration, a controversy developed around the proper form for Christian baptism.

Three members of the church ignited the controversy by requesting that they be re-baptized by immersion. In so doing, these three were rejecting infant sprinkling as an unscriptural mode of baptism. The discussions that ensued about this topic were incapable of convincing the three icono-clasts that the tradition of infant sprinkling could be reconciled with bib-lical baptism. Thomas, therefore, agreed to immerse the three, though he and Alexander had been sprinkled as infants and had never actually wit-nessed an immersion. At this juncture in their lives, the Campbells had little concern about the mode by which baptism should be performed. Of far greater significance to them was that their questions about the mode

(Courtesy of Disciples of Christ Historical Society, Nashville, Tennessee)

Figure 2 – Alexander Campbell (c.1815)

By 1815, Alexander Campbell (1788-1866) had already gained a reputation for his preaching abilities and had published numerous essays in the *Washington Reporter*, a local newspaper. Many of the religious convictions that would later guide his movement and stoke his adamant opposition to skepticism had already been formulated by this time.

of baptism not be permitted to fracture the membership of the fledgling Brush Run congregation.[34]

The question of baptism was again brought to Alexander's attention when his first child, Jane, was born on March 13, 1812. Campbell's original indifference to the subject of baptism turned into an intense study of the topic as he questioned the scriptural authority for baptizing his infant daughter. Convinced that the Bible gave no authority for infant baptism or for the practice of sprinkling, Alexander refused to allow his daughter to be sprinkled as an infant. Furthermore, he and seven others—including his father—elected to be rebaptized by immersed on June 12, 1812.[35]

Campbell's immersion "was not a simple change of views on baptism," but the release of his mind "from all its former moorings." "I was placed on a new eminence," he wrote, "a new peak of the mountain of God, from which the whole landscape of Christianity presented itself to my mind in a new attitude and position." With a newfound approach to biblical interpretation, Campbell began an earnest investigation of the traditions and practices of the church. Having accepted the New Testament as the sole source of authority for the church, Campbell now began to question the meanings of the ideas expressed in the Bible. Did baptism constitute infant sprinkling, as he had always been taught, or adult immersion? "I must know now two things about every thing," he wrote, "its *cause* and its *relations*." As a result, he delved further into the Bible in his quest to understand the original meanings of scriptural teachings and practices rather than the meanings that had been inculcated upon him throughout his early life. "It became my duty," he went on to explain, "to set forth the causes of this change in our position to the professing world, and also to justify them by an appeal to the oracles of God."[36] This pursuit of Christian primitivism, by which Campbell believed the divided ranks of Christendom could be united, became the hallmark of the movement that developed around Campbell's call for a "current reformation" within Christianity. Later proponents of Campbell's views would refer to themselves as the "Restoration Movement" because of the Campbellian insistence on restoring Christianity to its New Testament form.

A NOTED CHRISTIAN LEADER

The Christian rationalism that emerged from Campbell's experiences combined the Enlightenment concepts of Baconian inquiry and Lockean empiricism with the practicality of Scottish Common Sense Philosophy.

Added to this mix were the concepts of American egalitarianism, which gave rise to his advocacy of nondenominational individualism and local church autonomy, and Christian primitivism, which led to his promotion of such early church practices as believer's baptism by immersion and the weekly partaking of the Lord's Supper. Throughout the remainder of his life, Campbell affirmed these standards as he implemented nearly every conceivable method of communication to advance the ideas of his movement throughout the nation and abroad. "We little expected, some thirty years ago," Campbell told the readers of his *Millennial Harbinger* in 1846, that these "principles ... could have been plead with such success, or have taken such deep hold of the consciences and of the hearts of multitudes of all creeds and parties, of all casts and conditions of society." Furthermore, he pointed out, the "characteristic principles" of the "reformation of the 19th century" have been spread to "some parts of Europe, and throughout almost all our American States and Territories."[37] Henry Webb estimates that the American Campbellite following—more commonly known as the Disciples of Christ in its early years—had grown to 350,000 by 1870 (less than sixty years after its beginning). By the turn of the century, Disciple membership stood at 1,120,000. "This impressive increase," Webb contends, "could hardly be matched by any of the religious bodies of the time."[38]

As Campbell's "reformation" gained momentum and his reputation as a debater and Christian leader grew, he was called upon time and again to defend revealed religion from the attacks of unbelieving antagonists. Confident that Christianity could be logically justified, Campbell became the nation's foremost opponent of natural religion and a leading figure in the defense of revealed religion. Although, as Robert Frederick West asserts, Campbell "sympathized with most of the criticism which the natural religionists raised against the established churches and their views of revealed religion,"[39] he refused to berate the undefiled ideals of biblical Christianity or revelation. "Convinced that no Christian ... need be ashamed of his faith and of the reasonableness of his cause in the modern world,"[40] Campbell stood toe to toe with the leading skeptics of his day. Much to their surprise, Campbell relied on the principles of Baconian inquiry and enlightened rationalism—the very tool his unbelieving adversaries employed in their opposition to revealed religion—as his weapons for battle against the enemies of Christianity, the church, and revelation.

3

DRAWING THE BATTLE LINES:
CAMPBELL'S EARLY OPPOSITION TO SKEPTICISM

When Elihu Palmer, the evangelist of American deism, unexpectedly died in 1806, the American freethought movement was left without leadership or direction. Lacking the guidance of Palmer or the impact of the caustic anti-Christian writings of Thomas Paine, skepticism fell into a period of decline between 1806 and 1825. Dying with Palmer was his dream of uniting freethinkers into societies that could more effectively promote the advancement of skeptical unbelief. Though freethought itself did not die, the hope for amalgamation did. Thus, the few lone voices of unbelief in this period were completely overshadowed by the surging expansion of evangelical Christianity during the Second Great Awakening.

The impetus for the revival of the freethought movement came with the 1824 immigration of Benjamin Offen (1772-1848) to America. Offen, a self-educated shoemaker from England, settled in New York where he began a lengthy career as a freethought propagandist. Soon after his arrival in the United States, Offen became one of the moving spirits in the institutionalization of the Thomas Paine Birthday celebration.[1] The first celebration in America was held in January 1825, when some forty followers of natural religion gathered in New York City to commemorate Paine's contributions to American unbelief.[2]

FIRST ENCOUNTER WITH SKEPTICISM

The resurrection of American freethought gained little attention from Campbell until a skeptic with the pen name "D." challenged Campbell to respond to his abandonment of the Christian faith. "Impelled by the death-bed injunctions of a beloved mother, and the necessity I saw for living a religious life," D. wrote, "I seriously determined on leaving my evil habits, while young, and endeavoring to have religion firmly seated in my heart." Nevertheless, he continued, "a coldness and apathy made me insensible to both the threatenings and promises of the gospel." Amid his feelings of indifference, D. stumbled upon a thought that changed his entire view of Christianity and the Bible. "The Deity," he reasoned, would not "have created any being and placed him in such a situation in which it was possible for him to make himself deserving of eternal torment." Because of this notion, he explained, "I was led strongly to doubt the divinity of the bible."[3]

With "further reflections," D. was convinced that the "greatest degree of happiness was the only object of creation," and that "the Almighty would have failed, if, as the scriptures authorize us to believe, a majority of mankind will be forever damned." Moreover, he exclaimed, "I thought the Deity was the first cause of all things, . . . especially for evil, as he possessed a greater power to prevent it than the immediate cause." If it is true that God created evil, he mused, then "he could not punish any of his creatures with eternal misery."[4]

Campbell's reply to D.'s skepticism took the form of six essays that he published in the *Christian Baptist*.[5] In these articles, Campbell addressed two primary issues: the source of D.'s contentions with Scripture, and the problem of explaining God and the existence of evil. The final article contained an overview of the gospel message and an exhortation for D. to embrace the gospel as presented in the Bible.

To Campbell, the source of D.'s arguments against the Bible was itself in opposition to his stated objection to divine revelation. "I cannot see how your difficulties could make you a Deist," Campbell wrote. "Your difficulties never could have existed except for the bible." In his essay to the *Christian Baptist*, D. professed to believe that there is a God, that this God created the world, that humans possess an eternal spirit, that there will be an end to the present world, and that there is a future state of punishment or reward that awaits each individual. Upon what evidence are these beliefs based, Campbell asked?

> Not by the testimony of your five senses—for they give no revelation of this kind; all they can tell you is that all nature concurs in attesting these truths. But, remember well, they do not

originate in your mind these truths. . . . All the ideas you have by the five senses are the mere images of sensible objects, or objects of sense; but on subjects that are not objects of sense they give you no information. Hence, the deaf know nothing of sounds— Hence the blind know nothing of colors. The reason is, the other senses give no information of any kind but what belongs to them, consequently all the senses are limited by things material and mundane; consequently [the senses] can give no information on things spiritual, such as God, human spirits, heaven, &c. These truths then, however Deists may boast, are all borrowed from the bible. Hence there is not a rational Deist in the universe.[6]

Campbell further disputed D.'s rejection of Scripture by questioning the source of his insights into the nature of God. "You doubt the divinity of the bible," he wrote, "because, as you understand it, it opposes or clashes with your views of the Divine character." Where, Campbell queried, did your personal insights into the divine character originate? Individual experiences divorced of revelation, he maintained, lead different people to divergent understandings of the nature of God. Therefore, "your views of the divine character independent of the divinity of the bible, are not worth one grain of sand."[7]

That deists could accept the idea of a creator God, a human spirit, heaven and hell, and other spiritual concepts, was beyond the scope of logical feasibility to Campbell. Spiritual truths, he argued, are "truths which no man without a revelation, either oral or written, ever knew." Therefore, "either Atheism, unqualified Atheism, or faith in Jesus as the Son of God are the legitimate stopping places on the principles of sound reason and good logic." Anything between atheism and faith in Christ, he claimed, is "besotted with a brutish stupidity."[8]

The second issue Campbell confronted was the correlation of evil with the existence of an omnipotent God. "Your capital difficulty," Campbell observed, "is 'Whether the Deity would have created any being, and placed him in such a situation, in which it was possible for him to make himself deserving of eternal torment.'" Such an issue, Campbell pointed out, is "purely theoretical" and beyond the scope of human answerability. Man is unable to state conclusively what the deity would or would not do with his creation. "Consequently," he continued, it "can be of no real importance in deciding either upon the evidences of revelation nor upon its meaning."[9]

Not wishing to evade D.'s concern so easily, however, Campbell confronted the issue that caused such turmoil for his skeptical reader. God could have "given birth to a system which in its very nature excluded the possibility of evil," he proffered, but "it would have also excluded the possibility of his being a governor."[10] In order for God to govern over the hearts and lives of humanity, Campbell explained, there must exist the possibility of both obedience and disobedience. "If a rational being was created incapable of disobeying, he must, on that very account, be incapable of obeying. He then acts like a mill wheel, in the motions of which there is no choice; no virtue, no vice, no moral good, no moral evil." Moreover, Campbell argued, there are some things that are impossible even for omnipotence. "Hills cannot be made without vallies [*sic*]; shadows, without substances; nor rational beings, without free agency." Likewise, he claimed, "it is impossible to create a being that shall be capable of obeying, and at the same time incapable of disobeying."[11] Thus a world created without evil could recognize God as the Creator, but could never know him as governor and could never experience the ultimate happiness of being under God's dominion.[12]

NEW HARMONY AND THE OWENITE FREETHINKERS

The response generated by Campbell's essays to D. inspired the editor of the *Christian Baptist* to turn his attention to the freethought resurgence that had recently started to sweep across the nation. Among the more noteworthy groups to advance the notion of freethought was the Owenite community of New Harmony, Indiana. Though not strictly an organization for the promotion of unbelief, the Owenite community at New Harmony viewed religion as a hindrance to their efforts for social reform. Based on the communitarian social ideas of Robert Owen (1771-1858),[13] New Harmony's settlers dreamed of creating a utopian community that would eliminate the ills and vices of humanity. To reform their world, Owenites were convinced that they needed only to establish a single successful community. By developing one functional association as a model, they believed the rest of humankind would recognize the benefits of their system and seek to copy the model. As a result, the world would adopt the Owenite system with the hope of creating a new and better social order.[14]

The New Harmony site of Owen's social experiment had been the home of an earlier millennialist group that also sought the establishment of a utopian society on earth. Led by George Rapp (1757-1847), a group of nearly five-hundred "Rappites" separated from the Lutheran state church of Germany and immigrated to America. Believing their efforts would culminate in the establishment of Christ's millennial kingdom on earth, the Rappites purchased a parcel of five-thousand acres in Pennsylvania and began the Harmony Society on February 15, 1805. Unhappy with their location in the shadow of Pittsburgh, the Rappites looked west for a more suitable location to build their idealistic society. In 1814, they purchased thirty-thousand acres of government-owned land along the Wabash River in the Indiana territory. By 1815, the entire population of the Harmony Society had relocated to the Indiana settlement they called "New Harmony."[15]

After ten years of toil in Indiana, however, Rapp and his followers chose to return to Pennsylvania. Their numerous viniculteralists found the Indiana soil unconducive to their vineyards, and the western market had few buyers for the large amounts of cloth produced by the community. When the Rappites returned to Pennsylvania to establish their new settlement of Economy in 1825, they sold New Harmony—buildings, equipment, and everything—to Robert Owen, a wealthy industrialist from New Lanark, Scotland.[16]

Upon his arrival in the United States from Great Britain, Owen met with the Rappites on January 3, 1825, and signed the final agreement for the purchase of New Harmony. He then embarked on a three-month speaking tour to disseminate his communal theories and enlist participants in his grand experiment. Owen's highly publicized tours gained notoriety for the New Harmony experiment and a considerable amount of respect for his social system. While in Washington, D.C., Owen gained a hearing from outgoing President James Monroe, president-elect John Quincy Adams,[17] and both houses of Congress. When he finally arrived at New Harmony in April 1825, Owen found eight-hundred people desiring to unite with him in building a visionary society along the shores of the Wabash River.[18]

The New Harmony communal society had its formal beginning on April 27, 1825, when Owen presented his recruits with a constitution by which the community would govern itself. In its initial stages, until it could operate on its own, the community chose Owen as the leader of the experimental association. To communicate the ideas and expected success of the society, Owen initiated the publication of a weekly newspaper, the *New Harmony Gazette*, on October 1, 1825. Frequent travels as an ambassador for the community, however, severely limited Owen's involvement in the daily operations of New Harmony. While engaged in one of his promotional trips to Pennsylvania, Owen made a positive influence upon a group of educational leaders that he invited to join him in his New Harmony enterprise. The celebrated "Boatload of Knowledge," traveling on the keelboat *Philanthropist*, made their way to the community in early 1826, giving additional notoriety to the society as a center for education and enlightened thinking.[19]

On July 4, 1826, in a widely distributed Independence Day speech entitled, "A Declaration of Mental Independence," Owen announced the inception of a new age in the existence of humanity. "I have calmly and deliberately determined, upon this eventful and auspicious occasion," he proclaimed to his New Harmony audience, "to break asunder the remaining mental bonds which for so many ages have grievously afflicted our nature, and, by so doing, to give forever FULL FREEDOM TO THE HUMAN MIND." Humanity, Owen claimed, has been enslaved "to a

(Courtesy of Indiana Historical Society, Indianapolis, Indiana, C2375)

Figure 3 – New Harmony, Indiana (c.1832)

When Robert Owen (1771-1847) purchased New Harmony in 1825, he envisioned the settlement in southwestern Indiana as the site for implementing a social plan that would ultimately bring universal peace and prosperity to the entire world. When Swiss artist Karl Bodmer (1809-1893) sketched the above image of New Harmony during an 1832-1833 visit to the area, the Owenite experiment had already ended and Owen had returned to Great Britain.

trinity of the most monstrous evils that could be combined to inflict mental and physical evil upon his whole race." The trinity of evil to which Owen referred was private ownership of property, individual marriage, and religion. "This formidable Trinity, compounded of Ignorance, Superstition and Hypocrisy," he insisted, "is the only Demon, or Devil, that ever has, or, most likely, ever will torment the human race."[20] With the attainment of mental liberty, Owen went on to say, "soon would rational intelligence, real virtue, and substantial happiness, be permanently established among men: ignorance, poverty, dependence, and vice, would be forever banished from the earth."[21]

CONFRONTING NEW HARMONY

Beginning on April 2, 1827, three months after the conclusion of his series to D., Campbell offered the readers of the *Christian Baptist* five essays critiquing Robert Owen's social system and its opposition to many of the values considered important to Christianity. "Out of this 'mental independence' has arisen the hostility to the Bible which so much characterizes the New Harmony Gazette," Campbell told his readers. "Free agency, responsibility, marriage, and every religious institute are exiled from the city of Mental Independence." Therefore, "if no abler hand will appear on the side of the Bible," he wrote, "I shall be compelled to volunteer in the service." Of interest is the fact that Campbell had no objection to Owen's communal system, but only to the fact that "Mr. Owen has found it necessary to the completion of his plans to abolish every vestige of the religion of the bible." "I will only add," Campbell wrote in his final paragraph, "that it is the deistical or rather atheistical part of Mr. Owen's system to which I am compelled at present to object."[22]

Campbell expressed a more strident opposition to the deistic philosophy of New Harmony in the second installment of his series against the Owenite system. As a result of the response he received from his correspondence with D., the prevalence of unbelief, and "the bold and open attacks of Deists on the Scriptures of Truth," Campbell saw it as his "duty to devote a few pages of [the *Christian Baptist*] to the Sceptics of the present day." Furthermore, he claimed, "The New Harmony Gazette, which, in this country, is the focus of the lights of scepticism, . . . merits a particular attention." "We have not seen a number of that paper," he observed "in which there is not either a popgun or a blunderbuss discharged at Revelation."[23]

Claiming "reason, argument, [and] persuasion" as the tools he would use to defend Christianity, Campbell challenged the New Harmony deists to a written debate. As an impetus for this debate, he proposed that his deist opponents explain and provide evidence for their belief or disbelief in the following questions: Is there a creator God, is there an eternal spirit in man, and is there a future state of reward or punishment? In return for the answers to these questions from "some enlightened Deists at New Harmony," Campbell promised to "reciprocate the favors." "If there be in this country a reasonable Deist," he announced to his readers, "I have not had the good fortune to become acquainted with him."[24]

In the August edition of the *Christian Baptist*, Campbell trumpeted the fact that his challenge had gone unanswered. "None of the Deistical Philosophers of the city of 'Mental Independence,' nor any where else, as far as I have seen, have as yet, either deigned or ventured to meet me on the premises submitted in my last."[25] Little did he know, a brief response to his queries from a correspondent identified as "W. R." had already been printed in the *New Harmony Gazette* of August 1, 1827. Campbell reprinted the comments of W. R., along with his reactions, in the September edition of the *Christian Baptist*. The substance of W. R.'s rejoinder to Campbell's questions is that he did not have enough evidence to affirm or deny the existence of a god, the soul, or a future state of reward or punishment. "If such existences and places do really exist," he wrote, they "can never, from their nature, become cognizable by the senses of man." Thus, "we possess no positive knowledge on any of these subjects."[26]

The answer of uncertainty, Campbell countered, has been the answer throughout the ages. "With all the improvements in philosophy for eighteen centuries," he wrote, "the world is no wiser with respect to God than it was when Paul lived." "The God that was unknown in Athens, is unknown in New Harmony, and to all who have no other lights than what philosophy affords." So, even though the people of New Harmony claim to be "mental independents" who are advantaged by their social conditions, they have "voluntarily extinguished the lights of supernatural revelation" and can do no better than repeat the aged answers given by earlier philosophers. "This is the identical conclusion to which I knew most certainly . . . they would be constrained to come," Campbell noted. "For, as I have frequently said, there is no stopping place between Deism and Atheism; and they are lame philosophers who, taking philosophy for their guide, profess to hold with Herbert, Hume, Gibbon, and Payne [*sic*], that there is a God, an immortal soul, a heaven, or a hell."[27]

Campbell's fourth article in this series addressed the argument that there is not enough evidence to support a belief in Christianity. Intending to "offer a few reflections upon the adjustment of the evidences to the condition of mankind in general," Campbell proposed to his reading audience that "the evidences of the truth of christianity might have been easily augmented if it had pleased the founder of it." God has "precisely crafted" the substantiating proofs of Christianity, "to the condition of man in this stage of his existence." Had God amplified the evidences of Christianity beyond their present state, he went on to posit, "all excellency in faith would have been destroyed." Therefore, rather than authenticating humanity's need to acknowledge God, an enhancement of the evidences of Christianity would eliminate the very concept of faith. Humankind would become nothing more than a mechanistic slave to God, forced by the preponderance of the evidence to conform to the standards established by the deity. Consequently, Campbell saw God's limitation on the confirmations of Christianity as essential to the preservation of human free will. Without free will, he added, humanity would be devoid of the capacity for morality and happiness.[28] Thus, "a race of beings created incapable of disobeying," as Campbell wrote in an earlier article to D., "are as incapable of moral good or moral evil; of virtue or vice; of rewards or punishments; of happiness or misery, as the stones of the field."[29]

A LOVER OF JUST REASONING

As the capstone essay of this series, Campbell responded to a letter composed by a writer identified as "A Lover of Just Reasoning." "I wield a young untutored pen—one in which it would be the height of presumption to undertake to vie with the masterly quill of the erudite A. Campbell," the author of this correspondence conceded. Nevertheless, he proceeded to contend with the editor of the *Christian Baptist* on two specific issues that were central to Campbell's opposition to deism: the reliability of Scripture and the question of whether God could be logically proven to exist without the benefit of revelation.

"You deny the possibility of the existence of a God being known without deriving that knowledge from the Bible," Campbell's opponent began. It is "strange," he contended, that "the all-wise Creator of the universe" would make the most fallible kind of evidence "the *only* possible vehicle through which he can be known to his creatures." Of the three kinds of evidence—intuition, experience, and testimony—testimony, this Lover of Just Reasoning argued, is the most fallible because it is based upon the veracity of others. Scripture, he continued, "because it is to us history, hearsay, or evidence resting on the testimony of others" resides within this most fallible classification of evidence. A far more reliable form of substantiation, he suggested, would be "the more durable work of [God's] own hand—the Book of Nature."[30]

Campbell readily agreed with his correspondent's classification of the three types of evidence, but claimed that Scripture is more than simply a matter of testimony. "The Revelation is addressed to the whole man," he countered, and "its claims are supported by intuitive evidence, experience, and testimony." Throughout the Bible, Campbell noted, intuitive principles are clearly presented. To examine the experiential evidence, he explained, one need only to encounter Christianity and decide for himself. "Jesus the Messiah puts it in the power of every person whom he addresses experimentally to prove the truth of his pretensions." Therefore, "whether he were an impostor, or the Messenger of the Great God, is submitted thus to be tested by our experience."

As to whether nature or Scripture is better suited to communicate the existence of God, Campbell wrote, we need only to ask one question: do those who read the Bible or those who study nothing other than nature "possess the more clear, consistent and rational view of Deity?"[31] The answer to this question, Campbell further stated, can be found in the very pages of the *New Harmony Gazette*. Citing an essay that had recently appeared in the *Gazette* as an answer to the questions Campbell himself had set before his Owenite counterparts, Campbell noted that an author identified only as "H." could only claim uncertainty—as did his earlier New Harmony colleague, W.R.—about the existence of God, the spirit of man, and the future state.[32] Thus, the students of nature, Campbell illustrated to his reader, cannot find in nature enough evidence to support three of the central tenants of Christianity that are revealed to the students of Scripture.

The certainty of God's existence, the Lover of Just Reasoning further claimed, could be more fully recognized through intuitive and experiential evidences. "We can, by our senses, and reasoning faculties," he wrote, "be as imperatively convinced of the existence of a God, as we can by the scriptures." Using the cosmological argument for the existence of a deity, the letter's author made a case for an eternally existent being who initiated the existence of all other beings. "What was not from eternity, had a beginning," he stated, "and what had a beginning, must be produced by something else." Therefore, he reasoned, there must be an eternal being who is the source of all beings, the origin of power, and the basis of all knowledge. "Thus, . . . our reason leads us to the knowledge of this certain and evident truth, that there is an eternal, most powerful, and most knowing being; which, whether any one will please to call God, it matters not."[33]

The problem Campbell raised to A Lover of Just Reason's cosmological argument is the starting point. Rather than showing "how a person without such an idea is to originate in his own mind the whole idea of a God," Campbell's correspondent began his argument with the idea of God already implanted in his thought. Both Locke and Hume affirm that humankind cannot create a single idea except through experience, Campbell noted. Therefore, he asked, how can the concept of God be formulated in a person except that God provide a revelation of himself to humanity? "That any man could logically infer that there is a first cause, which is the effect of no antecedent cause from any thing he ever saw or heard outside of the bible," wrote Campbell, "no philosopher has yet shown." The very concept of a being "creating or producing something out of nothing, or forming any thing essentially unlike itself," he explained, is contradictory to the teachings of nature. "So soon as the bible words and ideas are proscribed," Campbell concluded, "man is left in total darkness, both as respects his origin and destiny, the two grandest and most sublime points ever imagined or expressed."[34]

In a separate article at the close of his final essay to the Owenite free-thinkers, Campbell posed a different question to the philosophers of New Harmony. How did the idea of God enter the world? "The christian idea of an eternal first cause uncaused, or of a God, is now in the world, and has been for ages immemorial. You say it *could not* enter into the world by reason, and it *did not* enter by revelation. Now, as you are philosophers and historians, and have all the means of knowing, *how did it enter into the world?*"[35] Although Campbell's query was printed in the *New Harmony Gazette* with an appeal for one of their adherents to reply,[36] no response to this question made its way into the pages of the Owenite periodical.

PRELUDE TO A DEBATE

Campbell's railings against the deistic philosophers of New Harmony garnered interest from both Owenite and Christian partisans. No less than seven letters—a mere sampling according to the editor—were printed in the *New Harmony Gazette* as challenges to Campbell's Christianity.[37] In addition, a Christian designated simply as "A." informed the editor of the *Christian Baptist* that Dr. Samuel Underhill, "an emissary of infidelity, of considerable talents," has been disseminating the deistic philosophy of New Harmony throughout Stark County, Ohio.[38] "He is going from place to place, and great numbers ... are converted to his new doctrine," the correspondent reported. Furthermore, "Dr. Underhill has challenged, boldly, every one who would be willing to question his views," but has received little response from the Christians of the area. Because of the imperative need for Christianity to be defended, A. told Campbell, "I wish you would be willing to enter the list with this man."[39]

Claiming Dr. Underhill as "too obscure to merit any attention from me on the Atheism or Deism of his philosophy," Campbell declined the invitation from A. to journey to the area and confront the Owenite free-thinker. He went on to say, however, that he would willingly engage Underhill's "great master, Mr. Robert Owen," in a public debate on "the whole system of his moral and religious philosophy." "In the armor of the bible, I feel prepared to meet the sage philosopher of New Harmony," Campbell wrote. "But in the mean time I will not draw a bow, save against the king of the sceptics of the city of Mental Independence."[40] The exchange between Campbell and A. was printed in its entirety in the *New Harmony Gazette*, along with a note from the editor stating, "We expect to receive from Robert Owen a reply to Mr. Campbell's proposition next week."[41]

By the time Campbell published his offer to debate Owen, the communal experiment at New Harmony had come to an unsuccessful conclusion. In a speech to the citizens of New Harmony, on May 6, 1827, Owen affirmed that "many who were here ... were unprepared to be members of a Community of common property and equality." Therefore, he continued, the "estate of Harmony" has been divided among its members so they can form their own communities. "Already eight independent Communities of common property and equality have been formed upon the New-Harmony estate," he reported, and this aside from the town of New Harmony and the Education Society of William Maclure.[42] In a subsequent address, published two days before Owen's departure from New Harmony, he offered the citizens of the smaller communities surrounding the site of his grand experiment an encouraging report on their progress.

The difficulties attendant on the commencement of this mighty change in the affairs of men, you are rapidly overcoming; the unavoidable, disagreeable rough work, which the nature of the country and of the materials, which first congregated here, rendered necessary, is daily diminishing, and the industry, economy, beauty, order, and good feeling, are silently and gradually growing up around you, and the right spirit of the system, not derived from imagination or enthusiasm, but from a real knowledge of your own nature and of your true interest, is gaining ground among you, and soon cannot fail to become general.

Thus, he further exclaimed, "your progress and success cannot fail to be certain."[43]

On June 1, 1827, Owen left New Harmony for England. As he traveled to New York for his exodus to Europe, he stopped in several cities to lecture on his social system and to paint a positive portrait of the conditions at New Harmony.[44] On the occasion of this departure, Arthur Bestor observes, "New Harmony as an experiment with Owen's system was dead."[45] Owen confirmed this death when he returned to New Harmony in April 1828, and lamented the demise of his social system in that community. "I tried here a new course for which I was induced to hope that fifty years of political liberty had prepared the American population[,] . . . but experience proved that the attempt was premature to unite a number of strangers not previously educated for the purpose, who should carry on extensive operations for their common interest and live together as a common family."[46] Owen ultimately sold the lands of New Harmony at a low price and extricated himself from the former community. His aggregate loss in the venture amounted to two-hundred-thousand dollars, just fifty-thousand dollars short of the entire fortune he possessed at the outset of the experiment.[47] Nevertheless, he refused to view his social system as a failure.

After Owen's trip to England and before his final separation from New Harmony, he set out on a propaganda tour attempting to vindicate his ideas and explain the problems experienced at New Harmony. While delivering a series of lectures in New Orleans, in January 1828 (previous to Campbell's debate offer), Owen suggested that the clergy of that city attempt to support in a public discussion the doctrines that they preach in their houses of worship. At the conclusion of his lectures, Owen inserted an advertisement in the local newspapers issuing a challenge of debate to any of the clergy in New Orleans.

> I propose to prove, as I have already attempted to do in my lec-
> tures, that all the religions of the world have been founded on
> the ignorance of mankind; that they are directly opposed to the
> never-changing laws of our nature; that they have been and are
> the real source of vice, disunion and misery of every description;
> that they are now the only real bar to the formation of a society
> of virtue, of intelligence, of charity in its most extended sense,
> and of sincerity and kindness among the whole human family;
> and that they can be no longer maintained except through the
> ignorance of the mass of the people, and the tyranny of the few
> over that mass.

In the postscript of his challenge, Owen haughtily added, "If this proposal should be declined, I shall conclude, as I have long most conscientiously been compelled to do, that the principles which I advocate are
unanswerable truths."[48]

Upon obtaining a copy of Owen's proposal to the clergy of New
Orleans, Campbell reprinted the challenge in the *Christian Baptist* and
agreed to meet Owen "at any time within one year from this date, at
any place equi-distant from New Harmony and Bethany." Moreover,
he stated, "[I] will then and there undertake to show that Mr. Owen is
utterly incompetent to prove the positions he has assumed, in a public
debate before all who may please to attend."[49]

At nearly the same time, and completely unaware of Campbell's
reply to his New Orleans challenge, Owen forwarded his own response
to Campbell's earlier disputation offer in the *Christian Baptist* of April
1828. "The time is indeed come," Owen wrote, "when religion should
be proved to be true or false." With a desire to discover the "truth upon
these matters," Owen suggested that he form a company of those who
are "conscientiously opposed to all religions" to discuss the issue with
Campbell and "the leading ministers of the religious sects in this western country."[50]

Campbell rejected Owen's invitation to form a committee to discuss
the issues surrounding the validity of Christianity, but reaffirmed his willingness to confront Owen and raised no objection to Owen's use of a
group to support the claims of skepticism. "I have accepted your challenge ... in the identical terms you proposed it in New Orleans," Campbell
wrote in his rejoinder to Owen's letter. Furthermore, he declared, "I take
the negative of every position embraced in your challenge—And now I

stand pledged to the public, to show that you cannot establish the positions which you have so repeatedly proposed, and attempted to do." A discussion of this nature, Campbell explained, "cannot fail to be pleasing and profitable to all concerned, and . . . cannot fail to be of some consequence to posterity." Therefore, he advised, we must "settle the preliminaries as soon as possible."[51]

Campbell's early confrontations with freethought had a dramatic impact upon his continuing efforts to oppose the advocates of unbelief. His essays responding to the skeptical views of D. and his articles attacking the assertions of the citizens of New Harmony solidified the apologetic tactic and philosophy that Campbell would use in his numerous encounters with freethinkers throughout the remainder of his life. Moreover, his correspondences with the *New Harmony Gazette* opened the door for Campbell's debate with Robert Owen, the champion of unbelief on two continents.

4

THE GREAT DEBATE: CAMPBELL, OWEN, AND THE EVIDENCES OF CHRISTIANITY

Desirous of meeting his future disputant face-to-face before departing for some months to England, Owen detoured from his journey to New York—from where he would sail to Europe—to make a stopover at the home of his opponent. From Wheeling, a natural stopping place on his excursion, Owen traveled the fifteen mile route to Campbell's home in Bethany. Their meeting in early July 1828 both settled the preliminaries of the debate and established a mutual respect among the two reformers. "Mr. Campbell found [Owen] to be a very affable and pleasant gentleman," according to his biographer, Robert Richardson.[1] Likewise, Owen noted in a letter written to a friend shortly after his stay in Bethany, "Mr. Campbell is an acute, clever, and I believe, sincere man, who will make the most of his cause." Nevertheless, Owen continued, "I have no doubt that truth will ultimately prevail."[2]

Though Owen's junior by seventeen years and a figure of considerably less notoriety at that time, Campbell did not fail to make a discernible impression on Owen in their initial encounter. While ambling upon the grounds of Campbell's estate and chatting about the final arrangements for their debate, Campbell's guest caught a glimpse of the family cemetery. "There is one advantage I have over the Christian—I am not afraid to die," Owen noted as they strolled beside the burial site. "Most Christians have fear in death, but if some few items of my business were settled, I should be perfectly willing to die at any moment," he continued. "Well," answered Campbell, "you say you have no fear in death; have you any hope in death?" After a solemn pause, Owen responded that he did not. "Then you are on a level with that brute," Campbell replied, as he pointed to a nearby ox. "He has fed till he is satisfied, and stands in the shade whisking off the flies, and has neither hope nor fear in death." Unable to reply, Owen could do no more than smile as he conceded the correctness of his new friend's logic.[3]

OWEN'S RISE IN THE INDUSTRIAL WORLD

Like Campbell, Owen was a product of the British Empire and a student of the European Enlightenment. Born on May 14, 1771, he was the sixth of seven children in the poor family of a saddler and ironmonger in Newtown, North Wales. Though he received only an elementary education, Owen developed a "strong passion for reading" and became an enthusiastic student of literature and philosophy.[4] From his studies, Carol Kolmerten suggests, Owen drew upon the ideas of numerous individuals to form a philosophy of his own.

> From Locke he took the idea that the character of man is a tabula rasa at birth; from Rousseau, that children collectively may be taught any sentiments and habits because humans are basically good and it is institutions that pervert this natural goodness; from the Utilitarians, the importance of happiness, which can be attained only by conduct that must promote the happiness of the community; from William Godwin, the notion that private property has to be eliminated in order for equality to exist; and from Adam Smith, the premise that wealth results from labor.[5]

The conviction "that the character of man, is, without a single exception, always formed for him,"[6] became the cornerstone belief of Owen's social philosophy and a mantra that he would never tire of repeating.

Owen's childhood life in Newtown ended at the age of ten, when he departed from his parents' home to become an apprentice draper with James McGuffog in Stamford.[7] After three years as his apprentice and one year as his assistant, Owen left McGuffog's company to accept a more profitable assistant draper's position in Manchester. By age eighteen, however, as new inventions were revolutionizing the methods of cotton manufacture, Owen and a partner set up a business of their own within that industry. When his partner left the business in search of a better opportunity, Owen successfully sustained the operation until a more intriguing position caught his eye. Though not yet twenty, when the managerial position of the modern steam-powered cotton mill of Lancashire became vacant, Owen pursued and received the job. At the age of twenty, Owen found himself leading some five-hundred employees in one of the largest and best-equipped cotton mills in England.[8] His success at handling the mill, coupled with a reputation for the production of fine cotton, advanced his career as an industrialist. At the behest of three potential colleagues, Owen left the Lancashire mill to become a partner in the creation of a new mill. The birth of the Chorlton Twist Company, in 1794 or 1795, was for the production of "cloths for printing, and . . . muslins" as needed by the manufacturers of Manchester and Glasgow.[9]

Because many of the customers for his new company were located north of Manchester, Owen often traveled to Glasgow to seek orders for the new mill. On one of these journeys he met Caroline Dale, the daughter of David Dale, a notable Glasgow businessman who owned the New Lanark cotton mills. Smitten with Caroline, but uncertain as to whether her father would permit her to marry him, the twenty-seven-year-old Owen approached David Dale about the possibility of purchasing the New Lanark mill. Through this tactic he gained a cordial acquaintance with Dale and soon received the permission he sought for Caroline's hand in marriage. In addition to gaining a wife through his visits with Dale, Owen and his partners agreed to purchase the New Lanark mill as a profit-producing enterprise. Shortly after his wedding and honeymoon in late 1799, Owen assumed the managerial position of the company.[10]

OWEN'S REFORMS AND THE REJECTION OF RELIGION

On the first of January 1800, when Owen instituted himself as the "government" of the New Lanark mill, he noted that his intent "was not to be a mere manager of cotton mills." "My intention...," he wrote, is "to introduce principles in the conduct of people . . . and to change the conditions of the people, who . . . were surrounded by circumstances having an injurious influence upon the character of the entire population of New Lanark."[11] Thus he commenced what he referred to as "the most important experiment for the happiness of the human race that had yet been instituted at any time in any part of the world."[12]

Manufacturers of the early nineteenth century often possessed a strong hold over the lives of their employees. In isolated locations like New Lanark, the long hours of factory work were but a minor part of management's control over the laborers. Employers frequently owned the houses in which workers lived, and the stores and shops that sold provisions to them. Well aware of his control over the lives of the workers at New Lanark, Owen began "to make arrangements to supersede the evil conditions with which the population was surrounded, by good conditions."[13] He improved the wages and working conditions of his employees, provided better housing, enhanced the quality of the food and other necessities sold by the village stores and shops, made the village of New Lanark a sanitary and pleasant place for his employees to reside, and restricted the use of child laborers at New Lanark while providing opportunities for children to gain an education. "No experiment," Owen was convinced, "could be more successful in proving the truth of the principle that the character is formed *for* and not *by* the individual."[14]

Not only did Owen's experiment at New Lanark produce improved lives for the mill workers and their families, but it made the factory into something of a showcase of profitability and social concerns. The principles of his experiment, "applied to the community of New Lanark, at first under many of the most discouraging circumstances, but persevered in for sixteen years, effected a complete change in the general character of the village."[15] Throughout his life, Owen would point to New Lanark as proof for the success of his social theories. Furthermore, in 1813 he published *A New View of Society* to further elucidate his beliefs on the formation of human character and to promote the amalgamation of his ideas into society at large.

In *A New View of Society*, Owen expressed the basic principles of his system. "Any general character, from the best to the worst, from the most ignorant to the most enlightened, may be given to any community, even to the world at large, by the application of proper means."[16] The "proper means" for forming the best character, Owen went on to explain, is to train children "from their earliest infancy" in good habits, provide them with a rational education, and prepare them for useful labor. "Such habits and education," he claimed, "will impress them with an active and ardent desire to promote the happiness of every individual, and that without the shadow of exception for sect, or party, or country, or climate."[17] Using New Lanark as a model for the success of his system, Owen argued that it could no longer be "said that evil or injurious actions cannot be prevented, or that the most rational habits in the rising generation cannot be universally formed." The experiment at New Lanark, he suggested, proves that his system "is not hypothesis and theory."[18] Thus, he remarked, "the members of any community may by degrees be trained to live without idleness, without poverty, without crime, and without punishment; for each of these is the effect of error in the various systems prevalent throughout the world."[19]

A central component to Owen's plan was the construction of a building at New Lanark, which he called the New Institution, as a center for training the village's inhabitants in his new system. The New Institution provided the inhabitants of New Lanark with the necessary facilities and administrators of the proper forms of infant training, recreation, childhood education, evening lectures, and church, all in accordance with the Owenite plan. The implementation of this system, he surmised, would result in the formation of characters "that in true knowledge, and in every good and valuable quality, will not only greatly surpass the wise and learned of the present and preceding times, but will appear, as they really will be, a race of rational or superior beings."[20]

The church established at the New Institution would not teach "uncertain legends of the days of dark and gross ignorance," according to Owen, but "universally revealed facts, which cannot but be true."[21] "A religion of this character," he wrote in an 1823 editorial, "must be devoid of forms, ceremonies, and mysteries; for those constitute the errors of all the existing systems, and of all those which have hitherto created anger, and produced violence and bloodshed throughout society." In the place of religious doctrines, Owen's religion would seek the undeniable and consistent truths of nature. "Such religion will possess whatever is valuable ... and exclude whatever is erroneous," according to Owen, "and, in due time, a religion of this character, freed from every inconsistency, shall be promulgated."[22]

While yet a child of age ten, Owen noted in his autobiography, his personal studies constrained him to believe "that there must be something fundamentally wrong in all religions, as they had been taught up to that period."[23] In an effort to discover "the true religion," Owen carefully studied and compared the various religions of the world. "Before my investigations were concluded," he wrote, "I was satisfied that one and all had emanated from the same source, and their varieties from the same false imaginations of our early ancestors."[24] All religions, he later commented, "contain too much error to be of any utility in the present advanced state of the human mind."[25] As a result, Owen claimed to have rejected Christianity and all other forms of religion.[26] His frequent references to natural law, rationalism, and the Creator, however, indicate that he was actually a deist who rejected all formal religious sects and organizations.[27]

Owen's animosity toward religion advanced beyond mere disagreement; he ultimately sought the total annihilation of religion. "There is no sacrifice at any period, which I could make, that would not have been willingly and joyously made to terminate the existence of religion on earth," he wrote.[28] "In everything I attempted for the advance and permanent benefit of the human race," he explained, "I was always checked and obstructed in my straightforward and honest progress by religion."[29] The doctrines of religion "create and perpetuate ... a total want of mental charity among men," and "generate superstitions, bigotry, hypocrisy, hatred, revenge, wars, and all their evil consequences."[30] Therefore, Owen argued, rational thought and permanent happiness can only be attained when "the human mind shall be cleared from all religious fallacies and all dependence upon religious forms and ceremonies."[31]

OWEN'S SOCIAL SYSTEM IN THE NEW WORLD

Certain of the ultimate success of his plan for social reform, Owen abandoned his normal activities by 1817 and began a crusade for the restructuring of British society into a series of "villages of unity and co-operation" modeled after the community he formed at New Lanark.[32] If the money used for public support of the destitute would be applied to the creation of self-supporting villages of between 500 and 1,500 residents, he insisted, his plan would be so successful that "no complaints of any kind will be heard in society" and "evils . . . will permanently cease."[33] Moreover, he asserted, "one of these new associations cannot be formed without creating a general desire throughout society to establish others, and . . . they will rapidly multiply."[34] Historian G. D. H. Cole contends that Owen's social system became "the germ of Socialism and of Co-operation."[35]

With little progress having been made in Europe by 1824, however, the news that the New Harmony settlement of the Rappites was for sale in America left Owen wondering whether a fresh start in a new land might be the impetus he needed to bring his system into reality. Robert Dale Owen (1801-1877), the second of Owen's eight children,[36] recounted in his autobiography the occasion when Richard Flower, an English agri-culturist who had emigrated to the United States, approached his father with information about the Rappite desire to sell New Harmony. "The offer tempted my father," the younger Owen recalled. "Here was a village ready built, a territory capable of supporting tens of thousands in a coun-try where the expression of thought was free, and where the people were unsophisticated." To the utter shock of Flower, who found it unfathom-able that Owen would surrender his wealth and position in Great Britain to move to the American west, Owen agreed to purchase New Harmony as the site for his social system. "My father's one ruling desire," Robert Dale Owen wrote, "was for a vast theatre on which to try his plans of social reform."[37] On January 3, 1825, the deal for New Harmony was sealed, and by April 1825 Owen's social experiment began at his newly purchased settlement in southwestern Indiana.

Though Owen's hopes for New Harmony came to a costly and miserable end in April 1828, his aspirations for reforming society and expectations for future success were largely left untarnished. During the summer of 1828—following both the demise of New Harmony and his agreement to debate Campbell—Owen considered an even grander experiment for his social system. In his *Memorial of Robert Owen to the Mexican Republic, and the Government of Coahuila and Texas*, published in September 1828, Owen requested that the Republic of Mexico award him the Provinces of Coahuila and Texas as the new proving ground for his ideas. From his past experiments in Great Britain, he explained, he had "ascertained the principles of the sciences by which a superior charac-ter can be formed ... and by which a superfluity of wealth can be created and secured for all without injury to any." Furthermore, his more recent experiments in the United States have shown him "the difficulties which the existing institutions and prejudices have created in the present adult population to make the change from the old to the New State of society under any of the existing laws or forms of governments." Therefore, to insure the success of his plan, Owen requested that the government of Mexico provide him with "a new country," independent of interference from the United States or Mexico, "in which the laws and institutions shall be formed in conformity with the principles on which the great ame-lioration is to be achieved."[38]

From England, where he had sailed in July 1828 following his meeting with Campbell to establish the preliminaries of their debate, Owen traveled to Vera Cruz, Mexico. Vincente Guerrero, the newly installed president of Mexico, and Antonio López Santa Anna, Mexico's military leader, met with Owen when he arrived in their country in December 1828. According to Owen's recounting of the incident, both Guerrero and Santa Anna were favorable to his proposal and promised him a large tract of land upon which his social experiment could be enacted. The dream of testing his system in Mexico, however, came to an abrupt end before it ever began. No land was ever offered to Owen by the Mexican government, and he soon had to depart for Cincinnati, Ohio, where he and Campbell agreed to begin their discussion on the second Monday of April 1829.[39]

PRELIMINARIES TO THE DEBATE

The months preceding the debate were no less hectic for Campbell than they were for his opponent. "Mr. Campbell had but little time to prepare for the approaching debate," his biographer wrote. "In addition to his editorial duties and his immense correspondence, as well as his ministerial and other engagements, he had on hand a new edition of the Testament in a more portable form, demanding great attention."[40] Nevertheless, Campbell did not regard Owen lightly. As a social philosopher and a champion of unbelief, Owen was highly acclaimed in both America and Europe, and Campbell recognized him as a capable adversary. "When we consider his superior opportunities from age, traveling, conversation, and extensive reading for many years, added to the almost entire devotion of his mind to his peculiar views during a period as long as we have lived," Campbell wrote, "we should fear the result of such a discussion." Nevertheless, he went on to say, victory will result from "the invincible, irrefragable, and triumphant evidences" for the Christian religion.[41]

Excitement ran high in Cincinnati as the two disputants made their way to the Queen City of the West. The week before the debate's onset, Cincinnati's newly elected mayor, Isaac G. Burnet, called a meeting of some of the city's leading citizens to make final arrangements for the event. Burnet appointed a committee of ten to request use of the First Presbyterian Church, the largest facility in the city, to house the debate.[42] Dr. Joshua L. Wilson, the church's minister and a leading figure among the Old School Presbyterians, however, forthrightly declined their appeal.[43] Frances Trollope, a British visitor to America who observed the debate, noted that Wilson's "refusal was greatly reprobated, and much regretted, as the curiosity to hear the discussion was very general, and no other edifice offered so much accommodation."[44] Application was next made to the Methodists for use of their largest structure to house the debate. Permission was readily granted for the event to be held in the Old Stone Church, a building with a seating capacity of approximately one-thousand people.

The widespread publicity that the debate received, when coupled with the topic and the noteworthy adversaries, brought spectators to Cincinnati from as far away as New York, Pennsylvania, Virginia, Kentucky, Indiana, Tennessee, and Mississippi. Overflowing audiences of "more than 1,200 persons" attended each session of the debate,[45] and Campbell reported that "many were forced to return to their homes in a day or two from the difficulty of getting seats."[46] Amid such a large audience, all of the available sources report that the spectators were courteous and attentive throughout the course of the debate.

Upon their arrivals in Cincinnati, Campbell and Owen each selected three moderators, who then selected a seventh moderator.[47] The propositions to be discussed were the five issues of Owen's challenge to the clergy of New Orleans:

1. That all the religions of the world have been founded on the ignorance of mankind.
2. That they are directly opposed to the never-changing laws of our nature.
3. That they have been, and are, the real sources of vice, disunion, and misery of every description.
4. That they are now the only real bar to the formation of a society of virtue, intelligence, sincerity, and benevolence.
5. That they can be no longer maintained except through the ignorance of the mass of the people, and the tyranny of the few over the mass.[48]

Preliminary to the debate's commencement, it was agreed that each of the disputants would alternately speak for half an hour. Owen, having taken the affirmative positions, would begin the discussion. Charles H. Simms, a stenographer from Cincinnati, was employed to record the arguments of the disputants for future publication.

THE DEBATE BEGINS

Owen's opening remarks on Monday, April 13, 1829, inaugurated eight days of debate that Trollope described as "a spectacle unprecedented . . . in any age or country,"[49] and which Timothy Flint referred to as "the combat, unparalleled in the annals of disputation."[50] "Dressed in Quaker plainness; wearing his customary, undaunted, self-possessed, good natured face,"[51] Owen imparted to the audience his reasons for believing in environmental determinism and the events that led to the present meeting between himself and Campbell. In rejoinder, Campbell read a manuscript—the only document he used in the debate that had been prepared in advance of the event—extolling the value and defensibility of Christianity. "For the present generation and the succeeding I have been made willing to undertake to show that there is no good reason for rejecting the testimony of the apostles and prophets," he exclaimed, "but all the reason which rational beings can demand for the sincere belief and cordial reception of the christian religion."[52]

In his second speech, Owen began reading a lengthy document that listed and described what he referred to as "the divine, unchanging laws of human nature." These twelve "fundamental laws of human nature"

Figure 4 – Robert Owen (c.1823)

In a famous Fourth of July oration to the inhabitants of his New Harmony settlement, Robert Owen (1771-1858) claimed there were three great evils that must be eradicated so that a universal period of peace and prosperity could be introduced to the world. Owen's three great evils were private property ownership, individual marriage, and religion. His objections to religion led to the 1829 debate with Campbell in which the evidences of Christianity were discussed.

(Courtesy of Indiana Historical Society, Indianapolis, Indiana, C2257)

Figure 5 – Alexander Campbell (c.1829)

At the age of forty-one, Alexander Campbell publicly defended Christianity against the skeptical attacks of Robert Owen in an eight-day debate in Cincinnati, Ohio. Campbell, at the time, was a relatively unknown leader of an antebellum movement to restore Christianity to its primitive form. His opponent, however, was the unrivalled champion of unbelief on two continents.

(Courtesy of Disciples of Christ Historical Society, Nashville, Tennessee)

(see Appendix A) were an outgrowth of Owen's doctrine of circumstance and the basis of his argument in the debate. If properly carried out, he believed they would "produce, in practice, all virtue in the individual and in society, sufficient to enable man . . . to 'work out his own salvation' from sin or ignorance and misery, and to secure the happiness of his whole race."[53] Using the phraseology of a Christian revival preacher, Owen further announced that the change that "can be wrought simply by acquiring a knowledge of these eternal and immutable facts" is that "you can be born again" and receive "the regeneration which you and past generations have been looking for."[54]

As the contest proceeded, Owen failed to address the issues raised by Campbell, but used his time to repeat, explain, and emphasize his twelve natural laws and their bearing on individual and social development. "These twelve fundamental laws of human nature (divine in every sense of the word)," he stated, "demonstrate that all the religions of the world have been founded in ignorance, and are opposed to our nature."[55] In the course of the discussion, Owen repeated these laws no less than twelve times, sending a wave of laughter throughout the audience each time he revisited his listing of these "gems" of human nature. "All that Mr. Owen said or read," an observer of the contest wrote, "was predicated upon these twelve laws."[56] Moreover, "to outline these twelve laws," Bill Humble contends, "is to summarize every argument made by Owen during the course of the entire debate!"[57]

Campbell reacted to Owen's inventory of natural laws by questioning his opponent's approach to debate and challenging the significance of the information he had imparted. To which of the five propositions, he asked, are the twelve laws offered as evidence? "What may logically prove the first position," he explained, "cannot, *ex necessitate*, prove the last."[58] The rules of debate require the disputants to provide logical argumentation upon each individual proposition. "The same matter cannot be received in evidence of each position," he contended, "it must apply to some one [proposition] in particular; it cannot [be applied] to all, unless they be identical positions." Furthermore, argued Campbell, even if all of Owen's laws were acceded to, it would still fail to offer a rational verification for his propositions. "All this time I should have been proving or disproving some position bearing upon the great question at issue," he stated. "Instead of this, I must hear Mr. Owen reading upon a variety of topics having no legitimate bearing upon the subject matter before us."[59]

During a midday intermission, the moderators discussed Campbell's concerns and agreed with his assessment of the debate's proceedings. Upon returning for the afternoon session, the chairman of the moderators announced that Owen's challenge contained five distinct propositions that should be individually addressed. "It is therefore expected," he continued, "that the discussion, this afternoon, will be founded on, and confined to, this first proposition, viz.: 'that all religions are founded in ignorance.'"[60] Their directive for the procedure of the contest, however, had little impact on Owen. He continued to expound his fundamental laws of human nature as the only argument he carried in his arsenal against religion.

Throughout the discussion, Campbell consistently appealed to a modified form of the Ontological Argument for God's existence—a classical Christian apologetic.[61] Campbell's philosophical defense of theism grew out of his epistemological belief that all knowledge and understanding derives from sensory perception and the operation of the mind upon these perceptions. Locke, Hume, and the metaphysical philosophers, he maintained, "agree that all our original ideas are the result of sensation and reflection." Thus, "our five senses are the only avenue through which ideas of material objects can be derived to us." With this in mind, he asked, "how can we have any idea, the archetype of which does not exist in nature?"

> We have an idea of God, of a Creator, a being who has produced the whole material universe by the bare exhibition of physical creative power. This idea, we contend, can have no archetype in nature, because we have never seen anything produced out of nothing. But we have the idea of the existence of this creative power. It is to be found in almost all religions. If we appeal to traditionary or historic evidence, we shall find that all nations had originally some ideas of the existence of a Great First Cause. But the difficulty is—how did the idea originate? By what process could it have been engendered? Where was the archetype in nature to suggest ... the remotest idea of a Creator, or any other idea concerning spiritual things?

While admitting with Locke and Hume that the imagination "can abstract, compound, and combine the qualities of objects already known, and thus form new creations *ad infinitum*," Campbell also noted that the imagination "borrows all the original qualities from the other faculties of the mind, and from the external senses." Therefore, "to form ideas concerning spiritual things, imagination has to travel out of her province." Carrying this argument further, Campbell proposed five questions that he requested his opponent attempt to answer:

1. Can man, by the exercise of his mental powers, originate language? And even suppose he could invent names for external sensible objects, could he also originate the terms peculiar to religion, for which he has no types in the sensible creation?
2. Must not the object or idea exist prior to the name or term by which it is designated? For example, the term "steamboat," a word invented in our time—was not the object in existence before this name was found in our vocabulary?
3. Must not the idea of the existence of any particular object, be prior to the idea of any of its properties? Or can we conceive of the properties of a thing, before we have an idea of that thing's existence?
4. How, then, do we become conscious of the idea of spirit, our consciousness being limited to the objects of sensation, perception, and memory; and, consequently, all our mental operation being necessarily confined to the same objects?
5. Does not our belief, as well as our knowledge and experience depend upon our mental operations?[62]

Claiming Campbell's questions were irrelevant to the issue at hand, Owen refused to even consider them, but continued to expound his twelve laws of human nature. Campbell countered Owen's assertion by stating that the questions he had posed in his previous address were the natural outflowing of the topic under discussion. "He proposed to prove all religions human," Campbell quipped, "therefore he must show that human beings could invent them."[63]

Campbell further responded to Owen's persistent exposition of his twelve laws of nature by calling upon his opponent to explain "who, or what is *nature*?" The skeptics claim "man is the work of nature," Campbell explained, thus he is bound by the "laws of nature." Yet, these same skeptics render nature to be nothing more than "an abstract being" consisting of "the great whole that results from the assemblages of different matter, of its different combinations, and of their different motion which the Universe presents to view." As nothing more than a combination of matter and motion, Campbell asked, can nature truly be a creator or a lawgiver?[64] Once again, Owen refused so much as even to attempt an answer to Campbell's question, but continued the delineation of his twelve natural laws. Campbell later explained that the one who created the matter and motion of nature is himself the "God of Nature" and the universal lawgiver who is found in the pages of the Bible.[65]

Aggravated by Owen's incessant repetition of his twelve laws and wanting to prod his opponent into a proposition-by-proposition discussion, Campbell responded to Owen's eighth address by conceding that his natural laws have some value. "They are true in very many instances," he admitted, "but are false in his universal application of them."[66] Owen, he went on to say, seems to believe that "the christian scriptures must tumble to the ground" if his twelve laws can be proven correct. "I have very little scruple or hesitancy in admitting all his facts, save one," Campbell claimed, "and yet I cannot perceive how they contravene any part of christianity."[67]

While Owen remained unwilling to enter into a proposition-by-proposition foray, he did, after another restatement of his twelve laws, begin an explanation of the social reform that he believed his system would introduce to humanity. Religion, he proclaimed, would be divested of its rites and ceremonies in his system, and truth would make itself known in the hearts of all men.[68] In addition, Owen suggested that his social system would render private property (which he deemed to be the source of all selfishness, poverty, and jealousy), human laws, wars, marriage, and government totally unnecessary. The enactment of this social system, he told his audience, would inaugurate a secular millennial society that would generate the characteristics of life that Owen considered essential for genuine human happiness.

MILLENNIAL OPTIMISM

Reflecting the optimism that permeated America's early antebellum period, both Owen and Campbell were certain that the reforming impulse of their society was laying the foundation for an approaching period of millennial perfection. To Owen, the implementation of his social scheme was the final component that would be necessary for the creation of a secular millennium throughout the world. He was convinced, however, that the world's religions "are now the only obstacles in the way of forming a society over the earth, of kindness, intelligence, sincerity, and prosperity in the fullest sense of the term."[69] Even so, Owen was confident that his contemporaries would reject religion and accept his plans for universal improvement. Thus, he unwaveringly declared his work and the other reform activities of his era as "the commencement of a search into the real nature of existing facts which will bring about the millennium."[70] He also noted that Campbell would ultimately accept the Owenite system and "assist in hastening [the millennium's] arrival, for he has a strong yearning after an improved state of society which he calls the millennium."[71]

With a similar optimism about society's advancements, Campbell saw his era of humanity progressively moving forward toward a golden millennial age. He refused, however, to accede to Owen's prophecies about the future. "How comes it that Mr. Owen talks with so much certainty about what will come to pass hereafter! No man can speak of the future, pretending any certain knowledge, but the christian. Here the infidel's candle goes out, and except he obtains some oil from the lamp of revelation, he must continue in perpetual darkness."[72] Campbell also refused to believe that the final and perfect millennial state could be inaugurated by anything other than the advancement of the Christian religion. Owen's belief that society could only reach its final stage of improvement with the demise of religion was fallacious to Campbell. "It is surely a novel species of logic," he insisted, "to argue, that, because we shall have better houses, and better schools, and must have new bridges, etc., therefore the christian religion must be false."[73] To the contrary, Campbell contended, "let the Christian religion be taught in its purity, and cordially embraced, and it will exalt man higher, and render him incomparably more happy than Mr. Owen has ever conceived of."[74]

In addition to identifying religion as the enemy of the millennium, Owen repeatedly criticized religion—with particular reference to Christianity and the Bible—as the enemy of nature and humanity. "The systems of religion ... are derived from the wildest vagaries of fancy; they are but the air-built fabrics of imagination," he claimed.[75] The devil, along with many other personalities and events recorded in the Bible, are merely "fanciful notions" accepted only by those whose circumstances have taught them to believe thusly.[76] As a result, religion's only real contributions to society, according to Owen, are vice, human disunion, poverty, insanity, ignorance, and anger. Should religion be extricated from society, the millennium would arise out of necessity, he claimed, because the problems of society would be abolished.

QUESTIONING OWEN'S DOCTRINE OF DETERMINISM

Taking Owen's doctrine of environmental determinism into consideration, Campbell asked his opponent to explain how he alone managed to escape his circumstances and recognize the rational and perfect system of nature that he propagates as the source of human happiness and fulfillment.

> Mr. Owen was himself educated in a family of Episcopalians; is he now an Episcopalian? We see that the circumstances of his education could not shackle his active mind. We see that he has broken his chains, and that his emancipated mind now walks abroad, as if it had never known a fetter. This shows that there are some geniuses formed to overcome all disadvantages, to grasp a whole system, as it were by intuition; that in some minds there is a renovating and regenerating power, paramount even to the influence of circumstances, omnipotent as my friend represents them to be. Now if this be true, in Mr. Owen's regard, why may it not be equally so with respect to countless other persons?[77]

Furthermore, Campbell solicited his adversary's clarification of the source of the "irrational and anti-natural" system that now prevails upon society. If man originated in and is governed by the rational and perfect laws of nature, as suggested by Owen, and man is unable to change the circumstances that have formed his character, then how did man enter into the present system of irrationality and unnaturalness? Christianity provides an explanation for this dilemma, Campbell explained, but the Owenite system cannot.[78]

Not only does Christianity provide an answer to the problems that Owen cannot handle, Campbell argued, but Christianity is also the fountainhead of many deistic principles and beliefs. While deists talk about the "light of nature" and "the great God of nature," Campbell went on to state, they have no basis upon which to establish their philosophical claims when they deny the validity of divine revelation. The very premises of their system, he insisted, show that their conclusions do not logically follow. Deists present their system as a philosophical midpoint that avoids the extremes of atheism or Christianity, he added, but "there is no stopping place between Atheism and Christianity."[79]

Keenly aware of Owen's background at New Lanark and the circumstances that influenced him, Campbell went on to ask if Owen's system was not actually a product of the Christianity that he condemns. Did the Owenite social system actually arise from the observations of human nature, he inquired, or did it originate in the Christian circumstances of Scotland? In response to his own question, Campbell alleged that "it was the christian benevolence of Mr. Dale which prompted him [Owen] to invent a plan for the education of the children of the poor. By instituting a system of co-operation, Mr. Dale was enabled to sustain five hundred poor children at one time, who were collected in the manufactories, which he controlled, and were there maintained and educated by his philanthropy. And to these circumstances, instituted by Mr. Dale, is Mr. Owen indebted for the origination of his new views of society."[80]

Owen conceded to Campbell's "surmise that the christian religion was the foundation of this system," but went on to suggest that it "was not founded in the *truth* of the christian religion." Upon studying Christianity and various other religions, he assured the audience, he became convinced that religion was not true and "that something else must be true, and it is highly important to discover what it is." This conviction, he explained, inspired him to embark on a search for truth that ultimately produced the social system and the twelve natural laws that he proceeded to elucidate yet again.[81]

CAMPBELL TAKES THE OFFENSIVE

Disappointed that Owen again returned to a listing of his twelve natural laws, Campbell announced in his sixteenth response to Owen that he would move from a defensive to an offensive posture. "I did expect to have matters of fact plainly, rationally, and logically presented," Campbell explained, and "I did expect to witness a powerful display of that reason which skeptics so much adore." Yet the only thing Campbell professed to have received from his adversary was "intangible verbiage." "I see plainly that there is nothing left for me but to proceed to avail myself of this opportunity of presenting the true grounds and solid reasons on which we christians build our faith."[82] The mere recognition of Owen's arguments as being worthy of notice, Campbell thought, was a deprivation of the "opportunity to advance any good arguments in favor of christianity."[83]

Having little more than his oft-repeated-and-explained natural laws to support his debate objectives, Owen concluded his twenty-second speech by giving Campbell permission to prosecute his arguments without interruption until he satisfactorily completed his case. At that point, Owen said, he would be prepared with a rejoinder.[84] This opened the door for what Jesse James Haley has obsequiously described as "the historic speech of the century, not only in duration but in illuminative and constructive power of solid and brilliant argumentation."[85] In a masterful twelve-hour discourse—delivered over three days in two-hour speeches from 10:00 a.m. to noon and 2:00 p.m. to 4:00 p.m.—Campbell displayed a vast knowledge of nearly every aspect of the debate's content.[86] At the outset of this lecture, Campbell told the audience that he would address four issues: the historic evidences of the Christian religion, the prophetic evidences of Christianity, the arguments formed from the "genius and tendency" of the Christian faith, and the faults associated with the Social System of Robert Owen.

So impressive was Campbell's address that even Owen conceded that his opponent "appears to me to have done his duty manfully, and with a zeal that would have been creditable to any of the primitive fathers of the church." "His learning, his industry, and some very extraordinary talents for supporting the cause which he advocates," Owen went on to say, "have been conspicuous." Most impressive to Owen, however, was Campbell's

> downright honesty and fairness in what he believes to be the cause of truth. He says to his opponent: "I am strong in the cause I advocate: it is from heaven; and I fear not what man can do against it. I am ready to meet you at any time and place, provided I may reply to you, and that our arguments shall go together to the public, to pass its ordeal, and await its ultimate calm decision." Now, this is a straight-forward proceeding in the investigation of truth which I have long sought for, but which, until now, I have sought for in vain. The friends of truth, therefore, on whichever side the question it may be found, are now more indebted to Mr. Campbell than any other christian minister of the present day.[87]

Nevertheless, Owen also made it clear that Campbell's arguments had failed to deter him from his mission to create a new society devoid of all religion. "Christianity is not of divine origin," he further stated, and "its doctrines are now anything but beneficial to mankind." Moreover, he proclaimed Christianity "the greatest curse with which our race is at this time afflicted" and said the weekly preaching of Christian ministers in the nation's churches is "the most despotic power in the world." Yet, in the midst of the grim circumstances that Owen accused Christianity of producing, he steadfastly maintained that his system would yield "the most mighty change which the world has yet experienced." "There is no power on earth that can resist its progress," he announced.[88]

Exasperated by Owen's indefensible claims and failure to tackle the issues of the debate in a logical discussion, Campbell lashed out at his opponent's tactics. "We met him on his own *five propositions*, on which he defied the world," said Campbell, yet "Mr. Owen has only repeated over and over the same dogmas" and "has *in every instance* refused joining issue either upon his own propositions or mine." Furthermore, he "has met all sorts of argument by mere assertions, by mere declamation." "We did most certainly expect," Campbell confessed, "that he would *reason* and not merely *assert*."[89] Because of Owen's inability to support his ideas or offer substantive responses to the arguments presented in defense of Christianity, Campbell acknowledged that he had been led to "entertain some hopes that when Mr. Owen arose, he was about to concede that he

Figure 6 – Campbell-Owen Debate (1829)

When British author Frances Trollope (1780-1863) embarked upon a three-year excursion through the United States, French artist Auguste Jean Hierveau (1794-1880) accompanied her to produce illustrations for a book she planned to write about her journey. Among the twenty-four lithographs Hierveau contributed to Trollope's book, *Domestic Manners of the Americans*, was an India ink sketch of the Campbell-Owen debate in progress. Hierveau's sketch portrays Robert Owen standing behind a desk, Alexander Campbell seated to Owen's left, and stenographer Charles Simms seated on the stage at Owen's right and taking notes of the debate's proceedings. Peering down from the pulpit behind the disputants is the ghostly face of Thomas Campbell.

had been mistaken; that Christianity is what it purports to be—a revelation from God."[90]

Unmoved by Campbell's allegations, however, Owen completed his part of the debate by yet again listing and describing the twelve natural laws. Campbell, on the other hand, brought the contest to its ultimate conclusion by providing a visual survey of the debate's impact. He first sought to show the success of his arguments by calling upon "all the persons in this assembly who believe in the christian religion or who feel so much interest in it, as to wish to see it pervade the world," to signify their belief by standing up. The response was "almost universal." He then demonstrated the failed contentions of his antagonist by asking "all persons doubtful of the truth of the christian religion, or who do not believe it, and who are not friendly to its spread and prevalence over the world," to indicate their belief in the same manner. Only three people rose to their feet.[91] Campbell and his supporters accepted the outcome of this maneuver as evidence of an overwhelming victory in the Christian battle against skepticism.

AFTERMATH OF THE DEBATE

Almost immediately, the media hailed Campbell as the victor in his debate with Owen. While the "Cincinnati papers" were silent on the arguments of the debate, according to the editor of the *Ohio State Journal*, they stated "that the public voice was unanimous in awarding the victory to Mr. Campbell."[92] In addition, the editor of the *Cincinnati Pandect* expressed his agreement "with the general opinion expressed, that Mr. Campbell had decidedly the advantage over his opponent and managed the defence [*sic*] of the Christian cause, in an able and interesting manner." Furthermore, the *Pandect* editor announced, "more than one individual previously inclined to skepticism, or confirmed in it, have, during the discussion, had their doubts and difficulties entirely solved, and now express a full conviction of the truth of Christianity."[93]

Noting that he was "not among those who anticipated any very beneficial results from this meeting," the editor of *The Cincinnati Chronicle and Literary Gazette* reported afterward that he envisions "a result from the controversy, more beneficial than was generally expected prior to its commencement." "All admit," the editor went on to claim, "that the talent, the skill in debate, and the weight of proof, were on the side of Mr. Campbell."

With an acute, vigorous mind, quick perceptions, and rapid powers of combination, he has sorely puzzled his antagonist, and at the same time both delighted and instructed his audience by his masterly defense of the truth, divine origin and inestimable importance of christianity. That Mr. Campbell would bring forward any new facts upon this subject was not to be expected, but he has arranged, combined, and enforced those already existing, in a manner well calculated, to carry, as we are informed it has in several instances, conviction to the doubting and skeptical mind.

Owen's adherents "appear to be sadly disappointed," the editor wrote, and "the disciples of infidelity, have either been shaken in their faith, or provoked, that their cause should have been so seriously injured by mismanagement and feebleness."[94] Furthermore, the editor of the *Washington City Chronicle*, when responding to a debate proposal by Robert Dale Owen, suggested that the Owenites reserve "their ammunition for the formidable enemy who has so signally triumphed over the founder of their system."[95] Even Timothy Flint, editor of the *Western Monthly Review* and one of Owen's choices as a debate moderator, concluded his analysis of the contest by writing: "Campbell left on the far greater portion of the audience an impression of him, of his talents and powers, and his victory over his antagonist, almost as favorable, as he could have desired."[96]

OWEN'S RETREAT TO EUROPE

Disappointed by his failed efforts at New Harmony, his inability to receive a land grant from Mexico, and the futility of his ideas at the public discussion in Cincinnati, Owen chose to return to Europe in the months that followed the debate's termination. Before his departure, however, Owen wrote a reply to Campbell that he hoped would rectify the abject perception of his debate performance.[97] Though largely a reprinting and more complete explanation of his addresses in the debate, Owen also included his observations about the contest and a narrative of his dealings with Mexico. Nevertheless, his book had little influence and added nothing new to the ideas he expressed during the discussion.

With his plans set for his return to Europe, Owen had little time or desire to participate in the publication of the debate. Consequently, he sold his interest in the discussion to Campbell, who immediately began the work of preparing the disputation for publication. Before departing

America, however, Owen made "a long visit to Bethany ... and wrote off or corrected several of his Speeches."[98] Prior to the conclusion of 1829, the written debate made its way through two widely distributed editions. It would ultimately go through five editions and twenty printings, with the last in 1957.

Upon returning to England, Owen continued to promote his social ideas and his certainty of the positive results his plans would have on society. Through an unrelenting barrage of publications and lectures, Owen persisted in his call for the establishment of his cooperative communities and the secular millennium that would follow. As his ideas gaining a hearing among the working classes, Owen's philosophy assisted the advancement of the trade union movement that swept across England's industrial centers in the early 1830s. Among his disciples was Frederick Engels, who eventually joined forces with Karl Marx to formulate the revolutionary doctrines of the *Communist Manifesto*. As an expression of his admiration for Owen, Engels later wrote that "every social movement, every real advance in England on behalf of the workers links itself on to the name of Robert Owen."[99]

Owen also maintained his attack on religion throughout the remainder of his life. Ever the foe of Christianity, Owen engaged himself in three additional debates with Christians after he returned to Great Britain. Opposed by Reverend John H. Roebuck in 1837, Reverend William Legg in 1839, and Reverend John Brindley in 1841, Owen repeated his oft-stated contention that religion is the source of all human misery and that his system would remedy all social ills. Ironically, however, Owen abandoned his total rejection of religion during the final five years of his life. To the surprise of many, he became an active spiritualist in 1853. Claiming to have communicated with the spirits of Benjamin Franklin, Thomas Jefferson, the Duke of Kent, and a number of the deceased members of his own family, Owen used his spiritual contacts to confirm "the correctness of his plans for the new moral world."[100]

Though disheartened by America's rejection of his plans at the time of his 1829 departure for Europe, Owen returned to the United States in 1844 with a renewed confidence and enthusiasm about the plausibility of his social schemes. In a published address that he delivered shortly after his arrival in New York, Owen declared that he had come "to effect in peace the greatest revolution ever yet made in human society."[101] Once again, however, his "revolution" failed to sway the course that the citizens of America had chosen to follow.

During his stay in America Owen had the opportunity to call on Campbell, who was in New York as he prepared for a preaching tour of Europe. Campbell provided a description of the visit to his daughter, who published her father's letter in the *Millennial Harbinger*. "The old gentleman shows as few of the scars of time upon his face as any man of his years that I know," Campbell wrote. Moreover, the failure of Owen's "ill-digested Socialism," he remarked, has failed to dim "his unyielding good nature and peculiar indifference as to public opinion." "He never alluded to the scenes of Cincinnati," Campbell observed, "but with the most perfect courtesy and kind feelings inquired after every thing interesting to me, and especially after the health and happiness of your grand-father."[102]

Owen returned to Europe in 1848, maintaining a rigorous schedule for the promotion of his social ideas throughout the remainder of his life. On November 17, 1858, Owen died in the Bear Hotel of Newtown, North Wales, next door to the house in which he had been born eighty-nine years earlier. Noting the death of Owen, Campbell wrote:

> for gentlemanly courtesy, good nature, and general candor and straight-forwardness as a debatant, Robert Owen excelled all other men with whom I have ever argumentatively discussed any religious question. In our protracted discussion of the evidences and claims of the Christian Gospel, and the Christian Scriptures, he never lost his equanimity or courtesy, and well sustained the character and candor of a gentleman and a philosopher. He spent some time at my residence in reading the proof sheets of the debate while issuing from the press—and not one discourteous or discordant word ever fell from his lips during his sojourn, and our corrections of the proofs. In this respect he excelled every Sectary with whom I presumed to dissent, or to discuss any religious or moral question.[103]

THE IMPACT OF THE DEBATE ON CAMPBELL

For Campbell, the debate with Owen would significantly influence the remainder of both his life and career. Prior to the contest, Campbell had a rather limited reputation in which he was viewed as a suspicious backwoods advocate of a new religious movement. After facing Owen, however, he gained an international reputation as a respectable Christian leader and a stalwart defender of the Christian faith. In 1843, when Robert J. Breckenridge, a prominent leader among the Presbyterians, was asked to defend his denomination in a debate with Campbell, he emphatically declared his admiration for Campbell, saying, "No Sir, I will never be Alexander Campbell's opponent. A man who has done what he has to defend Christianity against infidelity . . . I will never oppose in public debate. I esteem him too highly."[104]

Campbell's debate with Owen also formalized his arguments against the opponents of Christianity. Not only did he use the same refutations of skepticism throughout the remainder of his career, but he frequently referred to the Owen debate and the value of the contest to Christianity. When an "occasional reader" of Campbell's "debates and periodicals" complained that he could not fully accept the Christian Scriptures, Campbell observed that the letter writer must have been only an "occasional" reader, "else the difficulties complained of would not at this time beset his mind." He went on to recommend "not an *occasional*, but a *thorough* perusal of the 'Owen and Campbell Debate' on the evidences of Christianity," among several other books.[105] Furthermore, when Campbell re-read the debate in 1852 to prepare it for a new printing, he noted that he had not read the book since his initial reading for its first appearance. "I must say, that I am better pleased with it than I expected to be," he announced to his readers. "It is yet as necessary to be read by sceptics of all schools, free thinkers, slave thinkers, and no thinkers, and perhaps, by weak Christians, and certain other persons who cannot be named, as it was when pronounced and first printed."[106]

Finally, Campbell's public discussion with Owen also opened the door for additional confrontations with the advocates of freethought. Claiming that the debate "will prove . . . that no christian has any reason to blush, or be ashamed of the foundation of his hope, or of his religion,"[107] Campbell confidently challenged the enemies of Christianity to bring their criticisms into the realm of public scrutiny. "I have invited any gentleman who may be in possession of any historic, philosophic, or logical objection to my argument, to adduce it either orally or in writing," he declared.[108] Thus the opponents of the Christian faith, provoked by Campbell's widely acclaimed victory over Owen and his fearless defiance of the advocates of skepticism, viewed Campbell as both the leading Christian apologist of his day and an obstacle that must be overcome if they ever hoped to challenge the claims of Christianity.

5

A LETTER FROM A "PRIVATE STUDENT": HUMPHREY MARSHALL'S RESPONSE TO THE CAMPBELL-OWEN DEBATE

In a single obituary notice contained in the September 1841 edition of the *Millennial Harbinger*, Alexander Campbell informed his readers of the deaths of two men "with whom I have wrestled in defence [*sic*] of our common faith." Along with an erroneous announcement of the death of Robert Owen—who actually survived, as we have already noted, until 1858—Campbell reported the demise of Humphrey Marshall (1760-1841), a former Senator from the Commonwealth of Kentucky. These "decided enemies of the Bible," Campbell wrote, "recently departed this life, and entered that state where the reality of the pretensions of Jesus of Nazareth never has been, and never will be, a matter of doubtful disputation."[1]

While the obituary printed in Campbell's periodical incorrectly linked Owen and Marshall in death (only Marshall had actually died), Campbell's fervent Christian convictions did forge a connection between the two men in life. For after the Campbell-Owen debate was put in print, Marshall became the first skeptic to attempt a public response to Campbell's contentions. In *The Letter of a Private Student, or an Examination of the "Evidences of Christianity" as Exhibited and Argued, at Cincinnati, April, 1829, by Rev. Alexander Campbell, in a Debate with Mr. Robert Owen* (1830), Marshall challenged Campbell's widely heralded victory over Owen, expressed his own arguments against the Christian religion, and elicited a response from Campbell in a series of essays that appeared in the pages of the *Millennial Harbinger*.

MARSHALL AS A POLITICIAN AND WRITER

Though few sources about Marshall's early life have survived, he is known to have been born in Fauquier County, Virginia in 1760, where his uncle, Thomas Marshall (1730-1802), dramatically influenced the future course of his life. In his uncle's home, and alongside his cousin John Marshall (1755-1835), who achieved prominence as a distinguished Chief Justice of the United States Supreme Court, Humphrey gained a rudimentary education and was indoctrinated in the principles of American nationalism and Federalism. Humphrey's adoption of his uncle's radical patriotism inspired him to both enlist in the Continental Army in 1778 and to embrace the thought and character of the leading patriotic voices of his day. Thus, the deistic notions that motivated so many of the early revolutionists made its way into the thinking of young Humphrey. Unlike Campbell's other skeptical opponents, Humphrey Marshall bridged the chasm between Revolutionary Era deism and the revived views of unbelief that appeared in 1825 and the years that followed.

As compensation for his role in the national struggle for independence, Marshall received a land grant of four-thousand acres in what later became the Commonwealth of Kentucky. He settled in the Lexington area in 1782, beginning a career in law and land speculation that ultimately made him a wealthy man. So lucrative were his professional endeavors that he sometimes boasted about his extensive land holdings and his need to count his silver money "by the peck" because he did not have the time to count it coin by coin.[2]

From the time of his settlement in Kentucky and throughout the remaining years of his life, Marshall displayed an unwavering interest in politics. Though an obstinate Federalist amid the overwhelmingly Jeffersonian population of Kentucky, Marshall managed to win a variety of elections to public offices and secure a national reputation as a politician. In addition to serving as a delegate to the Virginia Convention for ratifying the Federal Constitution, participating in the Danville Conventions that led to Kentucky's statehood, and serving numerous terms in the Kentucky State Legislature, Marshall was elected to the United States' Senate from 1795-1801.

As a writer, Marshall was a regular contributor to the pioneer newspapers of Kentucky. He was, according to his contemporary, Colonel Samuel I. M. Majors, persistent "in the Quixotic effort to inoculate the Capital and the State with his peculiar Federal views in politics and his infidel views in religion."[3] Upon failing to win re-election to the Kentucky State Legislature in 1810, Marshall began his own newspaper, the *American Republic*. With a coiled rattlesnake in the striking position printed on its masthead, the *Republic* taunted Marshall's political opponents for their Jeffersonian views. Marshall wielded a "blistering tongue and a biting pen" as he attacked his Jeffersonian enemies and their anti-Federalist views.[4] Though a Federalist newspaper in the Jeffersonian-dominated Commonwealth of Kentucky, the *Republic* amassed nearly eight-hundred subscribers in its first year and flourished under Marshall's editorship. Within a couple years of its inception, Marshall changed the publication's name to the *Harbinger*, which he ultimately sold in 1825.[5]

Marshall may be best remembered for writing *The History of Kentucky* (1812), the first formal and comprehensive history of the commonwealth. Though politically biased and controversial in many of its claims, Marshall's *History of Kentucky* provides a wealth of information about nearly every aspect of early Kentucky. Much of it was designed to vindicate his views and belittle the ideas of his enemies.

"Old Humphrey," as he was often referred to, made his final foray into political life in 1823, when he was again elected to the Kentucky State Legislature. Though more popular than he had ever been as a politician, Marshall chose to retire to Glen Willis, his Frankfort estate, after serving his one-year term in the state legislature.[6] After his wife's death in 1824 and the sale of the *Harbinger* in 1825, Marshall retreated from public life, taking up his previously active pen on only a few distinct occasions to publish his views on contemporary issues. One such occasion was his 1830 publication of *The Letter of a Private Student* in response to Campbell's support of Christianity in his debate with Robert Owen.

MARSHALL THE SKEPTIC

For most of his adult life, Marshall opposed the ideas of revealed religion. "It was said of him by one of his enemies," Marshall's biographer wrote, "that 'he feared neither God, man, nor the devil.'" Not only was he candidly outspoken in his disbelief, but Marshall was also an active and aggressive enemy of religion. In his efforts to combat religion, Marshall wrote numerous pamphlets that he published and distributed at his own expense. "The doctrines of these [pamphlets] perhaps rankled like poison in the breasts of a people then sincere, serene and undisturbed in their faith," Quisenberry commented, "and doubtless in many instances made for him enemies of people who might otherwise have been his warm friends."[7] The most significant of Marshall's pamphlets was his opposition to Campbell in *The Letter of a Private Student*.

Figure 7 – Humphrey Marshall

When Senator Humphrey Marshall (1760-1841) supported a Federalist measure in Congress, his anti-Federalist constituents in Kentucky pulled him from his home with the intention of "ducking" him in the nearby Kentucky River. As the mob approached the river, Marshall requested the opportunity to "give my experience before you proceed to my immersion." Amused by the well-known skeptic's reference to his treatment as his baptism, the captors offered him a moment to relay his "conversion experience." Upon explaining his vote and reprimanding the riotous crowd for their actions, Marshall narrowly escaped the ducking.

Although the majority of Marshall's remaining writings provide little insight into his own beliefs about religion—other than to display his contempt for organized religion—he aligned himself with the traditional ideas of deism in his *Letter of a Private Student.* "It is time," he argued in this tract, "the people were taught the TRUTH, as it exists in God, and nature; so far as the *first* can be known by the study of the *latter*; so far has the Creator, permitted, but no farther."[8] Not contented with that, he went on to tell Campbell that "God makes no . . . personal revelation. His works of creation; man himself; reveals God, to man. The human intellect, as much a part of the constitution as his corporeal frame, reveals God to each man." This "human intellect," he further stated, is the human soul. "Its immediate organ is the brain, its more remote the spinal marrow, or medullary and the nerves, which connect the brain with the external senses of seeing, hearing, tasting, smelling, feeling." Through these senses, he explained, mankind is led "to a *conception* of the great first cause, whose 'eternal power and Godhead,' though not seen, are made manifest by the things which are seen."[9]

Marshall opened his rambling and repetitive *Letter of a Private Student* by noting that he "avowedly entered the lists as *anti-christian.*" In addition, he claimed to have taken a "new ground" in the examination of the Christian faith by using the "scriptures to refute and destroy themselves, by their own disclosures and contradictions."[10] "If . . . the scriptures . . . are not consistent with themselves," he contended, "they will not pair with TRUTH, but with UNTRUTH, or FALSEHOOD: For both parts of an *inconsistency*, or *contradiction*, cannot be TRUE!"[11] Thus, Marshall proposed to scrutinize the scriptural testimonies as if they were the witnesses in a judicial hearing. Observing that Campbell had "seized on the *resurrection of Jesus Christ* as 'the capital item in the Apostolic testimony,'" Marshall vowed to make the resurrection the primary issue for his analysis of scriptural veracity.[12]

By examining and cross-referencing the gospel accounts of Jesus' resurrection, Marshall claimed to have uncovered a conspiracy that had been formulated between Jesus and John the Baptist. In this "half digested—half formed" scheme, he argued, Jesus aspired to gain the position of "Messiahship" and thereby "attain the government [of the Jews], which was to have been a kingdom; and was in fact the kingdom of Heaven."[13] "This kingdom," he goes on to say, "was to have been an everlasting kingdom; therefore, the king of it was to be free from death." As a result, Jesus and his associates "were totally ignorant of any intended resurrection."

"The Messiah . . . was not to die; consequently, he could not rise from the dead."[14]

When Jesus' crucifixion thwarted his plan to attain Messiahship, Marshall hypothesized, two of his disciples, Joseph of Arimathea and Nicodemus, stole his body from its sepulcher and buried it in a secret location. At that point, Mary Magdalene became *the author of the resurrection of Jesus Christ*, by making the first suggestion of the fact." Even though Mary's resurrection stories were "*utterly false*," according to Marshall, they became "the origin of all the *scripture*, on the subject."[15] Furthermore, when the resurrection idea was suggested to the disciples, who had no hope for their late Lord to rise from the dead and did not believe the reports of Jesus' resurrection, "they found how they could make the idea subservient to their fondest hopes." Though their ambitions of reigning with Jesus in an eternal kingdom had been destroyed by his untimely death, Marshall proposed that the resourceful disciples were convinced that they could use the story of Jesus' resurrection as a tool for their personal gain.[16] So the disciples gathered for a "grand *caucus*, at which, it was agreed by the Apostles, to assert, and support the idea of his resurrection."[17]

Noting that Campbell sought his evidence for the resurrection from Paul during the debate with Owen, Marshall continued his study by pursuing "an investigation into the truth or falsehood, of Paul's assertion of his seeing Jesus after he had risen from the dead."[18] Calling Paul's testimony "incredible and unworthy of rational belief,"[19] Marshall interpreted Paul's encounter with Christ on the road to Damascus[20] as nothing more than a drunken seizure. "Paul, recollecting the apoplectic attack he experienced on his way to Damascus, full of pagan heat and zeal, probably inflamed by wine," he wrote, construed his experience "into a vision of Jesus Christ, and to this vision, without doubt, he alludes, when he asserts *that he had seen him.*"[21] As a result, he went on to explain, Paul never saw the risen Christ and although he was "an artful preacher, he was no less an uncandid witness: perfectly unworthy of credit, in this case. And one who said what he thought convenient."[22]

"Such are the scripture accounts of the *resurrection*," Marshall concluded. "They contradict each other, therefore they are false!"[23] He then proceeded to put forward three arguments opposing the very idea of divine revelation. The first, he maintained, is that God equipped man with the ability to know the deity "by means of the senses, and of the sensible objects," which reveal what "his maker intended him to know."

Secondly, "God, is impartial to mankind," and does not impart personal revelation to particular individuals. And, last of all, declared Marshall, the only voucher for a revelation from God is man's word, but "there never was a man who asserted a revelation from God, that rationally, deserved to be believed, upon a comparison of the probable, and improbable, of the assertion."[24] As such, Marshall dismissed Campbell's contentions for the resurrection and his case for the Bible as God's revelation to humanity. In addition, he invited Campbell, whom he called the "*christian champion*," to respond to the biblical contradictions that he had exposed.[25] "Talk no more of your twelve witnesses, nor of Mark, nor of Luke, nor of Paul, nor of Peter, until you reconcile their stories: then let the world see it in print." Upon receipt of such information, he continued, "if I cannot demonstrate a fallacy, in your testimony, or your application, I will have faith."[26]

CAMPBELL'S RESPONSES TO MARSHALL

"I have no doubt, sir," Campbell wrote in the first of his seven essays of reply to Marshall, "but you have strong objections to the truth of the christian religion, much stronger than you have either reason or argument to sustain." And though you and your associates like to style yourselves "Free-thinkers," Campbell noted, you "are not more free from prejudice and passion, from enthusiasm and infatuation, than those whom [you] denounce as dupes and imposters." Thus, "when I see you reason against the accumulated weight of evidences, from all sources, in attestation of the resurrection of Jesus from the grave ... must I not suppose that some passion, or prejudice, beclouds your reason?"[27]

"You believe and disbelieve what you please," Campbell remarked, and you prove facts historic with nothing more than "your own conjecture." Paul's "apoplectic fit on his way to Damascus," the plot of Nicodemus and Joseph to steal Jesus' dead body, and Mary Magdalene's invention of the resurrection account are nothing more, according to Campbell, than the "chimerical assumptions" of Marshall. "The freest piece of reasoning, which I recollect to have seen from the pen of a senator," Campbell told Marshall, "is your reasoning about the robbery of the sepulchre." Furthermore, he argued, "I know of no christian writer who ever demanded more credulity from his readers than you demand in this instance."[28]

Campbell also dispelled Marshall's conviction that he had successfully waged war upon the main point of his resurrection arguments by stating that the former senator had "not even glanced at it." "You rely upon the contradictions which you have imagined you have found in the narratives of the Evangelists," Campbell explained, but "we shall . . . calmly and dispassionately examine your '*reasons*,' if such they may be called, by which you would disprove the fact of Christ's resurrection." "How successful you have been in finding *contradictions* the sequel will disclose."[29]

"You have in your old days, at the close of a pretty long life," Campbell wrote, "thought good to leave behind you a monument of your hatred against the Author of the Christian Religion." As such, you have "put forth all your powers and all your influence, your last and best efforts, to rob the christian of his hope in God, and to weaken all that restrains the arm of violence and the heart of wickedness, by denying the facts on which that purest and best of all systems of morality and virtue rest." In its place, Campbell concluded, you offer "not a single ray of light or information on all that most interests man to know, viz. what he is, whence he came, and whither he goes."[30]

Campbell's second response to *The Letter of a Private Student* challenged Marshall's approach to determining the reliability of the facts surrounding the resurrection. The claims of Christianity, he argued, can not be judged by a court of law, nor can they be judged in the same way one might consider "a poem, a fine painting, a piece of architecture, a question in algebra, in physics, or in metaphysics." Nevertheless, should the biblical assertions about the resurrection be tried "by all the same rules, canons, and regulations which you can bring to bear upon any question of fact on record," Campbell maintained, the resurrection would indeed be proven true.[31]

Furthermore, Campbell declared Marshall in error for attempting to "try historical facts in the same court and before the same laws by which you would try a question of fact, the witnesses to which are all living." "Some of our laughing Sceptics, of the most fashionable schools, with an air of superior wisdom," he wrote with a hint of sarcasm, "inform us deluded christians that we could not recover a shilling in any court of law upon such testimony as we have to offer for our confidence in God and our faith in Jesus." Conceding that the testimony of the resurrection of Jesus may not be sufficient to gain a settlement before a court of law, Campbell proceeded to ask if there were any testimonies about historical facts that could be proven true with absolute certainty before a court.

> Could a person recover a shilling in any court of law or equity
> upon such testimony as he has to offer for any historic fact

which happened from the Creation to the Year of Grace 1700? Could you, sir, recover a shilling in any court in the United States by such testimony as you have to offer for your belief in the existence of such persons as Newton, Boyle, Bacon, Locke, Columbus, or any other person or event of whose existence you are assured? If, then, you could not, why discredit the resurrection of Jesus by objections drawn from such reasonings—by conclusions from such premises!

Name any historical fact that you believe, Campbell went on to say, "and I will undertake to show that you have better reasons to believe the fact of Christ's resurrection from the dead than that fact, whatever it may be."[32]

The historicity of the resurrection, Campbell contended, ultimately boils down to one question: "Can we act with certainty upon any testimony, or is testimony of any character capable of giving us assurance?" A negative answer, Campbell reasoned, precludes any objections to the character of the resurrection testimony, because the testimonies surrounding all historical facts must then be viewed as inadequate. A positive response, on the other had, would require Marshall to prove that the apostolic testimony is inferior to the testimony offered on behalf of those historic facts that he believes. "But this," Campbell insisted, "we presume to assert you cannot do."[33]

In his third article responding to Marshall, Campbell argued in support of the apostolic testimony for the resurrection. The essence of Marshall's contention, Campbell wrote, is that the followers of Jesus designed a plan to tell the world that their dead leader had risen from the grave. Even though they knew his body had been stolen, they spent the remainder of their lives circulating a resurrection story that contained enough contradictory information to prohibit its belief by any rational human being. The real miracle "which passes with you as a reasonable and credible miracle," Campbell satirically explained, is this: "Ten or twelve men, of no education, and of the humblest pretensions as to genius, and consequently the freest from *ambition, the characteristic and accompaniment of genius,* concerted, after the Jews killed their master, to propagate the belief that he rose from the dead, so soon as they heard the body was missing; and purely for the sake of imposture agreed to sacrifice every thing, life itself, and all future hope of reward, for the noble design of imposing an unprofitable lie upon the world, and yet had not sense enough to tell a feasible story about it." "This is your reasonable faith,"

Campbell told Marshall, "and that which you oppose to the unreasonable faith of all christians of all ages."[34]

Campbell also remarked about Marshall's assertion that only two of the apostles, Matthew and John, have left a testimony to Christ's resurrection. In reality, Campbell noted, you mean to say that only two of the twelve have left written memoirs of Jesus Christ. Must all testimony, he inquired, be written in the form of a memoir? "Are not the labors, preachings, punishments, and deaths of the other Apostles in asserting what they saw and heard, a testimony to the resurrection of Jesus?" To further illustrate his point, Campbell asked a question that was certain to resonate with Marshall because of his status as a Revolutionary War veteran. Within a few years, Campbell inquired, will there be "no other proof of the American Revolution, save the two or three histories of it written by those who lived contemporaneously with the progress and issue of that struggle?"[35]

Why, Campbell pondered, do you find the resurrection of Christ to be beyond the capacity of your acceptance? "You say that no testimony can prove the resurrection of Jesus, because the thing is itself *incredible*." Yet, as a deist, you believe that a divine being created the first man and endowed him with life. Why do you find it so difficult to accept that God can "raise from the dust a dead man, when he raised a living race out of inanimate dust, as you believe?"[36]

Antagonists of Scripture, Campbell noted in his fourth article to Marshall, fail to study the Bible "with half the attention necessary to understand geometry, astronomy, or even the grammar of a living language." And "I am sorry to see," he added, "that you are as superficially acquainted with the book against which you write, as were David Hume, Thomas Paine, and our own Jefferson."[37] To prove Marshall's faulty understanding of Scripture, Campbell reviewed his exposition of I Corinthians 15, the basis for his allegation that Paul himself did not believe in the resurrection of Christ.

Using Paul's statement, "But if there be no resurrection of the dead, then is Christ not risen,"[38] Marshall resolved that Paul "shows conclusively, that he does not believe himself."[39] The error in such a conclusion, Campbell noted, is that Marshall has failed "to ascertain the exact meaning of the words employed" by Paul. "Had you ever struck on the most obvious sense of the Apostle in the 15th chapter of the 1st Epistle to the Corinthians," he informed his opponent, "you would have blushed to make the assertions you here offer to the public." Paul's comments,

Campbell went on to show, were made to a group of Christians in Corinth who had no doubt about the authenticity of Christ's resurrection, but questioned the literal resurrection of the dead saints. Thus, Paul was merely telling his audience that their belief in Christ's resurrection is negated if they refuse to believe that the dead saints will also be resurrected. "You will, perhaps, yet see," Campbell apprised the former senator, "that all your reasonings and your alleged contradictions and weaknesses, as you call them, in the original witnesses are of a character similar to those I have now noticed."[40]

At the close of his fourth essay, Campbell poignantly asked, "What is there in the hope of immortality so repugnant to your happiness as to cause you to contemn and oppose it?" "It is the most mournful spectacle which this debased world has to present to a rational benevolent mind—an old man tottering before his fall, bereft of every hope beyond the grave, fighting against him who alone can save him from irremediable ruin, and defying Omnipotence to arms—putting forth his last efforts to rob others of their trust in God; and wishing not only himself, but all whom he can influence, to be accursed from Christ!. . . . Might I entreat you, to retrace your steps, to examine the causes which have led you to this dread alternative, and to ponder well the foundation of your reasonings against the last best hope of a dying man!"[41]

Campbell's fifth article addressed Marshall's frequent assertion that the Bible contains numerous contradictions. "By the term 'contradiction,'" Campbell explained, "I mean not merely a verbal difference, nor even a verbal opposition, but *an irreconcileable* [sic] *contrariety of statement.*" Terms and ideas may have more than one meaning, he noted, so "to constitute a contradiction in fact, it appears to be incontrovertible that all the terms must be used in the same sense, and that the statements made must be irreconcileable [sic] upon every conceivable possibility." As to this type of contradiction, he insisted, "there is not one instance in the New Testament."[42]

Campbell also pointed out that "Thomas Paine and most of his admirers have licensed themselves to call omissions *contradictions.*" A fact recorded by the four Evangelists, but omitted by another ancient writer, he exclaimed, does not constitute a contradiction. Nor does a fact recorded by an ancient writer, but omitted by the four Evangelists. Therefore, he argued, "it is intolerable on our part to hear you boast of 'plenty of contradictions,'" when in actuality you can find none. "If, sir, you could find only one real contradiction in the whole volume," Campbell challenged, "we might allow you to presume that there are others."[43]

Campbell wrote his sixth letter to Marshall with the expressed purpose of calling attention to his adversary's "state of mind" as he approached his "'private studies' upon the evidences of christianity." The examination of testimony by one who believes it is quite different from the examination of one who rejects it, he explained. "The one imagines contradictions and errors where they do not exist, while the other is only intent to have those things which appear contradictory explained." After exposing Marshall's use of "ridicule," which Campbell described as "no test of truth," and illustrating how he had studied Scripture with the intent of condemning it, rather than accepting it, Campbell repeated his invitation for his opponent to put forth one genuine contradiction in Scripture. "Whenever you can furnish me with one, and only one contradiction in the New Testament . . . I will engage to show, according to right reason, that there is no contradiction in it."[44]

A CONTRADICTION EXAMINED

Marshall replied to Campbell's challenge by clarifying his belief that "a contradiction consists of an affirmative on one side, and a negative expressed or implied on the other." He then used the gospel accounts of Jesus' prediction that Peter would deny him on the night of his crucifixion as the contradiction he wanted Campbell to address. In Matthew 26:34, Jesus told Peter, "Verily I say unto thee, That this night, before the cock crow, thou shalt deny me thrice." Mark 14:30, however, has Jesus saying, "Verily I say unto thee, That this day, *even* in this night, before the cock crow twice, thou shalt deny me thrice." "Here the *contradiction* relied on consists in the contrast between once and twice, referring to the crowing of the cock," Marshall noted. Since "each of these holy men give us, as the *very words* of Jesus, a recital variant from one another in *matter of fact*," one must be in error. He then asked Campbell to identify which of the reports was actually true?[45]

If you can sustain this alleged contradiction, Campbell responded, "we shall admit, without a trial, that you can sustain others." If you cannot sustain it, he continued, "we must conclude, without trial also, that you cannot sustain any one whatever." Agreeing that Marshall's definition of a contradiction, "though vague," was "sufficiently relevant to the case," Campbell began his analysis of Marshall's proposed discrepancy. Mark did not dispute Matthew's affirmation that Peter would deny his Master three times before the cock crow, Campbell explained. In addition, to say that

Peter would deny Jesus "*before the cock crow twice, does not* IMPLY *that it shall not be done before the cock crow once; and most assuredly it does not* EXPRESS *that it shall not be done until the cock crow twice.*" Therefore, using Marshall's own definition of a contradiction, Campbell deduced that "*there is not the semblance of a contradiction*" in the tendered scriptural passages. Not content to simply use Marshall's definition in explaining the passage, Campbell went on to reconcile the time differences by providing a scholarly exposition of the ancient Jewish methods of marking time and showing how the gospel passages correspond with those methods. Had you examined the incident more closely, he told Marshall, "you would never have selected [it] as a *contradiction*, and still less as *the most palpable one in the book!*"[46]

Some months later, Campbell published a brief notice stating that Marshall had "forwarded nearly nine pages of closely written manuscript on the subject of *contradictions* and *falsehoods* in the narratives of the Evangelists." Though an extant copy of this document no longer remains, Campbell described it as "a defence [*sic*] of his contradiction" and an introduction to "a number of new alleged falsehoods and contradictions, mingled with much low and vulgar abuse." Claiming to have already paid considerable attention to Marshall, Campbell decided against publishing the new manuscript. He has "no ground to expect that I would become the publisher of every thing he might hereafter write upon the subject," Campbell noted. Nevertheless the Bethany editor warned, "should he . . . or any other inventor or discoverer of contradictions furnish any thing worthy of notice, while we control a press we hope to be found faithful at our post."[47]

CLOSING THE FORAY WITH MARSHALL

After Campbell's refusal to publish his latest essay, Marshall appears to have abandoned his dispute with Campbell in order to take up a newer issue that captivated his interest. The 1831 appearance of George D. Prentice's laudatory *Biography of Henry Clay* inspired Marshall to write a scathing attack of both the book and his long-time foe, Henry Clay. The four articles of Marshall's review, appearing in the *Kentucky Gazette* during January and February of 1832, represent his final appearance in print.[48]

Marshall continued to reside in his Glen Willis estate until 1840, when age and illness forced him to move to Lexington with his son, Judge Thomas A. Marshall (1794-1871). On July 3, 1841, Marshall died in his son's home at the age of eighty-one. His body was removed to Glen Willis and buried on the grounds, but the location of his grave has been lost to history because his family failed to erect a marker over his burial site.[49] In Marshall's death, the last of the Revolutionary Era deists and Campbell's most recognizable disputant—with the exception of Robert Owen—passed away. The notable correspondence between Campbell and Marshall served to underscore Campbell's reputation as the 'Christian champion,' and brought additional challenges from lesser individuals who thought they could build a reputation for themselves by toppling Campbell from his position as the leading Christian apologist of his day.

6

"WHET YOUR SWORD ANEW": AN OWENITE CHALLENGE FROM DOCTOR SAMUEL UNDERHILL

Nearly eleven months before the commencement of his discussion with Campbell, Robert Owen received a letter of admiration from a zealous young "devotee to the Social System." Describing the prosperous conditions of the Kendal Community in which he was a leading figure, Dr. Samuel Underhill requested that the philosopher of New Harmony visit the society and see its success for himself.[1] Owen responded with a note of encouragement and a promise to "spend some days" with Underhill and his companions. He then proceeded to tell his admiring disciple about his upcoming debate with Campbell. Portraying himself as "incompetent" to do justice to his own principles, Owen made it clear that he did not relish the thought of participating in a public discussion with Campbell. "I wish a meeting had taken place between you and him as you proposed,"[2] Owen wrote, "but as he had declined doing so and challenges me so openly[,] I cannot fear that such discussion will be otherwise than beneficial to the cause of *truth*."[3] From these few words Owen inspired Underhill to develop a seething animosity toward Campbell that would be repeatedly displayed throughout much of the 1830s.

BACKGROUND AND DEVELOPMENT
OF SAMUEL UNDERHILL

In many ways Underhill characterized the average adherent to the Owenite system. Born into the modest home of a blacksmith on November 14, 1795, in Crum Elbow, New York, Samuel was the second of James and Clara Underhill's ten children.[4] Among his earliest memories, Underhill wrote in 1836, was that his parents were devout Quakers and that they had reared him in the Quaker tradition from the beginning of his life.[5] So earnest were his father's religious convictions that when Samuel was but an eight-year-old schoolboy, his father "obeyed the advice of the Quaker minister" and removed Samuel from the local school amid rumors that the teacher was a deist. "He was an excellent teacher," Underhill went on to write, "and I never could see the propriety of this movement."[6]

Noting that he had been "fond of the Bible" from his "earliest recollection," Underhill confessed that his attendance at the Quaker church had a profound influence on him by his thirteenth year.[7] As a youthful adherent to the teachings of the Society of Friends, Underhill learned "to believe in the infallible teachings of the Spirit" and to listen for the Spirit's "premonitory and approving voice." Moreover, he "sought an intimate and friendly acquaintance with that inward something which has inspired the prophets, illuminated the Apostles, proved the sustaining prop to the martyr at the stake, and the guide and glory of the proclaimers of every creed."[8]

At fifteen, Underhill found himself attempting to investigate the "great variety of religious sects and opinions into which even the believers of the Bible were divided." In characteristic Owenite terminology, Underhill explained how he was unaware that his "desires, thoughts, and feelings, were all under the control of irresistible circumstances." Thus, his exploration of religious diversity, he later suggested, was nothing more than an attempt to search "for arguments to prove those dogmas, in which I had been trained from my birth." As a result of his studies in theology, literature, science, philosophy, and the Bible, he boasted, "few enjoyed better success in defending the dogmas of their own church than myself!"[9]

After serving as a blacksmith's apprentice, probably with his father, Underhill worked the family's farm. His father's death, following an "epidemic fever" in the early spring of 1813, forced him to assume control of the farm for the remainder of the year. In December of that year, shortly after his eighteenth birthday, Underhill added the community schoolmaster's position to his list of responsibilities.[10] Amid his farming and teaching duties, Underhill somehow managed to attend the Medical College of Albany, New York, graduating as a physician in 1814. Furthermore, he was able to develop a romantic relationship with Deborah Story, whom he ultimately married on June 7, 1815.[11]

Underhill's interest in studying the Bible grew in the years previous to 1821, but his views of Scripture became increasingly less orthodox. The liberal ideas of Elias Hicks, a renegade Quaker who eventually caused a schism within American Quakerism,[12] led Underhill astray from the orthodox ideas advocated by the Society of Friends.[13] Though he had served as a preacher for "many years without pecuniary reward,"[14] Underhill's association with the Quakers was terminated in 1821 when he was excommunicated because of his "doubts of original immortality and the existence of the Devil."[15] By the winter of 1822, Underhill had abandoned Christianity altogether and embraced the claims of deism. As an outspoken advocate of the religion of nature, Underhill became one of deism's "earliest missionaries since the days of Elihu Palmer."[16]

UNDERHILL'S INDOCTRINATION INTO OWENISM

At roughly the same time that Underhill's allegiance to Quaker theology began to wane, Dr. Cornelius C. Blatchly, a New York physician, launched a campaign that ultimately landed Underhill in the Owenite camp. Blatchly unwittingly prepared the way for America's acceptance of Owen's social system when he formed the New York Society for Promoting Communities in 1820. Like Owen, Blatchly called for an end to private property ownership and the creation of communitarian societies. Not until 1822, however, when he had completed a pamphlet that defined his ideas, did Blatchly come in contact with Owen's social plans as expressed in *A New View of Society*. Welcoming Owen's book "as corroborative of his own ideas," Blatchly "incorporated portions of it in the pamphlet," and published it as *An Essay on Common Wealths* (1822).[17]

Blatchly's pamphlet and work through the society ignited a popular interest in social communities that gained further impetus when Owen arrived in the United States. Among the early readers of Blatchly's essay was Underhill, who examined the writing in late 1822 or early 1823 and was then "awakened to the subject" of social communities. "For three years before engaging [in a social community]," Underhill explained to Owen in an 1828 letter, "it had been a subject of reflection."[18] This reflection turned to action on December 16, 1825, when Underhill convinced three local families to join with his family in forming the Forestville Commonwealth of Coxsackie, New York.[19]

As the leading figure in the community, Underhill led the group's members in the development of a constitution and the purchase of a nearby farm as their residence. Even with the modest amount of growth the society experienced in its first year, they failed to generate the income needed to provide for the organizational expenses and routine costs of communal life. Saddled with debt and lacking a "few good men to steer things right," the Forestville leadership discussed the possibility of selling their land and reestablishing their community in Kentucky. This proposal was rejected, however, as they thought Kentucky "too far south for [their] constitutions." Instead, they arranged to join forces with the Kendal Community of Massillon, Ohio.[20] The Forestville Commonwealth was brought to its conclusion on October 23, 1827, when the residents sold their property and prepared for their relocation to Massillon.[21] Following a harrowing late fall journey, the twenty-seven refugees of the Forestville Commonwealth were unanimously approved for membership in the Kendal Community.[22]

Like Forestville and each of the other Owenite societies, the Kendal Community was launched with the grandiose dream of creating a utopian social order. A formal constitution, approved on March 17, 1826, incorporated the community as the "Friendly Association for Mutual Interests at Kendal, Ohio," and identified their work as the development of "a system of greater liberality and justice."[23] Early growth bestowed upon the association a confident hope for long-term success. This optimism was quickly dispelled, however, as financial hardships prompted discussions of ending the experiment throughout the summer and fall of 1827. The arrival of the remnant members of the Forestville group in early December, 1827, offered renewed enthusiasm to the Kendalites by providing the largest numerical increase they would ever have and supplying them with Underhill's zealous leadership.

Underhill's obvious passion for the Owenite system immediately elevated him into a position of prominence in the Kendal Community. Not only was he elected to serve as one of the community's five commissioners,[24] but he also became an active proponent of the Owenite system through public lectures and letter writing. "Our lectures go to elucidate and defend the doctrines of circumstances," Underhill wrote in a letter to the *New Harmony Gazette*, "and we, like Mr. Owen, invite discussion and allow opposition." Consequently, he noted, "truth gains a pretty fair hearing."[25]

As evangelistic efforts for the Kendal Community, Underhill's public addresses proved to be remarkably unsuccessful. His railings against the "individual system" of society and the superstitious nature of religion raised an uneasy level of animosity between the Kendalites and the Massillon residents. While the records fail even to hint that a single person was added to the community as a result of Underhill's orations, numerous letters objecting to the content of his speeches made their way into the local newspaper. Furthermore, at least one local citizen sought the assistance of Alexander Campbell in confronting Underhill's anti-religious tirades. Though Campbell declined the invitation to oppose Underhill, the letter he published in rejection of the offer eventually led to his 1829 debate with Robert Owen and his future confrontations with Underhill.[26]

The latter half of 1828 saw a steady decline of inhabitants in the Kendal Community as debt increased and disappointed members of the society petitioned for dismissal. Recognizing the impending demise of the association, even Underhill and his colleagues from the failed Forestville Commonwealth abandoned the society in early October.[27] On January 3, 1829, the few remaining members of the community unanimously agreed "to discontinue business as a Company and ... sell off the personal property of the Company," thus bringing the Kendal Community to its conclusion.[28]

With the collapse of the Kendal association (coupled with the earlier demise of the Forestville Commonwealth), Underhill's efforts to establish a flourishing Owenite community also faltered. His opposition to Christianity and convictions about the correctness of Owen's philosophy, however, remained undaunted. Over the next six years, Underhill maintained a medical practice in Massillon, but traveled throughout northeast Ohio (and possibly further) to present lectures on "Mysterious Religious Emotions,"[29] "Thomas Paine," and numerous other similar topics that he used to attack the teachings of Christianity and "priestcraft."[30] He also kept a close watch on Owen's activities, recording in his journal that "R. Owen & A. Campbell debated in Cincinnatta [*sic*] on the truth of religion" and that Campbell would be publishing the debate.[31] Having purchased a copy of the debate by early 1830, Underhill appears to have begun an initial reading of the contest at that time. In his journal he jotted down a summarization of Owen's fundamental laws of human nature, then observed that "Owen's first law is too plain to need proof."

Because the Christian religion advances a belief that is contrary to Owen's first law, he added, Christianity "is false."[32]

CAMPBELL REFUTED

After a more careful reading of the entire debate text, Underhill composed a letter to Campbell in which he hoped "to introduce a correspondence" with him in the pages of the *Millennial Harbinger*.[33] Claiming that he was willing to respond to Campbell's "boasted syllogisms in proof" of Christianity, Underhill asked only that he first be informed as to whether his articles would be accepted into the pages of his editor-opponent's periodical. "I am intimately acquainted with the scriptures," he noted in his letter to Campbell, and "your evidences do not remove my doubts of their authenticity." "Open your columns Mr. Campbell—put on your helmet and whet your sword anew," he challenged. "You complain of Mr. Owen 'no syllogisms[,] no therefores'[;] you shall complain no more."[34]

Campbell responded by observing that Underhill and his "fellow-laborers" are the subjects "of an irreligious frenzy." "All that I have heard, and read, and seen, of your school," he remarked, "convinces me that you are objects rather of commiseration . . . than serious argument." As such, Campbell questioned the ability of his adversary to present a logical, syllogistic argument. If you could "put three logical therefores together," Campbell wrote, "it would either restore you to right reason, that is if you ever possessed it, or it would dissipate the whole scheme, which like an incubus, is now impelling your life." Until such time as "three syllogisms [can be] fairly drawn upon any one question in religion," he further stated, "I never can consent to consume one gill of ink in giving publicity" to your "distempered reveries."[35] Campbell clearly saw Underhill as nothing more than an insignificant follower of Robert Owen seeking a conflict with the noted defender of the Christian faith in an effort to make a name for himself.

Underhill understood Campbell's publication stipulations as being tantamount to a refusal to include his articles in the *Millennial Harbinger*. As a result, he elected to print his objections to Campbell's debate in a pamphlet. Along with his introductory letter and Campbell's reply, Underhill included seven further letters to his foe from Bethany in the booklet he entitled, *Campbell Refuted: Being a Correspondence Between the Rev. Alex. Campbell, of Va. and Dr. Sam'l. Underhill, of Ohio; on the Subject of the*

Debate held in Cincinnati between the Celebrated Robert Owen, and Mr. Campbell, in April, 1829.[36] Furthermore, on May 7, 1830, before he had even finished writing the remaining essays of his tract, Underhill sent a letter to Josiah Warren, a resident of Cincinnati who had formerly lived at New Harmony, seeking a printer for the document. "I am far from a good press," he told Warren, as he explained the objective of his writing. "Will some printer of your city offer to print these letters and give me 200 copies for myself and my friends[?]"[37]

Of the eight essays Underhill wrote for *Campbell Refuted*, only the initial correspondence appears to have actually been forwarded to Campbell. The other articles were written as if they were letters that had been dispatched directly to Campbell's attention, but were ignored by the recipient because he was unable to provide an adequate response. In his second letter of the *Campbell Refuted* tract (the first of the seven articles written after Campbell's response), dated May 5, 1830, Underhill pledged to "prove" that Campbell's debate arguments were false. He also chided Campbell for being "afraid to risk a controversy" and announced that his letters to Campbell "will go before the public," even without the use of his opponent's periodical.[38] In a final jab, he noted that he had "learned the fact" of how Campbell sold a "blind Negro child in the night" and refused to make restitution for the deed.[39]

The third letter in Underhill's pamphlet was designed to refute Campbell's argument that all knowledge is derived from sensory perception and the mind's operations upon these perceptions. On the basis of this belief, Campbell had challenged the editors of the *New Harmony Gazette* and Robert Owen to explain the origin of the idea of God.[40] Because people are incapable of creating original ideas that are outside of those that they sense and reflect upon in nature, according to Campbell, they are unable to produce the archetype for God except through God's self-revelation.[41] To illustrate humankind's inability to produce original concepts, Campbell defied Owen to develop a sixth sense that was not a mere reconfiguration of the senses he already possessed.[42] Furthermore, in a footnote that he later added to the debate, Campbell suggested that humans are aware of three worlds. The first is the material world, which is known through the senses, and the second and third are the worlds of heaven and hell, which are known through faith. "I ask all the atheists and sceptics of every name," he continued, "to fancy any other world—a fourth world—and to give us a single idea of it, not borrowed in whole, or in part from the three already known."[43]

Failing to recognize the difference between an original idea and the description of such an idea, Underhill charged that the biblical writers used the elements of the present world in their portrayal of heaven and hell. Furthermore, he claimed that the Christian God is characterized as nothing more than "a combination of the powers of man multiplied." If the authors of Scripture did not refrain from using descriptive concepts from the world around them, he surmised, then Campbell has no basis for directing others to abstain from using the attributes of this cosmos in developing a sixth sense and a fourth world.[44] So, rather than submitting an *original* sixth sense or fourth world, Underhill felt justified in merely proposing a reconfiguration of familiar elements as a *description* of a sixth sense or fourth world. In so doing, he utterly misunderstood Campbell's call for original creativity and did nothing more than redefine the senses and worlds with which he already had familiarity.

So, in a total abandonment of the typical Lockean empirical epistemology of both Campbell and most Owenites, Underhill attempted "to humor the Great Appollus Magnus of Christianity" by suggesting that he could indeed produce an original sixth sense and fourth world. As an example of a sixth sense, Underhill offered "the sense of longitude" as something of a direction-orienting sense. Stating that the earth is "one great magnet" filled with "magnetic fluid," his "sense of longitude" would enable a person to "perceive this fluid" and "set off at right angles with its course." As to fourth worlds, Underhill offered a "Hell Clericus," for roasting "those priests who seek to curse the world with more new imaginary systems of religion," and a "Hell Usurpus," for those who are "oppressors of the poor." He also suggested "a heaven for good old horses," and "a heaven for good old dogs." Revealing the methodology of his thought, Underhill exclaimed, "I could give every word in the English language as a name of a hell or heaven."[45]

Noting Campbell's claim to "rest the whole merits" of his debate with Owen upon his "ability to prove the three leading facts on which christianity is based,"[46] Underhill's fourth letter attacked the principles Campbell used to support the historical authenticity of Christ's death, burial and resurrection. In the contest with Owen, Campbell acknowledged the existence of "certain *criteria* by which we are enabled to decide with certainty upon all questions of historic fact." The Bible, he further argued, must also be able to withstand the rigorous tests that are administered to measure the veracity of other ancient documents. There are, he told Owen, four criteria that he believed essential to "discriminate between the truth and fallacy of testimony":

1. The facts relied upon were sensible facts.
2. They were facts of remarkable notoriety.
3. There now exist standing monuments in perpetual commemoration of these facts.
4. These commemorative attestations have continued from the very period in which the facts transpired, up to the present time.[47]

The historical narrative of Christ's life, death, burial, and resurrection, Campbell went on to show, are clearly supported by these standards.

To discredit Campbell's criteria, Underhill attempted to apply them to "the supernatural acts of the witches in New England." The belief that there were actual witches in Salem who performed paranormal feats, he argued, is nothing more than "the feverish dreams of bewildered fanatics." In his effort to prove the correlation between Campbell's principles and the Salem witches, Underhill showed that "the acts and facts related of these witches were sensible," and that "they were facts of remarkable notoriety." He also pointed to the Salem court records and to Cotton Mather's history as "standing monuments in perpetual commemoration" of the Salem episode that "have continued from the very period in which the facts transpired up to the present time."[48]

Once again Underhill failed to grasp the full scope of Campbell's line of reasoning. In describing the second of his four criteria, Campbell insisted that valid testimony must have withstood the test of "severe scrutiny."[49] Upon scrutinizing the claims of Jesus' death, burial, and resurrection, Campbell explained, the Apostle's were so thoroughly convinced that they willingly suffered and died on behalf of the testimony about Christ.[50] The Salem witchcraft trials, on the other hand, were not able to withstand a thorough inspection. As news of the events in Salem gained a greater audience, authorities ultimately called for an end to the witch-hunting hysteria. Moreover, the apology of one of the judges in the episode confirmed that it was a misguided event.

Though his comparison fell short of meeting the criteria established by Campbell, still Underhill wrote, "Mr. Campbell, your sophistry is unraveled; and he that runs can read that you are far from having even your four criteria." Additionally, he contended, the testimony regarding Jesus is nothing more than "old legends presented as evidence." "Had you met me as you were invited to, it would have saved you all your late boasting," Underhill decreed. "Not because Mr. Owen did not establish to intelligent minds what he promised, but because I should have met you on the ground you wished, and where the people expected, and broke your own lance over your own steel-cap."[51]

The four concluding letters of Underhill's tract contained fewer substantial arguments than the earlier essays, while exuding a far greater sense of personal animosity toward Campbell. In his fifth letter, Underhill promised to "review the story of the resurrection." Even if the resurrection of Jesus could be undeniably established (a fact he was unwilling to concede), it cannot be inferred that other people would come to life as he did, insisted Underhill; thus, "the resurrection . . . has no manner of relevancy to our happiness any more than other curious historical relations."[52]

The sixth letter from Underhill's pen accused "all christian leaders" of "requiring a renunciation of the reason of every true believer." Though he complimented Campbell for brushing away "many cobwebs" from traditional Christianity, Underhill went on to say that he retained "some of the worst." "You have the unblushing audacity," he wrote, "to declare the bible, a full, clear, unerring guide" but, in so doing, you have cast aside "the touch stone of reason" in favor of "implicit faith."[53] Furthermore, he commented in his seventh essay, you have accepted free will in opposition to "the absurdity that follows Calvin's system." Yet it is irrational to accept the notion that "a benevolent, all-knowing, powerful, even Almighty, God, should make a hell and create a race of beings, and give them the power of acting independently of motives, (which constitutes free-will,) whilst he knew at the time, that the greater part of these beings, acutely sensible to pain, would wander into hell." The fear associated with religion "never produces virtue," Underhill declared, but rather makes humans the most "wretched" creatures in existence.[54]

The final letter in Underhill's pamphlet questioned Campbell's integrity as both a disputant and the editor of the Campbell-Owen debate. Claiming that Campbell tried "to impress the audience with a belief that religion is true, whether such was or was not the fact," Underhill called on Campbell to admit that he did not "attempt a candid examination on the subject of discussion." And commenting on Campbell's performance as editor of the debate, he wrote, "you availed yourself of every means that you dare use to prejudice your readers against your opponent."[55]

RELOCATED TO CLEVELAND

Undaunted by Underhill's pamphlet, Campbell made only a few brief remarks about it in the *Millennial Harbinger*. In pointing out that this tract was not a correspondence, as suggested by its title, Campbell alleged that its author was "as deceitful as his pretensions to reason." With the exception of "a note declining any correspondence with this 'apostate preacher,'" he further explained, "the *correspondence* is all on his side." Nevertheless, he wrote, the initial letter declining a correspondence "is from me a suitable and perfect answer to all he has written, and all he may hereafter write, on religion, morality, or common decency, as long as he may *vegetate* in this self-existent globe."[56]

The minimal amount of notoriety Underhill gained from his tract against Campbell had almost no impact on the activities of his daily life. From his residence in Massillon, Underhill continued both his medical practice and his frequent anti-religious lecture tours. Not until December 1834 did his routine change, when he was offered the Chair of Chemistry at Willoughby University of Lake Erie, in Willoughby, Ohio. Underhill's professorship was extremely short lived, coming to an abrupt conclusion in February 1835. Insisting that the charge of "incompetency" that was leveled against him was totally spurious, Underhill offered his irreligious views as the genuine issue that evoked his dismissal from the institution.[57]

From Willoughby, Underhill relocated to nearby Cleveland, Ohio, where he resumed his practice of medicine, first in association with Dr. W. F. Otis, a theological conservative who dissolved their alliance when he learned of Underhill's anti-Christian sentiment, and then on his own.[58] To supplement his work as a physician, Underhill opened a small printing business with his son, James, and was elected a Justice of the Peace for Cleveland.[59] The larger population of Cleveland also gave Underhill an expanded audience to whom he could advance his anti-religious teachings. Within a year, Underhill was acknowledged as one of the leading defenders of skepticism in northeast Ohio, a region widely recognized as a hotbed for unbelievers.[60]

Still intent on supporting his Owenite skepticism against the charges made by Campbell during the Owen debate, Underhill sent a letter to Campbell in early April, 1836, inviting him to Cleveland for a discussion of his religious views. Campbell replied with an April 18, 1836, letter in which he conveyed his intention to be in Cleveland during the first week of June. Noting his plan to "address the sceptics" of the city, Campbell also stated that he advocates a "free and full discussion on all subjects" and would "certainly hear and consider any objection they have to make to my discourses." Campbell further explained that he did not wish to address Cleveland's unbelievers with "the spirit of banter, but of homage and reverence for the truth, and of good-will even to those who deny my Lord and Master." By so doing, he hoped that he might "honorably endeavor to persuade all men to do homage to the prince of all the benefactors of mankind."[61]

SKEPTICISM IN NORTHERN OHIO

Along with Underhill's invitation, the rising tide of skepticism in northeast Ohio most certainly had an impact on Campbell's decision to embark upon a preaching tour that would take him through the area in the late spring of 1836. Never fearful of confronting his unbelieving adversaries, Campbell and his associates chose Ravenna, Ohio, as the site for their first stop. "Ravenna," Campbell later wrote, "is the seat of justice and of infidelity for the county of Portage." He also identified Ravenna as the publication site of the *Ohio Watchman*, a skeptical magazine edited by John Harmon. In "some half dozen of discourses" that Campbell delivered against the proponents of unbelief in Ravenna, he felt confident that he had gained "a fair, a full, and ... a pretty candid hearing."[62]

At the conclusion of their preaching campaign in Ravenna, Campbell and his associates determined to next confront the enemies of the gospel in Cleveland. Following a "tiresome and protracted journey," in which the group's stagecoach "barely escaped the disaster of being upset," they arrived at their destination in early June. "Cleaveland [*sic*] is ... the most flourishing and the most beautiful town in Ohio," Campbell told his readers. Yet, "like many other towns of the West in their first settlement, the village has been, and still is, greatly infected with the spirit of infidelity." So Campbell "thought it expedient ... to deliver a few lectures on the evidences of our religion." Making use of Cleveland's courthouse, which was idle through the weekend, Campbell gave a Saturday address and three Sunday addresses to the large crowds that assembled to hear him.[63]

Among the spectators at the first of Campbell's Sunday morning discourses was Irad Kelley (1791-1875), a local businessman and skeptic. Following Campbell's lecture supporting the claims of Christianity, Kelley inquired as to whether he might be able to offer an objection to the speaker's evidences in support of the Christian religion. With Campbell's consent, Kelley called attention to "the remarkable silence of all antiquity on many of the extraordinary facts reported by the Apostles and Evangelists." Campbell responded to Kelley's contention by explaining that the history of Jesus Christ could be observed even if the New Testament documents were unavailable.

> From the writings of Josephus, Tacitus, Suetonius, Pliny the Younger, and the decrees of the Emperors Trajan and Adrian who lived in the first century, together with certain references

(Image reproduced from W. Scott, Robison, ed. *History of the City of Cleveland: Its Settlement, Rise and Progress* (Cleveland: Robison and Crockett, 1887)

IRAD KELLEY.

Figure 8 – Irad Kelley

During Alexander Campbell's 1836 tour of Cleveland, Irad Kelley (1791-1875) initiated a discussion with him about the evidences of Christianity. Kelley soon bowed out of the debate to permit Dr. Underhill to continue his opposition to Campbell's position, but Kelley was himself well known throughout the Cleveland area for his irreligious views. Kelley was an early Cleveland postmaster, merchant, and real-estate investor. In 1833, Kelley and his brother began purchasing Cunningham's Island in Lake Erie. By 1840, they had purchased the entire island and renamed it Kelley's Island. The popular tourist area still bears his name.

found in the reigns of the two Antonines, and in the writings
of Lucian of Samosata, in the first half of the second century,
sustained by the direct attacks of the three first writers against
the Christian religion—viz. Celsus, Porphyry, and Julian the
Apostate; we could make out a very full statement of all the leading and important facts and events written by Matthew, Mark,
Luke, and John.

From both friend and foe of the gospel, he further stated, the early historical sources provide the same unique story of Jesus' death, burial, and
resurrection.[64]

The interest in Campbell's defense of Christianity evoked a call for
further examination into the objections raised by local skeptics. Because
the courthouse would resume its normal schedule on the following day,
making it unavailable to house additional discussions, it was agreed that
the assembly would meet at the First Presbyterian Church on the following morning. At the outset of the next day's meeting, Irad Kelley
"demanded a full hearing."[65] Campbell consented to provide Kelley with
one hour to present his case, but only if the skeptics of Cleveland would
then put forward the leading advocate of their cause. By contending with
their commissioned leader, Campbell explained, it could not "be afterwards said that his sceptical brethren had no confidence in him."[66]

Kelley's one-hour monologue on Monday morning questioned
God's cruelty throughout the Old Testament, the parts of the Bible that
are "not fit to be read in families and before mixed assemblies," and the
incompatibility of sound philosophy with the Mosaic account of creation
and the miracles of the New Testament. Unable to respond because he
had "contracted a severe cold and hoarseness," Campbell called upon his
brother-in-law and associate, Matthew Clapp (1808-1871), to provide
the rejoinder to Kelley's claims.[67] "Brother Matthew Clapp," Campbell
later wrote, "fully obviated the objections alleged by Mr. Kelley."[68] In
showing that God's actions are characterized by mercy as well as judgment, Clapp insisted that the removal of those who are unwilling to
reform is sometimes best for society at large. He also argued that the sins
to be prohibited must be explained without modesty, and that the biblical
records do not interfere with Newtonian philosophy. To Clapp's credit,
Campbell concluded, he "fully proved his ability to sustain the Christian
cause against any spirit which the infidels of that section can bring into
the field."[69]

CAMPBELL AND UNDERHILL IN CLEVELAND

During Clapp's address, the previously absent Dr. Underhill made his first appearance at the gathering. Having been out of town tending to a patient, Underhill returned to Cleveland on the first day of the discussion and was quickly apprised of the day's events. Wanting to have his ideas included in the discussions, he hastily made his way to the church and solicited a hearing from the assembly. In compliance with Campbell's desire to confront only that skeptic who had the full confidence of his like-minded brethren, Underhill claimed to be the city's greatest representative for unbelief. Because there was no association of infidels in Cleveland, he explained to Campbell, there was no organized method of selecting a champion for their cause. He went on to affirm, however, that he so fully had the backing of the city's unbelievers "that they would not choose any other person in case he failed to do them justice, or to sustain their views." The parties then agreed to meet on the following day with Campbell and Underhill speaking "alternately for half an hour" on "some two or three strong points" which Campbell left open to Underhill's choosing.[70]

On Tuesday morning, July 7, 1836, Campbell opened the discussion with a review of Kelley's speech from Monday afternoon. Underhill followed with a few introductory remarks and an assault on the consistency of Moses' account of creation with Newtonian philosophy. Both Underhill and Kelley, Campbell reported, "rallied their powers" behind "the creation of the earth three days before the sun." In response, Campbell explained that "a *day* is that period in which the earth revolves upon its own axis; which motion is wholly independent of the sun; and, therefore, could have been as well performed before, as after its creation." He also pointed to the fact that "the most celebrated geologists," along with "Newton[,] himself the father of philosophy, and Sir Humphrey Davy, the prince of chemists, were firm believers in the divine mission of Moses and his history of the creation of our earth." Upon hearing all of the evidence, Campbell wrote, Underhill candidly acknowledged that the Mosaic history contained "nothing incompatible with true science."[71]

Underhill's second objective was to attack Campbell's statement that "no man can say that he believes the gospel to be false." Without testimony, Campbell insisted, there can be no actual belief (i.e., conviction or certainty of knowledge). Thus, with "no contemporaneous contradictory testimonies against any gospel fact," the best that an enemy of Christianity could logically suggest is that "he *doubted* whether it were true." On the contrary, argued Underhill, many important decisions within society have depended upon circumstantial evidence. Belief in the falsehood of the gospel, he continued, may also be supported by circumstantial evidence. That circumstantial evidence has shaped society's decision-making process, Campbell readily admitted; nevertheless, circumstantial evidence, by its very definition, remains uncertain. Any rejection of the gospel based on the ambiguity of circumstantial evidence, Campbell argued, continues to be nothing more than a doubting of its truth.[72]

Amid "some eight or ten half hour speeches," at least seventeen different subjects were raised in the first two days of the meeting. "The Doctor seemed to delight in the opportunity of saying every thing he could against the Bible in a meeting-house," Campbell wrote. Yet, instead of "forming an issue" on his points, he ignored any arguments against his claims and continued to thrust additional topics before the audience. In an effort to end this tactic and bring about a more thorough discussion, "some gentlemen" decided that Campbell should be afforded as much time as he needed on Wednesday evening to formulate a complete argument on the subject of miracles. Underhill, it was also decided, would then be awarded with an equal amount of time for a response.[73]

In a monologue of one hour and twenty-five minutes, Campbell proceeded to give "a full development of the use of miracles, and of their precise weight and value in the establishment of the mission of Moses and of Christ." At the close of Campbell's address, Underhill "had scarcely begun [his reply], and had not spoken more than a few minutes, when the congregation, almost to a man, evinced a disposition to adjourn."[74] Underhill was forced to give his response to a much smaller crowd on Thursday morning. Some months later, Underhill accused both Campbell and the Rev. Samuel C. Aikin (1790-1879), minister of Cleveland's First Presbyterian Church, of arranging the evening so that he would be unable to respond to Campbell until the following morning. The purpose of this "cowardly manouvre" [sic], he explained, was to prevent the "mechanics" of the city from hearing his rejoinder to Campbell's pronouncements about miracles.[75]

On Thursday morning, Underhill commenced his speech of one hour and twenty-five minutes to counter Campbell's comments of the previous evening. Relying on the writings of Robert Taylor (1784-1844), a radical English deist whom Campbell described as "the most celebrated for blasphemy of all the Atheists of this day,"[76] and Thomas Paine, Underhill attempted to undo the case made by his opponent.

Campbell, however, suggested that his adversary "could not find how or wherein to assail the only positive argument I offered during the discussion." "Whether the argument of the preceding evening, or whether Mr. Taylor or Mr. Paine perplexed the Doctor, I cannot say," Campbell went on to explain, "but so it is, he never once glanced at the point or reasonings of this argument."[77]

REPORTING THE CAMPBELL-UNDERHILL DISPUTE

The contest came to a close on Thursday afternoon, June 9, 1836, after a few additional comments by both Kelley and Underhill. Campbell acknowledged the courteousness the two men extended to him throughout the debate, while also stating his confidence "that both these gentlemen think better of the Christian religion as found in the New Testament than before we met."[78] A report of the dispute in the *Cleveland Daily Herald* avoided naming a winner, but it did portray the contest as a very positive event for the city. "One thing is certain," the author of the article proclaimed, "the fund of valuable information upon the subjects of history, philosophy, astronomy, and indeed in almost every department of natural science, which has been imparted in the course of this controversy, will not be lost upon the community."[79]

Underhill's recounting of the dialogue—written between three and seven months after the event transpired—was markedly different from Campbell's. To launch his new publication, the *Cleveland Liberalist*, on September 10, 1836, Underhill announced that he would run a series of articles designed to "give a plain unvarnished account of the discussion as it actually occurred."[80] Stating that he had jotted down the propositions of the debate, but not the actual language of his opponent, Underhill wrote that he hoped "to do [Campbell] justice" with his coverage of the discussion.[81] Throughout a string of nine essays, however, he appeared more intent on vindicating his performance and slandering Campbell than in providing an accurate chronicle of the event as it actually transpired.

Upon learning about Underhill's review of the discussion, Campbell wrote that the doctor "lectures and writes with the zeal of a missionary." Nevertheless, he commented, Underhill's articles contain "nothing ... but the proof that his memory, as well as his understanding, is by no means extraordinary." Not only did Campbell find Underhill's assertions about the debate incredible, but he insisted that "no person who has heard me deliver one lecture on that subject, or read any thing I have written on the Christian religion, can for a moment imagine that the Doctor has fairly represented or met one of my arguments on the authenticity and inspiration of the Bible."[82] Campbell's allegations about his opponent's coverage of the debate appear to have been further supported by an anonymous letter to the *Cleveland Liberalist* that Underhill commented upon but refused to print. The unknown correspondent, whom Underhill identified as "Fairplay" and whose remarks are known only through Underhill's commentary on his letter, dismissed Underhill's professed victory over Campbell. In answer, Underhill repeated his declaration of triumph and challenged Campbell to another debate.[83]

Analysts of a more pious persuasion conferred upon Campbell a remarkable triumph in the dispute. Reverend Samuel C. Aiken, according to Disciples of Christ minister A. S. Hayden, credited Campbell with "the downfall of infidelity in the city of Cleveland."[84] Robert Richardson also noted that Campbell's debate performance "was very marked in checking the progress of infidelity" in Cleveland.[85] Perhaps a most revealing insight

Figure 9 – 1836 Advertisement for the Cleveland Liberalist

Dr. Samuel Underhill advertised the *Cleveland Liberalist* as a tabloid "devoted to free enquiry." Within the pages of the *Liberalist*, Underhill criticized Christianity and what he believed was its detrimental impact upon American culture. Underhill also published numerous articles in opposition to the views of Alexander Campbell within the pages of his periodical.

into the contest's influence in the community is Campbell's report that, in the midst of the discussion, he was "called to the river to hear the confession of six converts who were immersed into Christ."[86]

UNDERHILL AFTER THE CAMPBELL DISCUSSION

Throughout the *Cleveland Liberalist*'s two years of publication, Underhill produced a steady flow of articles aimed at Campbell's positions and activities. Aside from the objection to Underhill's recounting of the Cleveland debate, these articles provoked little notice or response from Campbell. On October 27, 1838, after having sunk fifteen-hundred dollars into the paper, Underhill published the final issue.[87] In addition to his failed attempts to gain further attention from Campbell and his loss of large sums of money that were expended on his publications, Underhill discontinued the *Cleveland Liberalist* to pursue his new-found interest in animal magnetism. Thus, in September 1838, one month prior to the final edition of his skeptical newspaper, Underhill began publishing a monthly periodical entitled *The Annals of Animal Magnetism*.

Animal magnetism, or mesmerism, was the brainchild of German physician Franz Anton Mesmer (1733-1815). Mesmer insisted that all animals, including humans, possess within themselves an unidentified magnetic fluid that is affected by a magnetic force created by the gravitational pull of various planets and the earth. Disease and illness, he argued, are the results of being out of harmony with the magnetic force. Using magnets and other devices, Mesmer claimed that he could restore health to his patients by manipulating the magnetic force and bringing his subjects into a renewed harmony with it. In an eventual abandonment of magnets, Mesmer implemented hypnotic trances—which gave rise to the modern term "mesmerize"—as a part of his healing technique. These trances ultimately led to an acceptance of clairvoyant communication with the dead and Spiritualism.[88]

Though Underhill's interest in animal magnetism lasted throughout the remainder of his life, his periodical on the subject survived only a few issues. Most Clevelanders alleged that mesmerism was little more than a hoax. "We are unbelievers in mysterious magnetic influence," wrote the editor of the *Cleveland Herald and Gazette*. Furthermore, he explained with a jab at the mesmerists' inclination toward putting their patients into trances, "a slight perusal of the ANNALS has set us to yawning."[89] The third issue of *The Annals of Magnetism*, from November 1838, was

Underhill's final printing of the tabloid. In its place he offered a bi-weekly paper called the *Bald Eagle*. Known for "plunging its talons promiscuously into people, without regard to consequences," the *Bald Eagle* proved to be Underhill's final journalistic venture. After Underhill disseminated some harsh comments about "City Clerk Curtis" in a mid-January 1839 edition of the periodical, the impugned official "seized a sledge-hammer and, rushing to the Doctor's office, proceeded to effectually reduce the primitive hand-press to metallic fragments."[90]

Underhill remained in Cleveland until 1844, promoting his belief in animal magnetism through public discourses and demonstrations.[91] From Cleveland, he relocated to La Salle County, Illinois, where he continued his lectures on mesmerism amid his farm work and medical practice. Like many other mesmerists, Underhill's interest in animal magnetism evolved into a fascination with Spiritualism. In his final writing, *Underhill on Mesmerism* (1868), he recorded that he and his wife traveled to Cleveland for six months in 1852 to investigate Spiritualism and spirit rappings.[92] During this time he discussed the phenomena with Horace Greeley, editor of the *New York Tribune* and an avid spiritualist, who also happened to be in Cleveland at the time.[93] Convinced of the genuineness of Spiritualism, Underhill proceeded to advocate its cause in the face of personal threats, fines, and imprisonment.[94]

On December 14, 1872, Underhill died at his farm in Illinois. The stubborn Owenite who had doggedly opposed Christianity and challenged Alexander Campbell in the 1830s, maintained a staunch affirmation of mesmerism and Spiritualism until the end of his life. It appears, however, that he did make one concession before his death. In 1859, Underhill "renounced his atheistic belief."[95]

7

CHARLES CASSEDY:
ALCOHOLIC, WRITER, AND INQUISITIVE SKEPTIC

As Campbell made his initial response to Robert Owen's opening address in their debate on the evidences of Christianity, he made it clear that the conversion of an adversary is seldom the outcome of such discussions. His decision to meet Owen "was not with any expectation that [Owen] was to be convinced of the errors of his system on the subject of religion," Campbell explained, but to influence "the wavering, doubting, and unsettled public, who are endangered to be carried off."[1] Though Campbell sought the conversion of each and every adversary with whom he discussed the merits and claims of Christianity and the Bible, he knew that his true audience was not the disputant with whom he argued, but the people who would explore the arguments of the debates in an effort to establish their belief systems. Consequently, Campbell made every effort to illustrate how his battles with unbelief resulted in both the rejection of skepticism and the acceptance of Christianity among the general population of the communities where his forays ensued. Men like Owen, Marshall, and Underhill, however, not only refused to abandon their unbelief after their encounters with Campbell, but continued to promote their objections to Christianity with the hope of winning converts to their cause.

In stark contrast to the confirmed unbelief of Owen, Marshall, and Underhill, however, was the curious uncertainty of Charles Cassedy (c.1782-c.1858). Though frequently unemployed as a result of his repetitious abuse of alcohol, Cassedy was a writer of some repute and an occasional newspaper editor in Tennessee. Unlike Campbell's earlier challengers who were overtly antagonistic toward Christianity, Cassedy could more easily be characterized as a non-Christian inquisitor who sought explanations about certain aspects of Christianity that he viewed as obstacles to a reasonable acceptance of the religion. When Campbell provided acceptable answers to the troublesome issues that vexed Cassedy, the Tennessee writer was only too willing to surrender his life to Christ. Moreover, he went on to become a contributor to Campbell's *Millennial Harbinger* and a supporter of Campbell's movement.

CASSEDY'S BACKGROUND

Cassedy's journalistic talent and addiction to alcohol are easily identifiable traits of his later life, but few items exist to provide glimpses into his childhood and early life. From the scant sources of information that survive, it appears that Cassedy was born in the state of New York around 1782, and relocated to Tennessee in about 1810. After serving in a secretarial position under General Andrew Jackson (1767-1845) for the final few months of the War of 1812[2], Cassedy entered into the service of Brigadier General James Winchester (1752-1826) of Sumner County, Tennessee. Winchester, whose military command was badly defeated at the Battle of River Raisin in 1813, procured the services of Cassedy to produce a written vindication of his actions at the battle and to rehabilitate his badly damaged reputation.

While preparing his exoneration of Winchester, Cassedy established a long-lived pattern of dependency upon the Winchester family's hospitality. His initial relocation to Cragfont, the General's stately mansion located some thirty miles north of Nashville, was intended to provide temporary access to the General's papers. The positive reception he received upon his arrival at Cragfont, however, instilled within Cassedy a sense of acceptance that would repeatedly drive him back to the General's home during the all-too-frequent low periods of his life. When debilitated and ill from his alcohol abuse, Cassedy found the General's doors open to him again and again. Though Cassedy was a strain on the Winchester family's finances and patience, the General seemed incapable of ignoring Cassedy during his recurring periods of need. Cassedy's "ever-redeeming quality," Walter Durham correctly affirms, "was an unyielding loyalty to General Winchester."[3]

By the summer of 1817, Cassedy completed his justification of Winchester's military actions. His defense of Winchester first appeared in the late summer and fall of 1817 as a series of eight articles in the Nashville *Clarion* and the *National Intelligencer* of Washington, D.C. In 1818, the articles were collected into a manuscript and published as *Historical Details Having Relation to the Campaign of the North-Western Army, Under Generals Harrison and Winchester, During the Winter of 1812-1813.* Although Cassedy's authorship of *Historical Details* is beyond question, the essays that comprised the book were made to appear as though Winchester wrote them himself. Any evidence to indicate Cassedy's authorship of the vindication of General Winchester fails to make even a single appearance in the publication. Nonetheless, the General's private records indicate that Cassedy was compensated for the services he rendered as Winchester's ghostwriter.[4]

Following the death of General Winchester on July 26, 1826, Cassedy appears to have drifted from one location to another in central and eastern Tennessee as he searched for an editor's position and a stable income. During much of this time Cassedy worked on a manuscript that he envisioned as a schoolbook for American students. His *North American Spelling, Defining, and Reading Manual of the American Language on a New Plan*, however, did not make its way into print until 1846. Toward the close of the 1820s, Cassedy found a job editing and rewriting a manuscript by Dr. John C. Gunn (1800-1863). *Gunn's Domestic Medicine or Poor Man's Friend* was ultimately published in 1830 as a home-remedy medical book. Its great success carried it through nine reprintings, but Gunn's deceitful handling of the book and its royalties prevented Cassedy and any other creditors from acquiring their pay from the doctor.[5]

On September 3, 1832, Cassedy wrote to James K. Polk (1795-1849), a Nashville lawyer, member of the United States House of Representatives, and future President of the United States, to ask if there was "any legal or equitable mode . . . by which [Gunn's] Copy-right, which is presumed to be valuable," could be acquired as payment for his services to the doctor. Apparently there was not.[6] Cassedy concluded his letter to Polk by asking if the congressman might forward "30 or 35 dollars" to be used for travel expenses to Pulaski, a small town in southwest Tennessee.[7] With the apparent aid of Polk, Cassedy made his way to Pulaski by October 1832 and became the editor of the *Tennessee Beacon*.[8] Shortly after his arrival in Pulaski, Cassedy sent his first letter to Alexander Campbell's *Millennial Harbinger*. Campbell published this letter in the January 1833 edition of the *Harbinger*, then began a series of four responses to Cassedy in the following month.

QUESTIONS AND ANSWERS

Having a familiarity with Campbell's writings and reputation, Cassedy noted his favorable "impressions respecting the intellectual character" of the editor from Bethany. This character, he explained, has induced "me to state . . . with *entire candor*, some of those prominent, and . . . insurmountable difficulties, which present themselves against an implicit confidence in the authenticity of all the doctrines of the christian religion." These difficulties, he went on to state, are "invincible barriers to implicit faith in the doctrines of christianity" for "thousands, perhaps *millions*," of nonbelievers. As such, Cassedy noted, "I do not wish you to refer me to the records of your public debates for the desired information." Instead, he sought Campbell's direct reply to the difficulties under consideration.[9]

Cassedy's objections to Christianity were posed to Campbell in a sequence of questions and statements that, as Campbell observed in his initial response to Cassedy, fall into three logical categories. First, Cassedy expressed his problem with the vast number of religious denominations and creeds. "Why are there so many, and such greatly diversified religious creeds among men," he asked, "whilst *reason*, and the *great interests* of mankind, would seem to require but *one religion*, capable of embracing the welfare of the whole human race?"[10]

Second, Cassedy questioned the narrowness and exclusivity of the Christian system when compared to the benevolent and philanthropic Creator of the universe. "Let it be supposed . . . that the doctrines of any *one religious sect* were to be made the rule of *judgment* and *condemnation* by the Almighty, at the GREAT DAY OF ACCOUNTS— and, I would ask these *exclusive* sectarians, what would be the awful condition of countless millions of the human race, who would have existed between the commencement and termination of time?" If God adopted but one of the many conflicting creeds or sects as the litmus for salvation in his "*divine* scheme of redemption," Cassedy explained, it would result in "*countless myriads*" of damned people; "*a Universe in ruins*—and an *almost* SOLITARY GOD!!*" He went on to insinuate that the creator of the universe differs from the God of the Bible, and expressed his desire to adopt "some religious faith and practice . . . capable of embracing the *whole human race*." "Exclusive partialities," he continued, "cannot *comport* with the wisdom, the justice, and the *all-absorbing love* of the ALMIGHTY, for his feeble and erring creature, *man!*"[11]

The third obstacle to Cassedy's acceptance of the Christian faith was "the Mosaical account of Creation, as it appears in the first book of Genesis, according to the present translation of the Bible." The immensity and complexity of the universe, Cassedy wrote, proves to all rational human beings "not only the existence of a GOD,…but also that this great *being* must possess infinity of wisdom, omnipotence of power, and perfection of design." Nevertheless, he asked, had Adam not fallen and the curse of death not been given, could the Garden of Eden, or even the entire surface of the planet, have afforded an ample space for the human race? Moreover,

> did the introduction of *death* into the world, by the *fall of man*, change the original conformation of the jaws of carnivorous animals, and make the earth, and the rivers, and the oceans of the globe, theatres of robbery, carnage, and bloodshed? In fine, did the original sin of Adam make the earth bring forth thorns, and briars, and noxious weeds—many, if not all of which, are calculated for the cure of the diseases of our race? And did that original sin produce all the physical, moral, and intellectual disorders, which we every where distinguish among mankind?

"These are some of the difficulties," Cassedy insisted, that inhibited his "selection and adoption of any particular code of Christian faith."[12]

"Your request to the contrary alone," Campbell wrote in his first reply to Cassedy, "prevents me from referring you to my Debate with Mr. Owen, for a rational consideration of some of the more prominent difficulties suggested in your letter." Addressing Cassedy's objection to the varieties of Christian groups and their contradictory messages, Campbell admitted the existence of "false gospels, corruptions, and apostacy" [*sic*]. These "defections" from the true gospel, he added, "are distinctly described and fully delineated by the Apostles themselves." Nevertheless, he reminded his correspondent, "the gospel and its counterfeits must always be regarded as *two* things, wholly and essentially different." The authentic gospel of Jesus Christ, Campbell explained, "is no more changeable with these sects, than is General Washington with the late 'Ordinance' of South Carolina, or with the wars of Bonaparte."[13]

Christianity, Campbell contended, cannot be charged with the problems associated with sectarian arrogance, illiberality, and division. All of these "justly lie" at the "respective doors" of the sects. "Not one of them can plead *Not Guilty* of the allegata, and sustain their plea in the presence of the Bible and right reason." Therefore, he told Cassedy, it is "illogical…to object against the gospel of Jesus, because of the follies and phrensy [*sic*] of sectarians in this cloudy and dark day."[14]

Campbell's second article addressed Cassedy's contention that the God of Christianity is far more narrow and exclusive than the deity found in nature. It is true, Campbell noted, "that some will be saved, and that some will perish with 'an everlasting destruction from the presence of the Lord and the glory of his power,'" but the Scriptures "are as silent as the grave upon the relative proportion of the saved and lost." Moreover, he explained, mankind's habitation of various locations and climates around the world "lays the foundation of ten thousand diversities in the constitutions, character, habits, and circumstances of man." Though all of humankind originated from the same stock, he wrote, nature has given rise to multiple variances as humankind has settled in sundry regions of the world. "From the shivering Greenlander to the sun-burnt Moor, what varieties of stature, figure, complexion, beauty, constitution, do we find!" If diversity is the rule of creation, Campbell asked, "should it be thought an insurmountable objection to the word of eternal life, that all will not— that all cannot embrace it? Does not creation, does not the providence of its Almighty author preach the same lesson in ten thousand varied types, figures, and analogies? Can all of any class become like one of that class, or like one of another class?" "Nature and the Bible," he observed, "speak the same lesson." When "attentively heard, and . . . fairly interpreted," he concluded, the "two witnesses" of nature and Christianity "concur exactly in their testimony concerning God."[15]

Campbell introduced his response to Cassedy's objection to the Mosaic account of creation by claiming that he "would travel on foot a hundred miles, at least, to converse with a sensible man, who had carefully read the Old and New Testaments without a preconceived idea on the contents of these volumes." As with most people, Campbell insisted, Cassedy's understanding of the Bible had been unduly influenced by the thought of some "pseudo-philosopher or priest." "I find you demurring at the narrative of Moses," wrote Campbell, "because his statements correspond not with the assumptions and dicta of the pseudo-philosophers, and of the patented soothsayers and sorcerers of the temple of reason." The crux of the problem in this third difficulty with the Christian religion, he told Cassedy, is that "some one, in some unpropitious moment, gave a false direction to your mind on this subject."[16]

Moses does not affirm that Adam and his descendents would have been confined to the Garden of Eden if sin had not entered the world,

Campbell argued. Furthermore, had Adam avoided the fall and spared mankind the necessity of death, humanity would not have been doomed to an overpopulated existence on this planet. In the Biblical account of Enoch, Campbell continued, God took Enoch out of this world without his experiencing death.[17] Thus, God demonstrated "a way of disposing of our race without the necessity of death or even the enlargement of Eden!" Finally, to Cassedy's query as to whether man's fall reconfigured the jaws of carnivorous animals and brought forth thorns, briars, and noxious weeds upon the earth, Campbell responded with a resounding "no." Instead, Campbell contended, man's fall merely "gave employment" to the aforementioned conditions and situations. They existed previous to the fall, but it was not until after man's fall that they took on their present characteristics and purposes.[18]

The fourth and final essay Campbell wrote in response to the skepticism displayed in Cassedy's letter was more evangelistic than apologetic in content. Noting that Cassedy had "as much at stake as any man living in deciding whether Jesus of Nazareth was an impostor, or the Son of God and the only Savior of the world," Campbell informed his correspondent that he must make a decision to either accept or reject Jesus as the Messiah. "Well attested facts—facts of immense moral power—sustained by the testimony which no honest and rational man, can, after full examination, doubt, constitute the materials of christian faith," he exclaimed. So Campbell asked, "why . . . should you, or any sensible man, hesitate on the question, whether it is more worthy of us to serve God than the Devil, or obey the gospel rather than our corrupt lusts[?]" Should you decide to make Jesus your savior, Campbell concluded, it "would afford me great satisfaction: incomparably more than to see you on the most renowned throne in the four quarters of the globe."[19]

TWO FURTHER QUESTIONS FOR CAMPBELL

Seemingly satisfied with Campbell's explanations for the objections he found in Christianity, Cassedy addressed two additional letters to the editor of the *Millennial Harbinger*. In the first letter Cassedy claimed that he had "perused, and ... reperused" Campbell's essays "with all the attention and depth of interest they so *vitally* and *richly* merit." Moreover, he remarked, "the manner in which you have treated the difficulties I stated to you, has induced me to peruse with attention your debate with Mr. Owen." Cassedy went on to commend Campbell for both his debate performance against Owen and his efforts to restore Christianity to its pristine state. "Your depth of historical research, and philosophic energy of argumentation in that debate, if they have ever been equalled, were, in my estimation, never excelled by any theologian of either ancient or modern days." Furthermore, he wrote, "your vigorous and unremitting efforts ... will probably and ultimately be successful, in bringing back the church of Christ to its primitive purity and simplicity."[20]

Cassedy's next letter questioned the relationship of the church and politics in the United States. The "sectarian theological journals," he stated, report that the Christian elements of society that wish to impose their will upon the country openly boast that they possess "the *wealth* and *numbers*, and would shortly possess the POWER to compel Congress to do as they pleased!" Do they wish to "establish a NATIONAL CHURCH," he inquired, "and enforce the collection of taxes (*tithes*) for this LEVIATHAN of their holy and misdirected zeal?" Moreover, he asked, "would they trammel the consciences of our citizens, and as far as *legislative influence* might be made to extend, compel them to attend their popular congregatings, and conform to their external rites and ceremonies? Can they possibly conceive, that the *human mind* may be *forced* into the belief and adoption of any theological creed, and compelled to direct itself heavenward by the anathemas of the church, or the energies of municipal law?" Responding to his own questions, he explained, "they have yet to learn, that although man may sometimes be made a *hypocrite*, he can never be made a *true believer*, by compulsory or even painful and cruel measures."[21]

Jesus explicitly told Pontius Pilate, Campbell wrote in his reply, "that his kingdom was not *of* this world, though he has a kingdom *in* it." Nevertheless, he explained, many of Jesus' adherents have attempted "to falsify, or at best nullify, this unequivocal declaration." Charging the Roman Catholic Church with turning Christianity into "a kingdom *of this world*," Campbell praised the leaders of the Protestant Reformation for laying "with great violence the axe to the root of the Papal tree." Yet, he claimed, they have failed to flee far enough away from the Church of Rome. In the carnal fashion of the Roman Church, he wrote, the Protestant sects have demanded worldly respect. When such esteem has not been afforded, they have "grasped the sword, after the manner of their old mother, and filled the incredulous with fear and trembling." Thus, Campbell stated, "the sages of the Revolution" were correct in their effort "to keep the civil government out of the church, and thus to remind the preachers that their Master's kingdom was not of this world." "The wisdom of our institutions is, that, irrespective of sectarian *opinions*, men of moral worth are eligible to every office, and that our government knows no man according to his faith," he concluded. "This is all we can expect or wish in the present state of the world."[22]

CASSEDY THE APOLOGIST

Cassedy resumed his letter writing to the *Millennial Harbinger* in July 1836 after a hiatus of nearly three years. Upon noticing an essay entitled "Sketches of the Life of Thomas Paine," which was reprinted in the *Millennial Harbinger* from the *Christian Observer*, Cassedy wrote his brief correspondence for "the correction of a historical error" in the article. Explaining that he had a personal friendship with Thomas Addis Emmet, the executor of Paine's estate, Cassedy noted that the essay incorrectly suggests that Paine, while in France, "seduced" Madame Bonneville from her husband and took her, along with her two sons, to America in 1802. To the contrary, Cassedy reported, Madame Bonneville followed Paine, a family friend, to America after her husband's death. Upon her arrival in America, she moved into Emmet's home and became "a teacher and governess to his daughters."[23] There was, Cassedy asserted, no impropriety in Madame Bonneville's relationship with Paine.

While claiming that he was not "the abettor or apologist of the follies or crimes of any man; and particularly not those of Mr. Paine," Cassedy insisted that the historical mistakes printed in the *Millennial Harbinger* be rectified. "The character of the *Millennial Harbinger*, and the general diffusion of the doctrines it advocates," he wrote, "forbid the supposition that its pages will be unnoticed and unread by posterity." For this reason, he claimed, its pages must be purged of error. Moreover, he argued, Christianity need not rely on false information to support itself against its opposition. "The pure and elevated character" of Christianity, he explained, "requires no *aid* but that of JUSTICE, no *logic* but that of REASON, no *faith* but that which is founded on RATIONAL TESTIMONY." Cassedy went on to chastise Paine for his denunciation of religion, and to suggest that genuine religion is a moralizing force that is essential to political freedom.[24]

Cassedy's objections to those who would contend with Christianity gained additional expression in a two-part article that appeared in the November and December issues of the 1836 *Millennial Harbinger*. "The scriptures inform us that God created man in his own image," the skeptic-turned-apologist wrote, but "irrational reasoners ... attempt to mould an infinite and incomprehensible God in the image of man." Their utter failure to "reduce an infinite Being to finite conceptions and human models" has caused them to "disbelieve in the existence of a God they cannot comprehend." As a result of this disbelief, he continued, atheists explain the visible universe by claiming that "dead and inert matter imparted to itself what it did not originally possess—motion, life, form, *organization*, and *intelligence*." Referring to such beliefs as "the absurd doctrines of Atheism," Cassedy countered them by arguing that "there is nothing ... in the aspect and economy of nature, that does not speak supreme wisdom and perfection of design." "Every thing in nature," he maintained, "demonstrates the existence of a God."[25]

Furthermore, he argued, "a belief in the immortality of the soul" is itself admissible as evidence of a divine creator. "The unquenchable desire in man to be remembered with gratitude and admiration by posterity, is but an emanation of the great sentiment of *immortality*, implanted in the human bosom" by the deity. Through the revelations of nature, he continued, humanity became aware of the existence of "an over-ruling and indefinable Power." This "original and crude idea of DEITY ... furnished the PAGAN with his idol gods of wood and stone." Yet, without Biblical revelation, Cassedy explained, "the pagan, the polytheist, the theist, and the atheist ... merely conceive of the existence and supremacy of *Gods*, which are the creation of their reason or fancy." Only by Scripture, he believed, could humanity fully understand the God that nature had revealed to mankind's intellect.[26]

The existence of God and the belief in an immortal soul that will be judged by God, Cassedy went on to suggest, provides mankind with a moral basis for individual and political government. "Without admitting the immortality of man, and his accountability to a supreme Being," he wrote, "the very foundations of society would be broken up, and present nothing but a bottomless vortex of degeneracy and crime!" Human laws and virtues, he added, would fail to provide humanity with the deterrents to evil that are found in an awaiting day of judgment. How many "secret murders" or "outrages against justice and humanity" would be committed, Cassedy asked, if "not for the deep and awful sentiment of accountability to God, and the apprehensions of the future inflictions of divine punishment?" Without the existence of God and the immortality of the soul, he declared, "the visible beauties and splendors of creation would darken around" humanity. Thus, he concluded, "the being and governing providence of a God, and the immortality of the *human soul*, constitute ... the very basis of the christian religion."[27]

THE VALUE OF EDUCATION

The waning years of the 1830s were an unusually productive period of writing for Cassedy. During his periods of sobriety, Cassedy's fertile mind and active pen generated a vast number of essays (primarily published in Tennessee newspapers) covering a wide array of topics. "The range of subject matter for Cassedy," his biographer notes, "seems to have been unlimited."[28] In addition to writing poems and epitaphs for deceased acquaintances, Cassedy presented his views on such subjects as "abolitionism," Sir Walter Scott, Aaron Burr, and William Henry Harrison, whom he admonished as a "second rate man."[29] Among the issues that most captivated Cassedy's attention during this period was his concern for educational reform, a concern that he shared with Campbell.

To Campbell's thought, education and religious reform were inextricably related. The Christian system, he believed, could only flourish in those areas where people are literate. Not surprisingly, Campbell's inaugural issue of the *Millennial Harbinger* embraced "the inadequacy of all the present systems of education" as one of the primary subjects to be addressed in his new periodical.[30] In addition to his frequent lectures and essays on the topic of education, Campbell established Buffalo Seminary, a short-lived academy that he operated from his home between 1818 and 1823, and Bethany College, which opened in 1841, as institutions of learning in which he put his educational theories into practice. "Next to the gospel," he recorded in an 1838 edition of the *Millennial Harbinger*, education "is the most important of human concerns and interests."[31]

Cassedy echoed Campbell's sentiment for educational reform in the final two essays that he submitted to the *Millennial Harbinger* in early 1839. The latter of the two compositions, a letter explaining his educational philosophy to General William Trousdale (1790-1872), sought the General's assistance in getting his "school book" published. Trousdale, a former state senator and future governor of Tennessee, kindly added a preface to the letter in which he offered a laudatory endorsement of both Cassedy and his ideas.[32] The earlier of the two articles was a rationale for Campbell's publication of the Trousdale letter, though it was not one "of a purely *theological*" nature.[33]

Education, Cassedy wrote in his initial submission, is "a subject which, next to *religion* and *morality*, is of the very highest importance to mankind." The American Revolution's loosening of intellectual and political restraints, he stated, "gave birth to a new era" in which the reform of Christianity could prosper. "All your *attempted* and *distinguished successes*, in reforming and purifying from corruptions and absurd superstitions, the vital and genuine religion of the true scriptural doctrines," he told Campbell, "have resulted from the *very same principles* of INTELLECTUAL IMPROVEMENT, which shed an unfading and imperishable splendor on the causes and events of the American revolution!" Nevertheless, he warned, "reformations in religious codes and abuses can go no further than the *moral* and *intellectual* freedom of the human mind can be protected and fostered by the liberal policy and tolerant spirit of popular political power." As such, Cassedy believed it was time for a national revolution "in the ancient and absurd systems of education."[34]

"Two-thirds—three-fourths of the education now given to the American youth," Cassedy alleged in his letter to Trousdale, "is not merely useless, but entirely *imaginative*." To revolutionize American education, Cassedy called for an end to instructing students in Greek and Latin—"the dead languages." Insisting that "a profound knowledge of language" is essential to the advancement and improvement of "the American national character," Cassedy made it clear that he meant a knowledge of "the language we speak, and that on which our best literary and political works are written, and THAT ALONE." Furthermore, he argued, a genuine educational reform must include mass public education.

Education, in this country, ought to be directed to the condition and improvement of the great mass of the people, because here, and here alone, the will of the people constitutes the basis of the government, the laws, and even the policy of our institutions: in truth, the government of this republic can alone be perpetuated by rendering the great body of the people sufficiently intelligent and virtuous to govern themselves. The privileged classes, by which I mean the *wealthy*, can educate themselves in any manner they please: it is not so with the great popular mass—and it is, therefore, that the means of education ought to be brought to their very doors.[35]

Cassedy continued his effort to reform American education, finally publishing his *North American Spelling, Defining, and Reading Manual of the American Language on a New Plan* in 1846, but his efforts fell far short of his desire to see an educational revolution that would sweep across the country.

CASSEDY'S FINAL YEARS

Little information exists about the final twelve years of Cassedy's life, though he was registered as a resident of the Sumner County poor house in 1850. At age sixty-eight, the document records, Cassedy was unable to walk because "his hips out of joint."[36] Two years later Cassedy made his final appearance before the public when he wrote a detailed report to Governor William Bowen Campbell (1807-1867) about the pathetic living conditions for inhabitants of county alms houses. Noting the graft, patient abuse, and corruption that characterize the "poor houses," Cassedy asked the governor to order an investigation of the management of the institutions. The "few rights of the poor," he argued, "ought to be strictly guarded by the laws of all countries."[37]

Though no records or details of Cassedy's death exist, he is known to have died between June 7, 1857 and May 30, 1858. Shortly after writing his report on alms houses to the governor, Cassedy took up residence with the A. R. Wynne family of Castalian Springs, Tennessee. On the evening of June 7, 1857, Cassedy dictated a poem to one of the Wynne children.[38] The next known reference to Cassedy is a May 30, 1858 letter to the Wynne family, in which "the late Charles Cassedy" is mentioned. As to his final resting-place, Durham reports that a tradition within the Winchester family suggests that "Cassedy's body was buried in one of two unmarked graves in the family cemetery at Cragfont."[39]

With the death of Cassedy, Campbell lost both a supporter who held him in the highest estimation and a convert who went on to assist him in his apologetic efforts. What is most remarkable about Campbell's relationship with Cassedy is that the Tennessee writer began his association with the Sage of Bethany as a critic who opposed the Christian system that Campbell so avidly embraced and adored. The fact that debates and controversies seldom conclude with a conversion from among the disputants did not escape Campbell's attention. Nor, one must surmise, did the fact that Cassedy abandoned his enmity toward Christianity. When Cassedy presented Campbell with his objections to Christianity and then reviewed Campbell's responses to the allegations, Cassedy ended up acknowledging the legitimacy of Campbell's affirmations and accepted the claims of the Christian religion. Cassedy did not merely agree to an ethereal metaphysical premise about the possibility of a divine being's existence, but he became an avid proponent of Campbell's Christian beliefs and ideas. In addition to writing an apology to uphold the claims of Christianity in the face of its enemies, Cassedy became a passionate advocate of the educational reform measures that he believed would benefit the advancement of Campbell's religious reform.

8

COMBATING THE NEW SKEPTICS: UNIVERSALISM, UNITARIANISM, AND SPIRITUALISM

Controversial beliefs about the nature of God and the doctrine of salvation appeared long before the development of America's Unitarian and Universalist denominations. The extensive legacy of the universal-salvation and anti-trinitarian groups of Christian history had an unmistakable influence on the appearance of the original Unitarian and Universalist churches in America. Nevertheless, as Paul Conkin aptly affirms, "the Unitarian and Universalist denominations in America were largely indigenous, rooted originally in New England puritanism and shaped doctrinally and institutionally by American religious innovators."[1]

The evangelical Christians of America's antebellum period generally associated Universalists and Unitarians with other forms of skepticism or unbelief. "Universalists," according to Albert Post, "were regarded as worse than infidels because they hid their unbelief under the cloak of Christianity."[2] Alexis de Tocqueville and Thomas Low Nichols expressed a similar disdain for Unitarians by referring to them as "deists" who maintained a semblance of Christianity only to deflect the opposition they would otherwise have received from the more orthodox strands of Christianity in their day.[3] Francis J. Grund echoed this sentiment when he suggested that Unitarians "either go further on the road to Deism, or retrace their steps, and become more dogmatical Christians."[4]

Like many of his contemporaries, Campbell regarded Unitarianism and Universalism as unmitigated forms of skepticism that attempted to shield their heretical ideas behind a thin veneer of Christian orthodoxy. "There is but a very narrow isthmus between absolute scepticism and [Universalism]," he told his readers in 1844.[5] He also insisted that the ultimate outworking of Universalism was unbelief. Orestes Brownson (1803-1876) and "some of the most prominent Universalists in the country," he wrote, have abandoned their Universalist beliefs for "the doctrines of Frances Wright, R. D. Owen, & Co."[6] Equally distasteful to Campbell were the anti-trinitarian ideas of the Unitarians. Claiming Unitarianism as "another name for deism," Campbell pointedly insisted that the movement "is not Christianity" because it attempts to "*undeify* the second Adam—the Lord from heaven, and the Lord of heaven!"[7]

From early on in his publishing career, Campbell made it clear that he opposed the doctrine of Universalism. "We are very sure that all the Universalists on earth," he wrote in 1825, "cannot produce one sentence in all the revelation of God that says any thing about the termination of the punishment of the wicked." Furthermore, "I am content to be assured that whosoever hears the gospel and believes and obeys it, *shall be saved*, and that whosoever hears it and disbelieves it, *shall be damned*."[8] Nevertheless, Campbell was frequently called upon to clarify his position on Universalism, and was occasionally applauded within the Universalist press.[9] In *The Sentinel, and Star in the West*, a weekly Universalist periodical published in Cincinnati, Ohio, the editors commended Campbell for his efforts to reform Christianity and wished him "God speed" with his further work.[10] The praise he received from the *Sentinel* was short lived, however, as Campbell soon became an object of contempt among many Universalists.

JONATHAN KIDWELL (1779-1849)

Campbell's contentions with the Universalists began in 1831 when he learned that the Unitarians and Universalists were claiming a unity of faith with him. In response to their assertions, the Bethany editor produced a brief essay explicitly stating the opposite: "We fraternize with none who preach that he that believeth not, shall be saved, nor with any called *Unitarians*, who give to Jesus no higher honors than to Moses."[11] The imminent reply of Jonathan Kidwell, the most vocal and immoderate member of the *Sentinel*'s editorial staff, touched off a lengthy dispute between the two editors that eventually led to further Universalist conflicts for Campbell.

As a native of Mt. Sterling, Kentucky, Kidwell was raised in the Methodist church, but converted to Universalism around 1815. He soon became a traveling evangelist and editor, and was among the earliest proponents of Universalism in Indiana and the western part of Ohio. Kidwell's well-deserved reputation as a radical Universalist emerged from his apparent delight in attacking the cherished doctrines of both the orthodox Christians and his fellow Universalists. He eventually rejected the biblical account of creation, the observance of Sunday worship, the inspiration of Scripture, and all supernatural occurrences. Kidwell was not only a lightning rod of contention among evangelical Christians, according to Russell E. Miller, but was also "a thorn in the side of 'respectable' Universalists everywhere."[12]

Kidwell responded to Campbell's "An Evil Report Corrected" by deriding the editor of the *Millennial Harbinger* for loving notoriety more than truth. "He knows universalism is not popular," Kidwell wrote, so he has distanced himself from this unpopular view and has misrepresented its ideas. Kidwell went on to invite Campbell to "justify his unfriendly insinuations," and promised that the *Sentinel's* columns would be "at his service" for the publication of his articles.[13] Campbell agreed to "expose the absurdities" of the Universalist system and "show its inevitable tendency to Deism or something worse," so long as Kidwell agreed to the following four conditions: he must maintain the openness of his paper until the argument is completed, define his ideas regarding "universal salvation," abstain from "scurrility" in his handling of the articles, and adhere to the established rules of scriptural interpretation.[14]

Campbell's acceptance of Kidwell's solicitation to sustain his allegations against Universalism provoked a perplexing response from the senior editor of the *Sentinel*. Rather than acknowledging Campbell's agreement to uphold his assertions, Kidwell informed his readers that Campbell had actually "invited us into the field of battle" and demanded "the use of our columns for his arguments." Nonetheless, Kidwell boastfully acceded to the challenge he attributed to Campbell and provided a rejoinder to the four issues of concern that his counterpart raised. First, he agreed to keep the *Sentinel's* columns open, provided Campbell would print his counter essays in the *Harbinger*. He then went on to define "universal salvation" as the belief "that all men, universally, will be saved by Jesus Christ." Next he consented to confine himself to "sober argument" if Campbell would do the same. Finally, he resolved to "abide by any rules of interpretation of scripture warranted by reason, scripture analogy, and the context," though he insisted that he was unaware of any "established rules of interpretation of scripture."[15]

In a followup article, Kidwell expressed his contentment with Campbell's willingness to grapple with the claims of Universalism. "One weighty consideration . . . which induces us to admit Mr. Campbell into our columns with no small degree of pleasure," he wrote, "is the fact that Mr. C. is the first man of talents who has had the moral courage to make a formal attack on us." Noting that Campbell had been "very successful in battle," Kidwell assured his readers that his opponent's "strength and skill in warfare has not been fairly tried." Campbell's contention with Universalism, he argued, will be "the first time he has attempted to lay siege to a fortified city." Moreover, he concluded, even "if it were possible for Mr. C. to convince us that our system of faith did inevitably lead to Deism, or even Atheism, we should feel bound to embrace it, unless he should be able to show us something better than orthodoxy."[16]

The first of Campbell's three articles to the *Sentinel* was little more than a reply to Kidwell's recriminations. In an effort to set the record straight, Campbell explained that he had not challenged Kidwell to a discussion, but had accepted Kidwell's invitation to present his reasons for opposing Universalism. Campbell also objected to Kidwell's demand for inclusion of the Universalist arguments in his *Millennial Harbinger*. Although he had "intended to publish the whole controversy . . . if it should be interesting," Campbell insisted that it was too late to make stipulations after the invitation had already been acknowledged. A further point of dissension was Kidwell's use of "Drury Lane or Grub Street Rhetoric," which does not, according to Campbell, "comport with the gravity and deliberation of religious discussion." Promising that he would not reply to Kidwell's use of such language, Campbell called for "argument and testimony" rather than "this species of ribaldry and buffoonery." Campbell concluded his essay by describing Kidwell's definition of universal salvation as "indefinite and ambiguous," and by suggesting a few standard works on the rules of interpretation for his opponent's consideration.[17]

Kidwell's verbose "Analysis of Mr. Campbell's Remarks" reiterated many of his earlier allegations against Campbell and repeated his claim that Campbell had actually been the aggressor of the argument. While describing Campbell as "slow of understanding," Kidwell charged that his adversary had no "tangible foundation" for his contentions with

Universalism. "If he was about to meet Mr. M'Calla or Mr. Owen, over whose systems he has such a decided advantage," wrote Kidwell, "he would not delay the blow; but he knows notwithstanding all his sneers and flouts about the logic and candor of universalism, that it is not easy to combat."[18]

Campbell's second critique of Universalism accentuated Kidwell's propensity for defamation rather than logical reasoning. Prior to viewing his first article's appearance in the *Sentinel* (and the extensive response by Kidwell), Campbell observed in his second essay that he had already received "four columns of abuse" from the Universalist editors.[19] Amid all of this, he insisted, the editors of the *Sentinel* have failed to suggest even "one proposition or argument in reference . . . to their peculiar system of universal holiness and salvation." "They pretend to be misrepresented and slandered," wrote Campbell, but they refuse to provide a "definite understanding" of their beliefs. Finding their incessant lament over his refusal to accept their "*ex post facto* conditions" for the discussion baseless, Campbell reminded his adversary that the leading Universalist in the nation, Hosea Ballou (1771-1852), proclaimed the terms of the dialogue "fair and equitable."[20]

In a final endeavor to get their discourse underway, Campbell acquiesced to Kidwell's complaints by offering him his own terms in the disputation. By allowing his counterpart to select the propositions he deemed most easily defended, Campbell recognized that he had granted very generous terms of debate to Kidwell. His willingness to do this arose from his conviction that Universalism could not be sustained because "it is wholly destitute of any countenance or support from the Author of the Christian Religion or any of his Apostles."[21]

Campbell's third and final essay to Kidwell analyzed a quote extracted from the April 21, 1832, edition of the *Sentinel*. Because the editors of the *Sentinel* refused to provide a proposition for discussion, Campbell selected their comments on Revelation 21:8-9 "as one definite exposé of their logic, grammar, and theology." As to their logic, Campbell noted, the editors of the *Sentinel* relied on Dr. Adam Clarke's (1760-1832) claim that "the bride, the Lamb's wife," of Revelation 21:9, refers to "the pure and holy Christian Church."[22] As such, they went on to contend, the "abominable characters" of Revelation 21:8 (i.e., the fearful, unbelieving, abominable, murderers, whoremongers, sorcerers, idolaters, and liars), are merely "excluded from the church of Christ *on earth*." In making their case, Campbell pointed out, the Universalist editors accept

Clarke's contention that the "Lamb's wife" (or the "New Jerusalem") is "the pure and holy Christian Church," while rejecting his conclusion that the "second death" is a place "from which there is no recovery." If "Clarke's views of *the New Jerusalem* are to be relied on in an argument, ought not his views on *the second death* to be equally relied on in the same argument?" Campbell asked. "Logic answers, Yes," he noted, "but the editors [of the *Sentinel*], in practice, say No."[23]

With regard to grammar, Campbell noted that his opponents' statement that the "abominable characters" of Revelation 21:8 "ARE excluded from the church of Christ *on earth*," changes the tense of the Revelation passage, which says these characters "SHALL HAVE their part in the lake which burneth with fire and brimstone." The difference between *are* and *shall have*, Campbell explained, is that "the one denotes the present only, and the other denotes all that is future." So, to state that "the righteous *shall have* their part" and "the wicked *shall have* their part" is not equivalent to saying that the "righteous *have* their part" and "the wicked *have* their part."[24]

As a theological "specimen" of Universalist thought, Campbell pointed to his antagonists' claims that the "abominable characters" of the Revelation passage will be excluded only from the church on earth. He then reminded them that they had stated in an earlier article that Universalists do not preach "that the unrighteous should inherit the kingdom of God; that he that believed not should be saved; [nor] that murderers, whoremongers, liars, &c. should have a part in the New Jerusalem."[25] The correspondence of these ideas, Campbell argued, necessitates the existence of some third church—"which is neither the church on earth, nor the church in heaven"—to which these abominable characters go after departing this life. That such a purgatorial place exists, he insisted, is totally foreign to the Bible.[26]

Kidwell responded to Campbell's third essay with a scathing attack on the Bethany editor and a statement of his decision to cease publishing any of Campbell's further writings. Declaring himself "quite out of patience" with Campbell, Kidwell told his readers that the most recent Campbell article would be "the last piece of his scurrility with which we will defile our paper." Kidwell's lengthy remarks endeavored to provide a rejoinder to Campbell's challenges to the logic, grammar, and theology of Universalism, but his primary objective was to vilify his rival rather than to answer him. In Campbell, he wrote, "we expected to find the dignified scholar, the candid critic, the sober reasoner, the gentleman, the christian, and a clergyman of deep research: but to our utter astonishment and mortification we find the man precisely the reverse of our expectations—a mere superficial polylogist—a quibbler—a sounding brass—a tinkling symbol; whose element is low wit, calumny, dull sarcasm, insult and abuse."[27]

Upon learning about Kidwell's announced decision to forego any of his future articles, Campbell immediately declared himself the victor over both Universalism and the editors of the *Sentinel*. Their reluctance to accept further essays, Campbell announced, "ends the boast of Messrs. Kidwell and S. Tizzard!!!!" Moreover, he explained, "any *gentleman*" who "thinks that he can sustain Universalism" will have the pages of the *Millennial Harbinger* "open to him under equal and impartial laws."[28]

By the time of Campbell's announced victory in late 1832, Kidwell had become busy with "an ambitious plan to establish a [Universalist] seminary of learning in the Midwest." Along with this he planned "to create a community which would become a center for Universalism and a rival to the unofficial headquarters of the denomination in the East." The location he settled upon for his Universalist academy and community was the abandoned town of Bethlehem, Indiana. In 1833, Kidwell renamed the town Philomath ("lover of learning") and relocated to the community with the editors of the *Sentinel*. From Philomath, Kidwell maintained his editorial duties with the *Sentinel* until 1836, as he recruited residents for his new town and established the Western Union Seminary in 1833.[29]

Amid his relocation and efforts to procure students and faculty for his seminary, Kidwell continued to express virulent opposition to Campbell in the pages of the *Sentinel*. To Campbell's claim of victory, Kidwell responded by stating that his opponent had actually "backed out" of the controversy and could in no way claim to have triumphed in the contest. "This mighty polemic, who has divided the Baptist church, made other sects to tremble, and defied the universalists," Kidwell wrote, "has played the coward . . . and retreated from the field of action, without ever attempting to come to an engagement." He went on to call for a renewed debate with Campbell, saying that he would "attack Mr. Campbell on his own ground" if he refuses a public meeting.[30]

Without so much as a notice of his rantings by Campbell, Kidwell zealously attempted to draw his antagonist into a heated battle. Not only did he issue a number of inflammatory articles about Campbell, but he also misrepresented Campbell and his beliefs to the audiences he amassed on his frequent preaching tours.[31] Not until 1837, when Kidwell produced a series of articles on the Campbell-Owen debate in his new monthly tabloid, the *Philomath Encyclopedia*,[32] did Campbell respond to the boasts and challenges of his antagonist. In his six-month run of articles on the Campbell-Owen debate, Kidwell insisted that the "wordy conflict" brought about no conclusive results. Nevertheless, he aligned himself with Owen's positions in the debate and "linked himself with Owen as 'a fellow infidel.'"[33]

Campbell replied to Kidwell's challenges by noting that he had declined a public meeting "because of the coarseness and abusiveness of [Kidwell's] style, and the vulgarisms of his manner as a disputant with those who dissented from him."[34] Kidwell maintained his effort to lure Campbell into a controversy, but the two men would never again have a formal confrontation.

For Kidwell, his Western Union Seminary ceased to exist after less that a decade of operation and his communal experiment at Philomath became an "unmitigated personal financial disaster."[35] He ultimately died in Philomath in 1849. For Campbell, the controversy with Kidwell was a stepping stone to a further discussion of Universalism with Dolphus Skinner, the esteemed editor of the *Evangelical Magazine and Gospel Advocate*.

DOLPHUS SKINNER (1800-1869)

What ultimately evolved into the written debate between Campbell and Skinner began with a letter to the *Millennial Harbinger* from an individual identified as "Spencer." Spencer's epistle questioned Campbell on the Greek terms *gehenna* (generally translated "hell") and *aion* (generally translated "eternal"). "It does not appear," he told Campbell, "that the term *gehenna* was ever used by the Jews to express future punishment . . . but was used by them in reference to the Valley of Hinnom, near Jerusalem." "Thus it seems that *hell fire* and *damnation of hell* simply mean temporal judgment, executed in the Valley of Hinnom." Spencer further stated that the term *aion* (and its Hebrew counterpart, *olem*) refers to indistinct periods of time that are not always unending in duration.[36]

Campbell's answer directed Spencer to recognize that "God has spoken in human speech to mortal man" and has thus used "the imagery of nature, and the costume of society," to convey his divine, spiritual, and eternal ideas to humankind. Therefore, Campbell argued, "the unfigurative delineations of things" must be "the landmarks of thought and inquiry by which the interpretations of metaphor, parable, and allegory are to be authoritatively decided."

Hence, when without figure, and with all the clearness and authority of supreme law, it is promulgated by the Christian Lawgiver, "He that shall believe and shall have been immersed shall be saved; and he that will not believe shall be damned, or condemned"—no allusion to ancient customs—no figurative representations through the imagery of nature, or costume of society, can have authority to make it read or mean, "He that shall believe, and shall have been immersed, shall be saved; and he that will not believe shall also be saved." *Saved* and *condemned* are opposites, and no reasoning upon any figure, custom, or form of speech, can make them identical. If *saved* is temporal, so is *condemned*; if *saved* is corporeal, so is *condemned*:

Figure 10 – Dolphus Skinner

As the influential editor of the *Evangelical Magazine and Gospel Advocate*, Dolphus Skinner (1800-1869) of Utica, New York, was among the most prominent and highly respected Universalists in the United States. When Campbell sought a credible adversary with whom to discuss the doctrines of universal salvation and eternal punishment, Skinner was recommended as the most competent of all American Universalists.

but *saved* and *condemned* are two states, fates, or fortunes, that
are perfect contrasts.

Amid all the debate about the meaning of *gehenna* or *aion*, Campbell
insisted, "eternal life and eternal death remain the immutable and invincible sanctions of God's last message to mankind." Moreover, he concluded, "he is no friend of Jesus who preaches that he who believeth not
shall be saved; or who infers that the righteous and the wicked shall after
death be equally pure, holy and happy for one moment or for duration
without end."[37]

From the pen of George W. Montgomery, a young Universalist minister from Auburn, New York, came a letter of reply to Campbell's epistle
to Spencer. Montgomery agreed with Campbell's contention that the
words "saved" and "condemned" are "direct opposites," but he argued
that their use in Mark 16:16 does not necessarily imply an unending
condition of existence. "If the passage does not refer to a future state,"
Montgomery wrote, "you will at once discover, that a person through life
may experience the miseries of unbelief [i.e., condemnation], and still,
by the chastising hand of God, become like the reformed prodigal [i.e.,
saved]." Furthermore, he maintained, the adjectives "everlasting" and
"eternal" do not always mean never ending, but they are "terms determined by the various subjects to which they are applied." Thus, just as
the word "tall" has differing interpretations when used to describe a man
and a tree, so "everlasting" and "eternal" must be defined in reference to
their subject.[38]

In addressing Montgomery's first item of dissent, Campbell pointed
out that the young Universalist concurred with his belief that the conditions of being "saved" and "condemned" are "two states essentially opposite." Yet "you will . . . have the believer and the unbeliever during this life
in opposite states, but in the same state hereafter." Universalist theology,
Campbell explained, places the believer in a state of salvation in both this
life and the afterlife. The unbeliever, however, resides in a state of condemnation in this life, but receives salvation in the next. Ultimately, he
therefore concluded, Universalists see no distinction between the words
"salvation" and "condemnation"—an absurdity that even Montgomery
has admitted.[39]

Addressing Montgomery's second issue of dissent, Campbell said he
agreed with the Universalist's contention that "adjectives sometimes . . .
take their peculiar meaning from the subjects to which they are applied."

Such a usage of the adjectives "eternal" and "everlasting," he suggested, explains the frequent application of these words in a limited sense. These words are "used *figuratively* . . . when applied to all things that *necessarily* must have an end," but not when the subjects to which they are applied do not require a limited sense. Therefore, to show a figurative use of "eternal" or "everlasting" for things beyond this life, the Universalist must show that "there is such a necessity existing as to preclude the possibility of its being used literally, or in its proper signification." And this "is a task that no living man can do." Because we cannot make an accurate judgment on the necessity of limitation with regard to things that are not of this life, "these words must be taken literally."[40]

Some four months after printing the Montgomery letter and his reply to it, Campbell had the opportunity to make the acquaintance of the young Universalist while on a speaking tour that took him through New York. At their meeting, Montgomery asked Campbell if he would engage him in a discussion of Universalism through the pages of the *Millennial Harbinger*. Campbell politely declined the youthful minister's debate invitation, but offered instead to confront one of the more notable members of the Universalist sect. "I would . . . rather encounter some of the older giants . . . of Universalism," he said, "for if I killed [Montgomery], these sons of Hercules would say I only killed a mere stripling, which would be unmanly and dishonorable." When asked for his opinion about the leading figures in the Universalist movement, Montgomery informed Campbell about "the mighty men in Boston," but "represented Mr. Skinner, of Utica, to be as competent as the best of them; nay perhaps, '*a more ready writer than any of them*.'" Thus, Campbell agreed to a dialogue with Skinner if he was unable to enter into a public discussion with any of the Universalists he would encounter on his preaching tour to Boston.[41]

After returning from his New England trip without an invitation for debate from the Universalists of Boston, Campbell soon received a letter from Skinner asking when the Bethany editor would like to resume the discussion on Universalism. "Mr. Montgomery," Skinner wrote, "says he transfers the controversy on the part of the Universalists into my hands for continuance."[42] Owing to his previously arranged commitment to debate the Roman Catholic Bishop John B. Purcell in January 1837, Campbell requested that they hold off their discussion until the spring. He also asked Skinner about having a "*face to face* discussion" that could be recorded by a stenographer and published for the world's inspection.[43] Skinner, however, opted for a written discussion, claiming that it would be "the freest from personalities, from passions, and from rash, hasty, and inconsiderate remarks."[44] Consequently, Skinner's epistle of February 10, 1837, began an exchange of forty letters between February 1837 and July 1839, in which the two men debated the tenets of Universalism. Both sides of the debate were published in each editor's respective tabloid throughout the duration of the correspondence, and at the close of the discussion the forty letters were compiled and published as *A Discussion of the Doctrines of Endless Misery and Universal Salvation: In an Epistolary Correspondence Between Alexander Campbell and Dolphus Skinner* (1840).

Though little has been written about Dolphus Skinner, he was a major figure among America's antebellum Universalists. Born on May 18, 1800, in Westmoreland, New Hampshire, Skinner spent much of his early life laboring on his father's farm and studying at a nearby academy. Around the age of twenty, Skinner and Lemuel Willis (1802-1878), a neighbor and friend, resolved to devote themselves to the Universalist ministry and began their theological studies under the guidance of Universalist minister Samuel C. Loveland (1787-1854). Upon completion of his education in 1822, Skinner traveled about New England as an evangelist, though he was not officially ordained by the denomination until September 1823. His itinerant preaching came to an abrupt end in September 1825 when he married Gratia Walker and settled into the located ministry of the Universalist church at Saratoga Springs, New York. After two years at the Sarasota Springs church, Skinner relocated to a ministry in Utica, New York, where he resided for the remainder of his life.

Shortly after his 1827 arrival in Utica, Skinner began his career as a successful editor of Universalist periodicals. His first publication, the *Utica Magazine*, scarcely existed for a year until it was merged with Lemuel Willis' *Evangelical Repository* to form the *Utica Evangelical Magazine*. Skinner and Willis co-edited the *Utica Evangelical Magazine* from April 1828 to March 1829, when Willis resigned his editorial position with the paper and Skinner shortened its title to simply the *Evangelical Magazine*. In 1830, Skinner purchased the *Gospel Advocate*, a Universalist paper issued from Buffalo, New York, forming a new tabloid, The *Evangelical Magazine and Gospel Advocate* Skinner led the periodical to "a circulation which no paper among Universalists had hitherto attained." He continued his association with this magazine until it was merged into the *Christian Messenger* in early 1851.[45]

In addition to the fame he gained from his editorial work, Skinner was widely recognized among Universalists as a popular speaker and a proponent of education. He was a renowned evangelist throughout New York, a prominent participant in many of the national Universalist gatherings, and a well-traveled lecturer on behalf of the anti-slavery and temperance movements.[46] Skinner also played a significant role in the 1831 founding of the Clinton Liberal Institute (1831-1900), a Univeralist-operated secondary school in Clinton, New York.[47] When financial difficulties threatened the school in 1858, Skinner again emerged as a champion of the institute and became the "principal fundraiser" who saved it from bankruptcy.[48] Until his death in 1869, Skinner remained a stalwart advocate of Universalism.

Skinner's primary contention in his debate with Campbell was that the doctrine of "endless misery" would essentially "transform our Creator into a fiend of infinite cruelty, clothe heaven in sackcloth and mourning, and fill the universe with sighs and tears."[49] Because God is omnipotent and all-loving, he further argued, his purpose is not to punish the wicked throughout eternity, but to reform them so that they can enter into his holy and eternal presence. To combat the belief in endless punishment, Skinner proffered ten philosophical arguments against it:

1. It would be *useless*, having no possible pleasure, honor, or profit for any being in the universe.
2. It is absolutely *pernicious*, making God an example of infinite malignity and revenge insatiable.
3. It *dishonors God* by suggesting that he could not or would not prevent it.
4. It denies the infinite *benevolence* of God, who is eternally good to every being he has ever created.
5. It denies the *mercy* of God, which cannot exist if any are left to suffer eternal misery.
6. It opposes the *wisdom* of God by suggesting that he did not have the foreknowledge to provide a means of preventing so great a misfortune to himself and his creatures.
7. It opposes the *power* of God by suggesting that his stated desire that all should be saved can not be fulfilled by him.
8. It opposes the *justice* of God in that it makes God inflict infinite and endless penalties for finite and limited transgressions.

9. It opposes the *veracity* of God, who declared that he will
   not contend forever, nor be always wroth (Isaiah 57:16),
   and that he will not cast off forever (Lamentations 3:31).
10. It opposes the general voice of revelation, and the numerous positive declarations of the Bible in favor of the final
   salvation of all men.

"Therefore," Skinner concluded, "endless punishment can not be true."[50]

In reply to Skinner's philosophical arguments favoring a curative punishment, Campbell explained that his opponent's view necessitates a reform in the lives of *every* chastised individual. Because Universalists teach that all human beings will gain access to heaven and God's chastisement is the method by which the wicked are reformed into holy beings worthy of heaven, it is essential that all people respond to punishment with reformed lives. Nevertheless, he persisted, "multitudes are often punished for drunkenness, licentiousness, and a thousand other vices, and afterwards die in the act of transgressing." Without any evidence whatsoever, exclaimed Campbell, one must "assume that what fails in this life will be successfully prosecuted in the next, and that punishment will be increased and perpetuated in another world till the incorrigible in this life shall become holy." Moreover, he scoffed, "satan and the rebel hosts are not reformed by six thousand years' banishment from the presence of God; and there is no reason to conclude that satan and all other imprisoned spirits are any nigher holiness and happiness now than they were thousands of years since."[51]

Campbell further questioned his opponent's view of the essential role Christ's death played in the redemption of humanity. If God can chastise persons only for their benefit, but never for the sake of his holy vengeance against evil then why did Jesus suffer and die on the cross? "Was it for his own good[?] Was it for his own reformation[?] Was it for an example to others to sustain sufferings when they were themselves holy, harmless, undefiled, and separate from sin[?] For what did he suffer through life, and for what did he die[?] Did he die to expiate the sins of men, or for his own sins, to magnify God's law and make it honorable; or merely to prove his own sincerity[?] . . . for what did he die?" The Universalist system, he added, professes no need for "Christ, or Holy Spirit, or Bible, or preacher, or faith, hope, and love, in order to [obtain] future happiness."[52]

In the conclusion of his twenty-sixth letter to the Universalist editor, Campbell offered three philosophical absurdities associated with Skinner's system of Universalism. The first absurdity was that they "make punishment annihilate itself." Punishment "ceases by its own operations upon itself," he explained. "In working reformation it kills itself. What else in nature," he asked, "annihilates itself?" The second absurdity was that Universalists "make the effect destroy its cause." "Suffering is not the cause, but the effect, of sin," he wrote, "yet you make suffering, the effect, destroy sin, its cause!!" In the last of his three absurdities, Campbell suggested that Universalists "represent the sinner as saved by obeying a broken law, inasmuch as you make his *post mortem* salvation the fruit of his obedience to the divine requisitions which on earth he contemned: for you teach that the sinner passes out of Purgatory upon his repentance, and obedience to that law, which, on earth, in his first state, he disobeyed. Thus you give to your law of justification a new power—the power of both condemning and justifying the same person!!"[53]

Robert Richardson awarded Campbell the clear victory in the contest, saying he "confuted the Universalist arguments, and proved the certainty of future punishment." He went on to state that the discussion "excited but little interest" because "much of it consisted in mere debates about words and criticisms upon translations of certain words." As a result of "Skinner's quibbling and abusive course in the discussion," Richardson further noted, Campbell regretted his willingness to provide space for Skinner in the *Millennial Harbinger*.[54] Therefore, when Campbell was satisfied that the contest had fairly run its course, he brought it to a close and freely offered the copyright for publication of the work to Skinner. "If you or your friends decline, I presume the right will be conceded to me?"[55] Campbell indeed wanted to see the dispute published, explained W. K. Pendleton (1817-1899), but "he preferred Mr. Skinner should publish it, as the surest way of getting it circulated among the Universalists, whom he especially desired to read it."[56] Skinner did, in fact, publish the debate and Campbell promoted its sale in his *Millennial Harbinger*.[57]

JESSE BABCOCK FERGUSON (1819-1870)

The uncivil nature of Campbell's controversies with both Kidwell and Skinner brought a significant turnaround in his attitude toward Universalism as a privately held opinion. While Campbell had never espoused Universalism himself, he had, as a young man, argued for the right of an associate to maintain a private belief in Universalism. In 1828, Aylette Raines (1788-1881), a young Universalist minister who converted to Campbell's fledgling movement, was in danger of being dis-fellowshipped because of his continuing belief in some of the tenets of Universalism. When the issue was raised before a group of ministers, both Thomas and Alexander Campbell argued for Raines' freedom to hold any opinion that is not expressly addressed in Scripture. Despite his philosophical differences with Raines, Thomas Campbell went so far as to say that he would put his "right hand into the fire and have it burnt off" rather than raise it in opposition to Raines. In wholehearted agreement with his father, Alexander Campbell "then made some remarks . . . defining the difference between faith and opinion." Raines' ideas belonged solely within the realm of opinion, he insisted, thus no one can cast judgment upon him.[58] By the conclusion of his conflicts with Kidwell and Skinner, however, Campbell no longer accepted Universalism as merely a private opinion, but as a heresy as dangerous as unbelief itself.

Campbell's acquired distrust of even the slightest hint of Universalist theology came to the fore in 1852 when Jesse Babcock Ferguson, a popular preacher and editor within the Campbellite movement, posited some of the same Universalist ideas that Aylett Raines had expressed in 1828. Ferguson's dramatic rise to prominence within the Disciples of Christ would later be matched by an equally dramatic demise and withdrawal from the fellowship. H. Leo Boles vividly compared Ferguson to "a meteor which flashes across the horizon, making a trail of glorious light behind it, and then suddenly disappearing and leaving nothing but darkness in its wake."[59]

Ferguson was born in Philadelphia, Pennsylvania, but his parents relocated to the Shenandoah Valley of Virginia shortly after his birth. At the age of eleven, the studious young Ferguson entered the Fair View Academy with a desire for future studies at the College of William and Mary. His father's financial misfortunes, however, dashed his dreams for a college education and prompted him to become a printer's apprentice during his fourteenth year. When his employer's bankruptcy brought his apprenticeship to an end after little more than a year, Jesse's father procured another position for his son with a book printer in Baltimore, Maryland. This job also ended quickly for Jesse when he came down with a sickness known as "white swelling" and was dispatched to the care of his home. After a three-month convalescence, Jesse was left a cripple for the duration of his life. Once he had recovered enough to carry on with his life, the young apprentice was placed under the direction of his brother, who had recently become the editor of a Virginia newspaper.

This position afforded Jesse the opportunity to study on his own and to complete courses of study in Greek and Latin.[60]

After settling in Logan County, Ohio, in 1838, Ferguson married Lucinda Mark, opened a small school, and embarked upon a career as an itinerant evangelist.[61] Though little is known about the influences that drew him into ministry, it appears that Ferguson was attracted to the Disciples of Christ from the start of his preaching career.[62] During this period Ferguson also began writing for the *Heretic Detector*, a periodical published by Arthur Crihfield at Middleburg, Ohio. Ferguson's first effort as an editor also came with the *Heretic Detector*, when he and Crihfield

(Courtesy of Disciples of Christ Historical Society, Nashville, Tennessee)

Figure 11 – Jesse Babcock Ferguson

Once the prominent preacher of the Nashville Church of Christ and the noted editor of the *Christian Magazine*, Jesse Babcock Ferguson (1819-1870) withdrew from Campbell's Restoration Movement after advancing the ideas of Spiritualism, Universalism, and Unitarianism. After his break from the Campbell movement, Ferguson traveled throughout the United States and Europe lecturing on spiritualism and holding séances. As the outbreak of the Civil War drew near, Ferguson repeatedly called for southerners to unite in defense of their cause. Slavery, he insisted, was a God-ordained institution for the benefit of the black race. Any inequalities that arise from slavery, he believed, would be recompensed after this life when all would have a "second chance" for eternal salvation.

served as associate editors for a brief time in 1841. With no explanation, the partnership of Ferguson and Crihfield was "dissolved by mutual consent" after only three months of working together.[63]

In 1842, Ferguson moved again, this time settling in Kentucky. Boles indicates that Ferguson established several churches in Kentucky and "soon became known over the State of Kentucky and was acclaimed as one of the best preachers in the entire state."[64] During his stay in Kentucky, Ferguson's affiliation with the Campbellites drew him into an 1842 debate with J. J. Harrison, a Methodist preacher. So convincing were Ferguson's arguments in the dispute that eighteen months after the contest ended, Harrison identified himself with the Disciples.[65]

At the invitation of an associate, Ferguson visited the Church of Christ at Nashville, Tennessee, where he held a two-week series of meetings in May 1842. The great success of the meetings led the church leaders in Nashville to ask the young evangelist to return to their city for another series of meetings in 1844. With the triumphs of the 1844 meetings, the members of the Nashville church implored Ferguson to accept the full-time ministry position of their congregation. When he declined their initial invitation, the church continued their pursuit of Ferguson until he finally consented and accepted the pulpit position of the Nashville Church of Christ in February 1846. The first five years of his ministry in Nashville saw "almost unexampled success" and he "enjoyed the fame of being the greatest and most eloquent pulpit orator in the South." In addition to being "the preacher for the largest congregation in the state" and "the most popular preacher in Nashville," Ferguson became the editor of the *Christian Magazine* in 1848.[66]

The untimely demise of Ferguson's popularity and influence among Campbellite churches began with the publication of an article in the April 1852 edition of his *Christian Magazine*. Under the title "The Spirits in Prison," Ferguson's exposition of 1 Peter 3:18-20 and 4:1-6 argued that Jesus Christ, while his body was buried in the tomb, descended "in the spirit" to an "invisible world" to preach the gospel to those since the days of Noah who died without a knowledge of Christ. Many of the dead, he explained, had "never heard of [Christ] while in the flesh, and, therefore, must hear of him in the Spirit." Christ's mission was not limited "to the comparatively few who hear of him and learn his ways, while they remain in the flesh." A second opportunity for eternal salvation, he insisted, awaits the dead in an invisible spiritual world.[67] Therefore, he concluded, "we never commit the body of a single human being to the grave, for whom it is not a pleasure for us to know, that his soul has already entered where the knowledge of Christ *may yet* be his."[68]

Campbell issued his reply to Ferguson's "posthumous gospel"—a phrase Campbell used earlier to describe Dolphus Skinner's beliefs—in the June 1852 edition of the *Millennial Harbinger*. Rather than simply commenting upon the Nashville editor's essay, Campbell reprinted the entire article and offered his remarks afterward. Insisting that the "posthumous gospel" is nothing more than Universalism, Campbell asked why any imprisoned spirits would not immediately accept salvation if Christ should appear to them in their torment and offer it. This postmortem preaching of the gospel, he declared, would consist of "a large congregation, a short sermon, and a universal conversion."[69] In a later article, Campbell argued that Ferguson's postmortem gospel also corresponds with Unitarianism because it diminishes the significance of Christ's atoning death.[70]

Campbell also objected to Ferguson's exposition of the biblical passages from 1 Peter in his initial reply to the young preacher's essay. Rather than accepting Ferguson's suggestion that Peter's "spirits in prison" are souls that have been incarcerated since the time of Noah, Campbell argued that they were actually the contemporaries of Noah who were imprisoned by their inability to escape the impending flood. He went on to explain that Christ, as the eternal Word of God, preached to these imprisoned spirits through the Holy Spirit that indwelled Noah. Though Noah offered them salvation on the ark, they were destroyed because they refused to heed his warning. When placed within its proper context, Campbell concluded, "there is not one passage, from the Alpha to the Omega of the Bible, intimating that ever Prophet, Apostle or Evangelist, at any time, preached to a disembodied spirit."[71]

While claiming that his confrontation with Ferguson was "one of the most painful duties" that he had ever been "called upon to discharge,"[72] Campbell relentlessly criticized the young Nashville preacher and appealed for him to retract his statements. Ferguson responded to Campbell's attack with a series of essays in which he tried to clarify his ideas and answer some of the objections that had been expressed about his views. His assertion that "literal and definite ideas of future punishment or reward are not attainable in this life,"[73] however, only led to further questions from Campbell about his beliefs regarding the duration of eternal punishment. "He, indeed, affirms that the 'duration' as well as the 'nature' of future punishment are not clearly revealed," Campbell wrote.

But "if *eternal* and *everlasting* do not define the duration of future punishment they cannot define the duration of future happiness." Therefore,
Campbell continued, "he has . . . taken away my hope as well as the sin-
ners fear!!" "To hint any ray of hope to a man, living and dying in his
sins," Campbell explained, "is as dangerous and soul ruinous a speculation as was ever spoken or written." For this reason, Campbell demanded
of Ferguson "an apology to the whole brotherhood" that "ought to be as
public as the offence against truth and good morals was spread over the
whole community."[74]

Ferguson's first formal rebuttal of Campbell's advances came with an
August 1852 article he entitled "The Attack of the 'Millennial Harbinger'
upon the 'Christian Magazine' and its Editor." His primary argument
in this essay was that Campbell had branded him a heretic for nothing
more than a personal opinion. "In this case, so far as doctrine is concerned," Ferguson wrote, "I have uttered an opinion, *that men who have
not heard the gospel, will hear it before they are condemned by it.* THIS
IS THE SUBSTANCE OF THE WHOLE MATTER."[75] Ferguson ada-
mantly contended that he had done nothing wrong in declaring this personal opinion.

In spite of Ferguson's persistent claim that he had the right to express
his personal opinions, Campbell intensified his resistance to the Nashville
editor's postmortem gospel. Had Ferguson's theory been expressed in
private, Campbell informed his readers, then so would "our remon-
strance" to the offense. But because Ferguson's exposition of the scriptural passages from 1 Peter was not private, Campbell argued that the
scriptural precedent to "publicly rebuke" such heretical teaching compelled him to make a response. "Were it a mere *speculation*, however
visionary, we should allow it to evaporate according to the laws of nature
in such cases. But such is not its character. It is an avowal of the want of
faith in a future state of retribution, and is as clear a nullification of the
terrors of the Lord as can be found in the English language. It places the
vilest rebels on earth under a new dispensation of mercy after death, and
opens a door out of hell to the vilest inmate that ever died." So nefarious
was this postmortem gospel, said Campbell, that "nothing can undo its
mischievous tendency but a formal renunciation."[76]

The continuation of this controversy ultimately consumed over one-
hundred pages of the *Millennial Harbinger* and over one-hundred-eighty
pages of the *Christian Magazine.*[77] Campbell's campaign against the
Nashville editor gained the support of the leading figures among the

Disciples and left Ferguson virtually isolated from the rest of the movement. By the close of 1853, subscriptions to his *Christian Magazine* had so drastically dwindled that Ferguson was forced to discontinue its publication. With little more than a majority of his Nashville church standing behind him,[78] the once-prominent evangelist turned to Theodore Clapp (1792-1866), the well-known pastor of the Stranger's Church in New Orleans, as a confidant and ally during his struggle with Campbell.

Clapp, a native of Easthampton, Massachusetts, was raised in the Presbyterian Church and educated for the ministry at Yale College and Andover Theological Seminary. After moving to New Orleans in 1823 to assume the pastorate of the First Presbyterian Church, Clapp soon found himself charged with heresy as a result of his growing approval of the beliefs of Unitarianism and Universalism. In 1832, when the Mississippi Presbytery finally excommunicated Clapp for his unorthodox beliefs, a significant majority of his parishioners favored his continued ministry in New Orleans and appealed for the congregation's separation from the Presbyterian Church. With their break from Presbyterianism completed in 1833, the newly formed "First Congregational Church" became an ecumenical house of worship that espoused no denominational ties or affiliations.[79] Under the leadership of Clapp, who freely referred to himself as both a Unitarian and a Universalist though he refused to formally unite with either of the denominations, the church opened its doors to numerous speakers from various ecclesiastical backgrounds. The growth of the church and the eloquence of Clapp progressively gained a national reputation.[80]

Ferguson's association with Clapp, whom he had probably first met during an 1851 preaching tour in Louisiana, was an obvious attempt to align himself with a noted religious leader whose theological ideas differed significantly from Campbell's. As early as 1839, Campbell had corresponded with Clapp and had even visited his church for the purpose of delivering a series of lectures to a large New Orleans audience. At the conclusion of his New Orleans orations, Campbell expressed an unlikely hope that Clapp might be persuaded to "stand firmly and unequivocally on primitive ground" and thus lead his congregation into the Campbellite movement. "Oh! That he may become [as] valiant for the truth, as he is to rebuke the follies and vices of the age," Campbell wrote in recollection of his visit with Clapp.[81]

The paths of Campbell and Clapp crossed again in 1847, when the two men boarded the same passenger ship for a voyage across the Atlantic

Ocean and in 1850, when they met by chance in New York City. By the earlier of these two meetings, however, Campbell no longer viewed Clapp as a potential convert to his movement, but as a dangerous advocate of heterodoxy and an opponent of biblical authority. To a querist who asked about the truthfulness of a rumor that pitted him against Clapp in a debate on Universalism, Campbell reported that no such plans had ever been proposed. Nevertheless, he continued, "if there could be a proper issue formed between us respecting our tenets on that subject, the question would more appropriately be, *Is the Bible the book of God or of man?*"[82]

(Image reproduced from Theodore Clapp, Autobiographical Sketches and Recollections, during a Thirty-Five Years' Residence in New Orleans (Boston: Phillips, Sampson and Company, 1857)

Figure 12 – Theodore Clapp

"Parson Clapp" (1792-1866) served for many years as the celebrated minister of the Stranger's Church in New Orleans. His rejection of the reformed teachings of his youth and indifference to denominational affiliation prompted Campbell to consider Clapp a possible convert to his movement in the late 1830s. Campbell soon lost all hope for recruiting Clapp, however, when the New Orleans preacher began to advocate the doctrines of Unitarianism and Universalism. When Jesse Ferguson's posthumous gospel left him disfellowshiped by Campbell's adherents, Ferguson turned to Clapp as both a confidant and advisor.

As reports of Ferguson's association with Clapp reached Campbell in early 1853, he interpreted the fraternal alliance as a watershed event that identified the Nashville preacher's separation from the Disciples' movement. To Campbell, Ferguson's affiliation with Clapp was comparable to an open rejection of Christianity and the endorsement of skepticism. "Were Thomas Paine, Lord Bolingbroke, Volney or Voltaire, my contemporaries and my townsmen," Campbell wrote, "I would quite as cordially commune with any of them, or with them altogether . . . as with my personal friend and acquaintance, Dr. Theodore Clapp." Moreover, he noted, "I am, perhaps, the only preacher in the Union with whom [Clapp] would refuse to commune."[83] Campbell went on to describe Ferguson's doctrinal views as "essentially Unitarian and Universalian—or, in other words, Deistical." He explained that "our friend Ferguson" has found "a more cordial brotherhood, in such men as Dr. Clapp, of New Orleans, and, in his view, a much more pious, enlightened, free and charitable paternity, in Boston or Cambridge, than amongst us."[84]

Campbell's objection to the Unitarianism of Clapp and Ferguson matched his contempt for their Universalism. Some years previous to his controversy with Ferguson, Campbell labeled a Unitarian as "one who contends that Jesus Christ is not the Son of God. Such a one has denied the faith," he declared, "and therefore we reject him."[85] Campbell further insisted, during an 1854 trip to Nashville with the expressed purpose of confronting Ferguson, that Unitarianism is "utterly at variance with the doctrines of Christianity."[86] There is no excuse, he later wrote, for "*undeifying* the Lord Jesus Christ." Even during his waning years, when he was wearied from an active life and frequently taken with illness, Campbell's unswerving confidence in the divinity of Christ rekindled a youthful desire to confront Christ's detractors in a public forum. Thus, in 1863, the aged disputant offered to uphold the divinity of Christ "in New England, or in Old England, against any man of character or reputation who assumes Unitarianism, Arianism, or Socinianism, with either tongue or pen." In the end, Campbell concluded, "Deism and Unitarianism are twin sisters."[87]

With an ever-increasing number of allegations circling around the Campbellite defector, Ferguson chose to clarify his theological positions in an 1854 address to his Nashville congregation. In this discourse, which he promptly published after its delivery, Ferguson confirmed his adherence to many of the tenets of Universalism and Unitarianism. Moreover, he validated suspicions that he and his wife had become active participants in the Spiritualist movement.[88]

While claiming that his earliest inclinations toward Spiritualism grew out of an 1842 study of mesmerism,[89] Ferguson refrained from publicly admitting his acceptance of the doctrine until after the "spirit rappings" of Kate and Margaret Fox gained the nation's attention in 1848. When Campbell journeyed to Nashville in November 1854 to confront Ferguson and his ideas in person, he was greeted with the news that his adversary would not meet him. Professing to have received a clairvoyant letter from the late Unitarian divine, William Ellery Channing (1780-1842), Ferguson said that he had been explicitly commanded to refrain from any association with the editor from Bethany. "It had been our cherished opinion, that Mr. Ferguson would manfully stand up in defence [*sic*] of his teachings at any time, in any place, and against any one who would presume to challenge the truth of his position," Campbell wrote. "But so strong was his faith in the ghost of Dr. Channing, and in his chirography, that he obeyed, not to the spirit only, but to the letter, his written message."[90]

Campbell addressed Ferguson's recently announced belief by referring to Spiritualism as a "new form of infidelity" and described it as one of the "follies of the current age" that "caps the climax of delusions." Why would any genuine Christian "consult the spirits of dead men, as if *more reliable, more credible, more enlightened, better informed* of the spiritual, divine, eternal, than were Jesus the Messiah and the Twelve Apostles of the Lamb!!" Not only did Campbell view Spiritualism as "blasphemy against the Son of God" and "the Father that sent Him," but he also saw the practitioner of Spiritualism as "an infidel at heart."[91] Throughout the ensuing years, Campbell repeatedly declared Spiritualism an anti-Christian activity and referred to the conjured ghosts of the dead as either the counterfeit fabrications of the spiritual mediums or untrustworthy demons masquerading as the souls of the dearly departed.[92]

The act of "evoking or imploring intelligence from the dead, as to their destiny or ours . . . is superlatively irreligious and immoral," Campbell argued in an 1860 article, "and is, in no respect, advantageous, but always disadvantageous to us."[93] Moreover, "the whole system, (or delusion, as some regard it,) of spirit rapping and spirit responding, of moving tables and chairs, is wholly destitute of one argument or evidence, declarative or demonstrative of celestial or divine origin or influence," he contended. "There has not been *one new truth* developed, not one *new fact* established, not *one idea* communicated of any fact to any human being, so far as the published documents have reached my eye or my ear."[94] Thus to Campbell, Ferguson's announced belief in Spiritualism provided further evidence that the young evangelist's speculative belief in a postmortem gospel was a dangerous heresy.

Ferguson's ministry with the Nashville church ended in 1857, when a small party of faithful Campbellites in the congregation filed a lawsuit to determine the rightful ownership of the church building. When the courts awarded his rivals control of the building, Ferguson resigned from his ministry and turned the edifice over to the Disciples in early April 1858. Within days of the church house's exchange of hands, however, the structure was mysteriously burned to the ground. Many of Nashville's citizens were convinced that Ferguson's admirers set the fire as retaliation for their loss of the building.[95]

In 1860, Disciples evangelist James Challen (1802-1878) visited the Nashville congregation and reported that it was well on the road to recovering from the turmoil surrounding the Ferguson episode. A few, he wrote, continue to "adhere to the fallen fortunes of J. B. Ferguson—who has no church organization, and no Christian influence." Furthermore, Challen noted, Ferguson "speaks in the Theater, without the exhibition of any thing Christian, reformative or saving."[96] Though once a respected Christian leader in Nashville, Challen made it clear that Ferguson's reputation had significantly diminished by 1860.

Finding little success with his efforts to redeem his reputation and build another congregation of believers in Nashville, Ferguson embarked upon a traveling lectureship throughout the South and into Europe. In addition to spreading his doctrines of Spiritualism, Universalism, and Unitarianism, he regularly called for support of the Southern cause in the era of the Civil War. Toward the close of the war Ferguson returned to Nashville, where he lived the remainder of his life in relative obscurity. On September 3, 1870, Ferguson died after a lingering illness at the age of fifty-one.[97]

Campbell's confrontations with Universalism, Unitarianism, and Spiritualism were distinct manifestations of his ongoing battles with the foes of the Christian religion and biblical revelation. Though each of these groups promoted themselves as genuine Christianity, Campbell firmly denied them a position within the Christian community. Their rejection of such orthodox beliefs as the eternal punishment of the wicked, the divinity of Jesus Christ, and the evil of necromancy forced Campbell to view them as nothing more than deists clothed in the garb of Christianity. Unwilling and unable to ignore these new infidels, Campbell openly confronted them in his efforts to uphold Christianity and the veracity of the Bible.

9

CONCLUSION:
"DEFENDER OF THE FAITH ONCE DELIVERED TO THE SAINTS"

Following a lengthy career of traveling, preaching, writing, and confronting the opponents of the Christian faith, Campbell's activities were drastically cut back by the outbreak of the Civil War in April 1861. His advanced age and failing health, along with the travel restrictions brought about by the national conflict, forced Campbell to spend much of the war at his estate in Bethany, West Virginia.[1] By January 1864, Campbell noted that his *"forty-one* long, laborious, anxious years" as "a hard-working Editor" had finally caught up to him. "I find myself, from many considerations . . . constrained to abandon the purpose, and to discontinue my responsible relation as publisher" of the *Millennial Harbinger*. Though he continued to submit essays to the *Harbinger* throughout the remaining few years of his life, Campbell surrendered his editorial responsibilities to his "long and well-approved associate and co-laborer in many works, Prof. W. K. Pendleton."[2] Following a brief illness in the early months of 1866, Campbell died at his home on March 4. His passing was widely recognized throughout the country as Disciples churches held memorial services in his honor and the nation acknowledged the passing of one of her greatest religious leaders.

Following a funeral service at his Bethany church, Campbell's body was interred at the nearby family cemetery he had named "God's Acre." Campbell chose the site as a family burial spot some forty-six years earlier when his infant daughter died in 1820. By the time of Campbell's burial, this picturesque location, secluded among the trees on a hillside over-looking his Bethany mansion, already held the bodies of his father and mother, as well as a number of other family members. An impressive marble monument atop a granite base was erected on Campbell's grave to commemorate the life and work of the "Sage of Bethany." Along with his name and the dates of his birth and death, the grave marker recognizes Campbell's accomplishments as a religious leader, a prolific writer, and the founder of Bethany College. Heading the list of accolades hewn into the monument, however, is a description of Alexander Campbell as a "Defender of the faith once delivered to the saints."

DWARFED PHILOSOPHERS

From his 1826 response to the resurgence of American deism until his death in 1866, Campbell repeatedly defended the claims of Christianity and defiantly objected to the reasonableness of freethought. Though the skeptics of the nineteenth century claimed unbelief as the natural out-growth of the Enlightenment, Campbell refused to concede this point. "Skeptics generally are more witty than wise, more pert than prudent, [and] more talkative than learned," he maintained. "I have not had the good fortune to meet with a learned, well read, and well educated infidel, in all my acquaintance." Furthermore, he noted, the intellectual offspring of Paine, Volney, and Voltaire are but "dwarfed philosophers, reckless declaimers, and arrogant dogmatists."[3] Despite skeptic portrayals of themselves as the standard bearers of enlightened rationalism, Campbell argued that the actual enlightened rationalists are the proponents of Christianity, and he insisted that his freethinking adversaries match his use of logic and reason in their contentions against religion.

Armed with such absolute convictions, Campbell repeatedly called upon the advocates of unbelief to represent their views in the public battlefield of ideas. Not only was Campbell convinced that the skeptical belief systems of the nineteenth century were constructed upon deficient philosophical premises, but he was certain they would crumble when confronted with logical examination. He was equally confident that Christianity was a rational and plausible belief system, and that it had nothing to fear from the challenges and investigations of science, skepticism, or philosophy. On the basis of these certitudes, Campbell readily accepted the opportunities he received to sustain the reasonableness of Christianity and to refute the claims of rationality from the advocates of unbelief. "I am always ready," he wrote, "to give a reason of the hope which I have in a crucified Christ, through whom I expect to live forever."[4]

ALWAYS READY TO DEFEND THE FAITH

Whether through print or in person, Campbell seldom passed an opportunity to defend his faith or to present what he deemed to be the irrefutable message of the gospel. In addition to his major conflicts with skepticism, as covered in this book, Campbell had a number of lesser opportunities to defy unbelief and advance his Christian convictions. No matter the person, the location, or the situation, Campbell appeared always intent on answering the biblical mandate to be prepared to make a defense for the faith.

During an 1829 journey through Richmond, Virginia, Campbell gladly dialogued with a certain Mr. Judah, an aged Jew and leader of a synagogue, about the differences between Christianity and Judaism.[5] Some months later, in early 1830, Campbell agreed "with all cheerfulness" to respond to C. Shultz's objections to the divine origin of the Bible and "to hear what [Shultz] or any other sceptic has to offer new upon the subject of deism, theism, or general skepticism."[6] Moreover, when Joseph Smith's Mormon movement began in 1830, Campbell referred to the group as "the snare of the Devil"[7] because it lured people away from genuine Christianity. Campbell also wrote one of the first reviews of the *Book of Mormon*, where he exposed numerous contradictions, grammatical errors, historical mistakes, and theological inaccuracies. At the conclusion of his review, which he entitled "Delusions," Campbell described Joseph Smith as an "Atheist" and declared the *Book of Mormon* "as certainly Smith's fabrication as Satan is the father of lies, or darkness the offspring of night."[8]

Campbell also dared to "beard the lion in his den," to use the expression of Albert Post, by confronting the leading freethought societies of both the United States and Great Britain. In 1833, Campbell delivered a series of addresses to the skeptics of the Society of Moral Philanthropy that had gathered at the Tammany and Concert Halls of New York City.[9] Some years later, during an 1847 tour of England, Campbell "addressed the Sceptics, or Socialists, in their Hall of Debate, on the great question, *Has God Ever Spoken to Man?*" After his lecture, he noted, "a vote of thanks for my address was unanimously tendered to me by the members of the Literary Hall."[10]

One further example of Campbell's unswerving intention to meet the detractors of Christianity head-on is his publication of essays from his correspondents about various groups of unbelievers. An 1841 article from "R. E." examined the Transcendentalist movement and declared it a "poisonous influence" that is "heartily to be dreaded."[11] Another essay, published in 1861, challenged the editors of "an Infidel Periodical" known as the *Boston Investigator*.[12] The *Investigator* had begun in 1831 under the editorship of radical freethinker Abner Kneeland (1774-1844). By 1861, it had fallen under the co-editorship of skeptics Horace Seaver (1810-1889) and Josiah P. Mendum (1811-1891), and was among the elite freethinker periodicals of the nation.[13]

Defending Christianity in an antebellum climate of irreligious expansion was a responsibility of primary importance to Campbell. For Campbell, the proclamation and defense of revealed religion in the Bible was considered "one of the most delightful duties in all the code of our moral obligation." He explained: "We . . . undertake with pleasure of the highest order the task of showing the gospel to be no cunningly devised fable, and of exposing the dark and dreary speculations of those visionary 'Free-Thinkers,' who, while they would banish from the world the name and the idea of God the Supreme, of Christ the Saviour, of heaven and immortality, have, as a substitute, to offer only utter annihilation and eternal night."[14] In the closing pages of the 1831 edition of his *Millennial Harbinger*, Campbell stated that he had "been fighting for many years . . . against the three great powers" of "Atheism, Sensuality, and Sectarianism." Noting that the proponents of unbelief—"whether called sceptics, deists, or atheists"—had never been "more insolent, rampant, and vindictive" than in the current year, Campbell asked if his readers were willing to join him in the "great controversy" against those who would stand in opposition to the truth claims of the Christian faith.[15]

PREPARING THE SAINTS FOR BATTLE

Campbell believed that all Christians had the responsibility of defending their faith against those who attacked it. When a reader of his *Christian Baptist* first informed Campbell of the irreligious activities of Samuel Underhill in northeast Ohio, Campbell responded by telling the reader that he was "doubtless more than able to drive off to the wilderness this wild boar who lies under your hills and sheep folds, seeking whom he may devour."[16] Nevertheless, Campbell made a concerted effort to both produce materials that would equip his fellow Christians for battle with the advocates of unbelief and to encourage the saints through stories of Christian victory in those engagements.

Along with the Campbell-Owen Debate (to which Campbell repeatedly referred his unbelieving correspondents) and the essays he wrote to his opponents that have been considered in this book, Campbell produced an apologetic volume to equip Christians in their inevitable conflicts with skepticism. Arguing that the Christian faith could be sustained by the "concessions, admissions, and statements of the ancient unbelieving Jews and Gentiles," Campbell published *The Christian Preacher's Companion, or the Gospel Facts Sustained by the Testimony of Unbelieving Jews and Pagans* in 1836.[17] By examining the assertions of "unbelieving Jews and infidels" from the first two centuries of the church's existence, he claimed to have created a treatise that "modern skeptics and infidels of every school" would find "rather difficult, if not impossible, . . . to dispose of." This small book, when coupled with the Bible, Campbell wrote, "will be all that is necessary for any person competent to preach the gospel, to prove it to be true, in the presence of the most learned and talented of the opposers of our faith in Jesus Christ, and our hope for eternal life."[18]

Campbell's labor to furnish his readers with the tools for combating the ideas of the freethinkers appears to have influenced at least one disputant, and probably many more. When Origen Bacheler (1800-1848), an evangelical writer and editor from New York, participated in an 1831 corresponding debate with Robert Dale Owen (the son of Campbell's earlier antagonist), he appeared to have used many of the arguments that had been used by Campbell in the earlier debate.[19] Though Bacheler does not credit Campbell for his line of reasoning, nor can it be proven with certainty that he borrowed from Campbell, his debating points are remarkably similar to those of the Bethany editor. In an 1838 essay, Campbell described Bacheler as "a gentleman of good standing as a professor of Christianity, an editor of religious and moral periodicals, and well read on the evidences of Christianity." He also noted that Bacheler was a "friend" with whom he had developed a correspondence.[20] Of equal interest is the fact that Bacheler, like Campbell before him, published an exposition on the Mormons that was very critical of the fledgling group.[21]

CAMPBELL'S APOLOGETIC OBJECTIVES

The theme that threaded its way through all of Campbell's apologetic writings, lectures, and debates was his support of biblical revelation and the legitimacy of the Christian religion. Nevertheless, the objective of his apologetic work was always to persuade his "fellow-citizens to lay down their rebellion against the Lord" and to surrender their allegiance to Jesus Christ. The fulfillment of this goal, he believed, would require an honest, open, and rational search for religious truth and an affectionate appeal to those with whom he dissented. With these convictions in mind, Campbell promised to "hear, examine and judge all things, touching the foundation of our faith and hope; and . . . honorably [to] endeavor to persuade all men to do homage to the prince of all the benefactors of mankind."[22] Amid all of his activities and enterprises, Campbell never lost sight of his desire to convince the non-Christians of his world to submit themselves to the lordship of Jesus Christ.

(Courtesy of Disciples of Christ Historical Society, Nashville, Tennessee)

Figure 13 – Alexander Campbell (1857)

During the latter years of Campbell's life, he was widely recognized in both the United States and Europe as a distinguished Christian scholar, a prominent educator, the leader of an American effort to reform Christianity, and the most significant Christian apologist of his age.

As "an advocate for free and full discussion on all subjects, and . . . especially on the most important of all subjects, Religion," Campbell deemed it essential that his arguments be weighed against those of his adversaries.[23] He sought well-reasoned dialogue in which both the positive and negative sides of a topic could be explored in the hope that truth would make itself visible to both the disputants and the audience. To Robert Owen he explained, "I am, on all subjects, open to conviction, and even desirous to receive larger measures of light; and more than once, even when in debate, I have been convicted of the truth and force of the argument of an opponent."[24]

Though Campbell's pronouncements against skepticism were often stinging and harsh, he generally treated his opponents with a moderate amount of dignity and respect. "I will . . . not [debate] in a spirit of banter," he told Dr. Samuel Underhill, "but of homage and reverence for the truth, and of good-will even to those who deny my Lord and Master, and hold him up to the derision of scoffers."[25] Campbell's considerate approach toward those with whom he disagreed was recognized after his discourses to the Society of Moral Philanthropy in New York. Benjamin Offen, a deist and leading figure in the Society of Moral Philanthropy, expressed his appreciation for Campbell's "friendly visit" and assured him that he was "always a welcome guest." Speaking on behalf of the trustees and members of the society, Offen also complimented Campbell for "candidly and ably" stating "some of the evidences of the Christian religion." He finally thanked Campbell for the "friendly sentiments" he "expressed towards Sceptics—appealing to them as men—as *honest men*, instead of treating them with contumely, as is the conduct of the Christian priesthood of New York."[26]

CAMPBELL AND THE ANTEBELLUM SKEPTICS

Campbell's confrontations with skepticism provide an insight into the freethought movement of America's antebellum period. His numerous experiences with unbelievers during an era that is generally recognized for the advancement of Christianity suggest that American infidels were very influential during this time. Contrary to Post's assertion that the infidels of the early nineteenth century "were concentrated in the cities and found most of their recruits from among the lower-class radicals,"[27] Campbell's encounters with the opponents of revealed religion indicate that their influence traveled well beyond the lower-class citizens of urban

America. Robert Owen and Humphrey Marshall, for example, were frequent associates of the upper tier of society, and both possessed an excep-
tional amount of personal wealth. At the same time, however, Dr. Samuel
Underhill and Charles Cassedy had meager, and often sporadic, incomes
that fettered them to lower social positions. What's more, only a few of
Campbell's irreligious foes actually confined themselves to urban areas.
Cassedy was a drifter, Owen and Underhill spent some time in social communes, Marshall resided in rural Kentucky, and even Jonathan Kidwell,
who began his work in the city of Cincinnati, took his radical Universalism
to the rustic setting of Philomath, Indiana. As with Christianity, antebellum skepticism managed to pervade every aspect of American society. Though the unbelieving population seemed to advance throughout
much of the 1830s (Campbell repeatedly complained about the growing
acceptance of the freethought movement), their numeric growth and cultural impact came nowhere near rivaling that of Christianity.

At the outset of Campbell's campaign against skepticism, most of the
orthodox leaders of American Protestantism viewed him as a radical out-
sider who attacked traditional theology and the ecclesiastical structures
of the day. This one-time fiery rival of Christian orthodoxy, however,
was drawn "inside the framework of the organized institutions of society
and religion which he had once bitterly fought" in an effort to rid the
nation more effectively of unbelief.[28] In so doing, Campbell gained the
respect and admiration of the religious community who once deemed
him little more than an iconoclastic, backwoods preacher. As a result of
his battles with skepticism and acceptance within the world of orthodox
Christianity, Campbell gained both a national and an international reputation. Along with this personal notoriety came acceptance for and added
membership to his movement to restore Christianity to its primitive New
Testament form.

Campbell's conflicts with skepticism were tremendously successful.
"By 1850," writes Post, "infidelity had ceased to be the great enemy of
American Protestantism."[29] Though the new manifestations of skepticism
gained added distinction after 1850 (and Campbell continued his fight
against them), the classical forms of antebellum unbelief had largely fallen
by the wayside. Obviously, Campbell did not labor alone in his resistance
to the antebellum opponents of Christianity, but had the assistance of
numerous others who complimented his struggles against skepticism.[30]
Amid the excitement and the revivals of the Second Great Awakening,
however, many of the antebellum clergymen appeared to be somewhat

oblivious to the growth of the freethought movement within their midst. So Campbell took center stage in the venture to rid the nation of skepticism. "No clergyman of his time," reports Martin E. Marty, "exerted himself more vigorously in combat with the infidels of the period." "Unlike Channing, [Campbell] named names; unlike Beecher he met freethinkers in direct encounter—at Tammany and Concert Halls in New York; at Cincinnati, Cleveland, and Ravenna, Ohio; in his home, in churches, on the pages of periodicals."[31] Because of his ceaseless struggles and lucid arguments against unbelief, Campbell established himself as the most significant apologist for the Christian religion in antebellum America.

Appendix A

ROBERT OWEN'S "TWELVE FUNDAMENTAL LAWS OF HUMAN NATURE"

Throughout the Campbell-Owen debate, Robert Owen repeatedly listed and explained his "Twelve Fundamental Laws of Human Nature." Nearly every aspect of Owen's debate argument revolved around a repetition of these laws or his attempt to further clarify them. Describing these laws as "indisputable," "unchangeable," and "divine," Owen suggested that they are the foundational elements of human nature that govern the characteristics of every individual. A complete understanding of these laws and a proper response to them, Owen contended, would pave the way to a utopian state of social bliss. The laws listed below are taken directly from Owen's initial espousal of them in his 1829 debate with Alexander Campbell.[1]

The "Twelve Fundamental Laws of Human Nature":

1. That man, at his birth, is ignorant of everything relative to his own organization, and that he has not been permitted to create the slightest part of his natural propensities, faculties, or qualities, physical or mental.
2. That no two infants, at birth, have yet been known to possess precisely the same organization, while the physical, mental, and moral differences, between all infants, are formed without their knowledge or will.

3. That each individual is placed, at birth, without his knowl-
    edge or consent, within circumstances, which, acting upon
    his peculiar organization, impress the general character of
    those circumstances upon the infant, child, and man. Yet the
    influence of those circumstances is to a certain degree modi-
    fied by the peculiar natural organization of each individual.

4. That no infant has the power of deciding at what period of
    time or in what part of the world he shall come into exis-
    tence; of whom he shall be born, in what distinct religion
    he shall be trained to believe, or by what other circum-
    stances he shall be surrounded from birth to death.

5. That each individual is so created, that when young, he
    may be made to receive impressions, to produce either true
    ideas or false notions, and beneficial or injurious habits, and
    to retain them with great tenacity.

6. That each individual is so created that he must believe
    according to the strongest impressions that are made on
    his feelings and other faculties, while his belief in no case
    depends upon his will.

7. That each individual is so created that he must like that
    which is pleasant to him, or that which produces agreeable
    sensations on his individual organization, and he must dis-
    like that which creates in him unpleasant and disagreeable
    sensations; while he cannot discover, previous to experi-
    ence, what those sensations should be.

8. That each individual is so created, that the sensations made
    upon his organization, although pleasant and delightful
    at their commencement and for some duration, generally
    become, when continued beyond a certain period, without
    change, disagreeable and painful; while, on the contrary,
    when a too rapid change of sensations is made on his orga-
    nization, it dissipates, weakens, and otherwise injures his
    physical, intellectual, and moral powers and enjoyments.

9. That the highest health, the greatest progressive improve-
    ments, and the most permanent happiness of each individ-
    ual depend, in a great degree, upon the proper cultivation
    of all his physical, intellectual and moral faculties and
    powers from infancy to maturity, and upon all these parts
    of his nature being duly called into action, at their proper

period, and temperately exercised according to the strength and capacity of the individual.

10. That the individual is made to possess and acquire the worst character, when his organization at birth has been compounded of the most inferior propensities, faculties and qualities of our common nature, and when so organized, he has been placed, from birth to death, amid the most vicious or worst circumstances.

11. That the individual is made to posses and to acquire a medium character, when his original organization has been created superior, and when the circumstances which surround him from birth to death produce continued vicious or unfavorable impressions. Or when his organization has been formed of inferior materials, and the circumstances in which he has been placed from birth to death are of a character to produce superior impressions only. Or when there has been some mixture of good and bad qualities, in the original organization, and when it has also been placed, though life, in various circumstances of good and evil. This last compound has been hitherto the common lot of mankind.

12. That the individual is made the most superior of his species when his original organization has been compounded of the best proportions of the best ingredients of which human nature is formed, and when the circumstances which surround him from birth to death are of a character to produce only superior impressions; or, in other words, when the circumstances, or laws, institutions, and customs, in which he is placed, are all in unison with his nature.

Appendix B

UNDERHILL'S "CAMPBELL REFUTED"

After the publication of the Campbell-Owen debate and Campbell's comments about Dr. Samuel Underhill's published oration, "A Lecture on Mysterious Religious Emotions,"[1] Underhill attempted to "introduce a correspondence" with Campbell about the Cincinnati debate on the evidences of Christianity. Hoping that Campbell would open the pages of his *Millennial Harbinger* to his letters, Underhill was disappointed when Campbell refused to do so. In response, Underhill decided to publish his claims against Campbell in the form of a tract. Even prior to completing his composition of the tract, Underhill called on Josiah Warren, a resident of Cincinnati and former participant in the New Harmony experiment, to find a printer for the document. "I am far from a good press," he told Warren. "Will some printer of your city offer to print these letters and give me 200 copies for myself and my friends[?]"[2] The pamphlet was ultimately printed for Underhill, and Campbell eventually came across a copy of the tract from which he printed excerpts for his *Millennial Harbinger*.

The original tract consisted of notes to the reader and publisher about the content of the leaflet, Underhill's original letter to Campbell and a reply from the Bethany editor, and seven additional "letters" Underhill wrote with the intent of forwarding to Campbell. Underhill's final seven letters in the pamphlet were written as an analysis of Campbell's reply to his initial correspondence. It is highly doubtful, judging from his comments on the treatise, that Campbell ever received the final seven letters of this writing until he was presented with a published copy of

Underhill's tract.[3] No extant copies of the original pamphlet are known to remain in existence. The following reprint of the tract has been re-created from Underhill's publication of the pamphlet in his weekly newspaper, the *Cleveland Liberalist*,[4] from a rough draft of the writing in his unpublished journal, "The Chronicles, Notes, and Maxims of Dr. Samuel Underhill," and from the few excerpts of the tract contained in the writings of Alexander Campbell.

The following pages provide the content of the tract, along with a few brief editorial comments and clarifications. For the most part, Underhill's spelling, grammar, word usage, and appearance have been retained, with the exception of a few bracketed insertions to clarify the text. The tract is presented in the format of a correspondence, much as it was likely to have been when it was initially published. Any editorial insertions are identified by a numeric note and the explanation will be included in the endnotes; an asterisk marks all of the notes that Underhill included in the original writing and they are included as footnotes within the text of this document.

CAMPBELL REFUTED

Being a Correspondence between the Rev. Alex. Campbell, of Va. and Dr. Sam'l Underhill, of Ohio; on the subject of the Debate held in Cincinnati between the celebrated Robert Owen, and Mr. Campbell, in April 1829.

> *"Rising above our nature does no good,*
> *We must sink back to our own flesh and blood"—*
> *'Fear made their Devils and weak hopes their Gods.'*
>
> POPE'S ESSAY ON MAN.

TO THE READER

These letters were commenced with an expectation that Mr. Campbell would publish them in his paper. He had said in his paper that if any person of writing ability who had perused the debate and was not satisfied with his arguments would attack them, they should find a place in his paper. His reply to my introductory letter proves that he was unwilling to be taken in earnest!

S. UNDERHILL

Kendal, May 29th, 1830

Mr. A. C. Howell, Editor of the E. and Working Men's Adv.

Sir:—The following letter was designed for Mr. Campbell's paper, but he thought proper to refuse it admittance. His reasons are given in the accompanying letter addressed to me on the subject.

This letter differs from an exact copy of the one I sent to Mr. Campbell only in a few words, except that it is more explicit as to the course of Letters, five of which being now written, enables me to say with more certainty.

ANNO REPUBLICO, 54TH, APRIL 8TH, 1830

Mr. A. Campbell,

Sir:—I see by the February number of your Millennial Harbinger, that you are still puffing your defiances and uttering your groundless apprehensions, that no free enquirer durst attempt an overthrow of your boasted syllogism in defence of your Diana, the making of shrines, to which yields you so plentiful a harvest. I know your apprehensions are as groundless as I believe your arguments illogical.

Nothing but the pressure of professional business has prevented me from forwarding this communication. It is, however, necessary that you first inform me whether you will admit me in your columns. You have doubtless perused my first effort for the press. I refer to the pamphlet from which you made an extract, ushered in by a body of very pious effusions of the spirit, furnished with a glossary which an uninspired man could not have written, and ended with a paraphrase dictated by the Holy Ghost.

I am pleased with your pleasantry, as it seldom dwells with a bigot; and then it is so like the language of the New Testament—who that loves the one can hate the other? Again, it is so convenient to laugh at arguments one cannot refute, that to one building castles in the air, and waging war against a gauntlet, at free enquirers on the other, many weapons are necessary. And, that I may not seem to reprove you, you who conceive yourself a peculiar favorite of him who ROASTS in FIRE and BRIMSTONE such as lack faith in Jesus, I also will indulge in a little humor. A seasoning of argument, however, I promise, and what I cannot prove absurd, I will not try to render ridiculous. I design, first, to show you my opinion on your sixth sense and four world queries, as found on pages 163 and 164 of vol. 1st of your edition of the debate. Secondly, overthrow entirely your historical criteria. Thirdly, review the dogma of the resurrection. Fourthly, review, and perhaps paraphrase on your peculiar tenets. Fifthly, review the subject of voluntary belief, and Mr. C's. ineffectual attempts to oppose Mr. Owen's views on this subject. Sixthly, examine Mr. Campbell's conduct at, and in the debate, and consider him in the character of editor of the discussion. Seventhly, give some detached specimens from the debate, to prove that, stript of their trappings, the veriest school-boy must perceive their ridiculous absurdity and entire irrelevancy to the subject on which they are designed to bear.

If you publish this you will add my name to your subscription list. I have purchased and have carefully read the debate. I am intimately acquainted with the scriptures, having read them from my youth and having preached them many years without pecuniary reward, and without alliance with, or allegiance to any sect. When I ceased to believe the scripture doctrines I ceased to preach them. When again convinced of their truth and utility, I will again teach them. Your evidences do not remove my doubts of their authenticity; and to me it seems evident that a foundation is wanting to your whole superstructure. I should be more certain that your debate convinced many sceptics and materialists, as your remark to Mr. Shultz intimates in the 2d No. of the Mill. Harbinger, would you give a few dozen of their names in your paper. None of the many who have read the debate, with whom I am acquainted, have been shaken by it in the least. On the contrary most of them believe that had Mr. Owen treated the saints and their dogmas with the same freedom of contempt that Mr. Campbell did the sceptics, the meeting would have broken up at an early hour of the discussion.

You complain of Mr. Owen, "no syllogisms, no therefores," you shall complain no more. Open your columns then, Mr. Campbell—put on your helmet and whet your sword anew. Whilst you contend that willing to find the murderer of Col. Sharp of Ky. was the immediate antecedent of the jury's belief of Beaucamp's guilt, I shall either in your paper or before an audience meet you without fear. Confiding in the case with which truth is defended and error overthrown, I shall forget the difference of mental powers so favorable to you, and your wide-spread popularity, and the popularity of your side of the question, with many, more powerful than argument itself, and meet you fairly. Wishing to fulfill my creed, "do all the good you can, and as little hurt as possible," I proffer you good feeling, and am respectfully yours,

SAM'L UNDERHILL

Bethany, Va. April 20, 1830

Dr. Underhill,

Sir:—I do most sincerely consider you, and many of your fellow-laborers, as the subject of an irreligious frenzy. Under the same sort of illusion as the bishop of Cloyne or any of the Idealists. All that I have heard, and read, and seen, of your school convinces me that you are objects rather of commiseration (if some of you were not so desperately wicked) than of serious argument. You talk of therefores as a poor fellow I once saw strolling about the country, talking about his mistress whose cruelty had deprived him of reason. My dear sir, if you were to put three logical therefores together it would either restore you to right reason, that is if you ever possessed it, or it would dissipate the whole scheme which, like an incubus, is now impelling your life.

The documents from your pen which I have seen, are proof positive that you have in your efforts to see your own back, to look at your own eye, and to analyze your own brain, lost the centre of gravity. You tell me you have read the bible, and you were once a preacher. This is a second proof of the physical malady which oppresses you—that you ever understood a chapter in the bible, or were under the influence of a persuasion of its truth, would require the verdict of twelve men to produce faith in me.

You think I could believe upon your mere testimony that you once knew something about the bible. I am not so credulous, sir, I assure you; you have quite too much faith if you think I could be induced to believe you are reasonable, or was ever religious. I would recommend the shower bath and the oxide of iron, and if you can at any time produce [for] me three syllogisms fairly drawn upon any one question in religion, I will insert it in the Mill. Harbinger, and send you a copy of it. But until I see a series of at least three therefores, I never can consent to consume one gill of ink in giving publicity to the distempered reveries of a mind as completely incurable, in my judgement, as a body which has lost its excitability.

If I could relieve you, poor fellow, I would do it.

A. CAMPBELL.

ANSWER TO A. CAMPBELL'S LETTER

LETTER II

May 5, 1830

Mr. Campbell—

Sir:—Unacquainted with you save by your communications in print I almost doubted if the abusive scrawl with your signature was truly from your pen. You had promised to admit any person of writing ability in your paper. Judging in your own favor you count me incompetent. Is it the same Mr. Campbell who says, "the bible is as easy to understand as a newspaper;" and again says "that you ever understood a chapter in the Bible or were ever under a persuasion of its truth, would require the verdict of twelve men to produce faith in me?"

You say that my confession, that I had read the bible, and was once a preacher, is proof of my being under an irreligious phrenzy. Your conclusion being doubtless drawn from the effect of reading the bible and preaching has on yourself, I feel it due to you to say that constitutions differ, and that the same effects only follow where the constitutions are the same. From this it seems that you can "see your own back, look at your own eye, and analyze your own brain."

An insane person reasons correctly from false data, and my letters on your debate will decide whether you or I gave this evidence. If I prove your historical data or criteria false, there will be a case in point; and I pledge myself to do it. How sceptical you become when it suits your purpose. You cannot, without a jury of twelve men, believe that Dr. Underhill ever understood or believed a chapter in the bible. But you can easily believe the stories of the Egyptian plague—of the clothes of the Isrealites not wearing out in forty years—of Joshua making the sun stand still—of the spring of water that broke out—of Samson's jaw bone of an ass—of Jonah and the whale—and of the men in the fiery furnace;—of the Holy Ghost begetting a child on a virgin, and of the child cursing a fig-tree for not bearing figs in the winter, and sending 6,000 devils into 2,000 hogs—these and many more such stories you can believe of evidence, (much less a jury of twelve men,) to enable you to name the writer of one of these legends. Astonishing credulity!!

That you are afraid to risk a controversy in your paper, is an evidence of some discernment. But, my dear sir, my letters to you will go before the public. I have replied to your 6th sense and 4th world queries, examined and refuted your historical criteria, examined the story of the resurrection, and shall continue my labors as I get time until justice is done to deceive people. That you thought me insane, would have appeared more evident had you printed my letter and left your readers a dish of fun at least? As, unless you have altered, you could have no objection, for I have seen your paper furnished with it, even at the expense of truth. Your refusal to publish has induced me set at once about obtaining a press. Did it vex you, Reverend Sir, to ask you to give a few dozen names as a confirmation of your assertion that many sceptics were converted by the debate? I guessed it would be a hard question. I defy you Mr. Campbell, to give the name, (and furnish a verdict of three men,) of one well informed, openly avowed materialist, who was brought to believe in the doctrine of atonement by Jesus, or the authenticity of the bible by your debate. Some weak, wavering minds may have been confirmed by your loquacity. [Since I heard the story of your selling the blind negro child in the night and refusing to make restitution I have supposed your mind capable of any species of twistification in securing that fame for which many of your acquaintances think you more eager than you are to obtain eternal felicity.]⁵

Hoping that before you become a magistrate, there will be no means by which you can persecute those who differ from you in opinion, I inform you that I shall publish your letter, and if you were intoxicated with either wrath or wine when you wrote it, and will inform me, it shall be inserted as an apology.

The "Poor Fellow" salutes you with good will, and hopes your case may require no severer medicine, as he writes for public good and not for private spleen. You say, "if some of you were not so desperately wicked" we should be subjects of commiseration. This insinuation, Mr. C. is as base as it is malicious;—vicious sceptics there may be, but I boldly declare that after long acquaintance with both Christians and sceptics, I am compelled to say, that though I highly esteem many Christians as honest men, yet for real integrity, pure benevolence, and genuine morality, even taking the precepts of the amiable and benevolent Jesus for a rule, none have surpassed, and few have equalled sceptics or materialists of my acquaintance. I touch this subject unwillingly, as it is not my wish to be personal. Wishing to hear no more of this, in order to convince strangers that the insinuation was not based on fact, I here declare that my whole life has, since I arrived to manhood, been a life of integrity, and that I am persuaded that my whole life will not suffer by a comparison with any person whose sphere of action has not been more extended than mine.

On a bed of death I should be unmoved with other than joyous feelings, should I be convinced that I was to live in another world, and that on my way there I should meet with and be tried by a just judge. That I am convinced that even malace itself has never reported that I availed myself of darkness to cheat a neighbor. I say not that I never erred, I only say that I persist not knowingly in error. In good will.

SAM'L UNDERHILL.

LETTER III

June 1, 1830

Mr. Campbell—I promised in my introductory letter to reply to your queries for a sixth sense and a fourth world—[will the printer be so kind as to insert here the note in Mr. Campbell's edition of the debate—vol. 1st, page 163 and 164.][1]*

The first enquiry that naturally suggests itself is, has Mr. Campbell established any proposition which warrants him in asking these questions? If he has not let him comfort himself with that scripture which says "If the prophet be deceived, I the Lord have deceived that prophet."**

Had his two deaf and dumb men been also blind, he could have brought them to prove that revelation is the medium by which we learn

---

* While reading over my debate with Mr. Owen which I see is a good deal in the style of my extemporaneous harangues, a good many repetitions and a too great diffuseness in the argument, (tho' I hope this defect will be advantageous to the common reader, as it will keep the argument longer before his mind, and relieve him from much abstract thinking;) I discover what I consider a more forcible proof of the argument against the deistical notion of natural religion, or the supposed power we have to originate the idea of God, Spirit, Angels, Heaven, a future state, &c. I gave one forcible proof, as I think, in merely asking Mr. Owen to originate the idea of a sixth sense. This, I think, is an irresistible proof, that the human mind, however cultivated, cannot originate an idea entirely new. But perhaps this puzzle will carry conviction farther and deeper than any argument yet adduced upon this subject.

** We know three worlds, one by sense, and two by faith—I say we are in possession of ideas concerning three worlds: The present, material world, possessing, as we think various combinations of forty elements. This is the mundane system.

that the sun exists. Hard must be the lot of him whose case requires the testimony of what men felt when they had not five senses.

Mr. Campbell, described your God, and tell us of what elements your heaven and hell are composed. And if you give us the idea of an element, a form, or an attribute, not derived in whole or in part from the things and beings around you, your questions stand fair. If not you had no right to ask them. Your God is a combination of the powers of man multiplied, to which you add your ideas of immensity and infinity excited by the unmeasurable space and innumerable particles by which you are surrounded. Particles by which you are surrounded.

Habituated to seek an antecedent to every effect, to every occurrence, we fall into the notion that every substance as well as every effect has an antecedent. But when the mind expands we begin to find that something must exist without an antecedent. It is perceived that though it be very difficult to conceive that matter exists uncreated and eternal, it is still more difficult to conceive that a being without substance or parts exists uncreated and eternal, and that this immaterial being made all things out of nothing. Matter we know exists. Of immaterial beings we cannot by possibility form any definite idea. The question which of these ideas is true? cannot be decided.

Mr. Campbell says something must necessarily be uncreated eternal. So says the materialist. So far then we are agreed. One step farther must settle the question. We both know that matter exists. I now ask all the wise, the learned and the ignorant, (for it is so plain that all can see,) whether a proposition can be affirmed of a substance, of the existence

---

The other two worlds are heaven and hell, or a state of future bliss and future woe. Besides these, from some expressions found in scriptures, concerning the intermediate state from death to the resurrection, some have fancied the state of purgatory. This is, however, only in part fanciful, because there is a state of separation of spirit and body, which was the data for this idea. But now I ask all the atheists and sceptics of every name to fancy any other world—a fourth world—and to give us a single idea of it, not borrowed in whole, or in part from the three already known. If, with all the intellect which science and philosophy has given them they cannot do this, how, in the name of common sense, can they say that savages, when they had but this globe, or knowledge of one world could originate two others.

If then any sceptic durst, or atheist in these United States will tell what a sense, or a fourth world be, I will then concede this philosophical argument is not conclusive; till then I must think it is; till then I must think it exterminates every system of scepticism in the world. . . . If this be not good logic on their premises I will consent to go to school again.

Will some of the club show us that the conclusion is illogical?

of which we know nothing. The materialist points to light and heat, to ponderable and imponderable substances and says these are uncreated and eternal. You say at the same time that you perceive only matter, that God is uncreated and eternal. I sought many years to understand how man was made in the image of God. I only learned that all men and every nation made their God in their own image. The Jews made him a wrathful tyrant. Jesus is made to paint a benevolent being, while christians represent him as so wrathful that he could not forgive mankind, without quenching his anger in the blood of his son; and that son as old and as almighty as himself. You ask, who made the universe? I answer, it has eternally existed. I then ask you who made God? You say, he is uncreated and eternal. And he made all things out of nothing, say you. Then something may come out of nothing. If you say this rather than attribute your idea of God, heaven and hell to revelation, say these ideas came out of nothing. I presume that you will admit that the following sentence conveys an idea of no actual occurrence: "witches have flown through the air astride a broom." This sentence may be said to contain a thingless idea, as it represents nothing real. So all your ghosts, gods, fairies, devils, genii, spirits, heavens, hells, haydes, &c. are thingless names. Not one of your senses ever came in contact with any such thing.

The scriptures are explicit in fixing the elements of heaven and hell, as you will find in the revelation of John—pearl, jasper, onyx, chrysolite, beryl, agate, &c. And hell has fire, brimstone, a lake, &c. all borrowed from this world. Are you not ashamed, Mr. Campbell, that you so triumphantly asked these questions?

You ask for the sixth sense. Since proving that you have no ground to ask, I might excuse myself, but I like to humor the Great Appollus Magnus of Christianity, and therefore suggest the idea of the sense of longitude. The globe is doubtless one great magnet, from pole to pole of which, passes in right lines, the magnetic fluid; this would require such an organization and arrangement of nerves as would enable us to perceive this fluid, and then we should be able to set off at right angles with its course.

Mineralogy being in its infancy when the inspired penmen wrote, they could not with Mr. C. say the mundane system is composed of about forty elements. Now of the many which they have left, I shall make some worlds. With stone-coal I shall heat a hell which I shall call Hell Clericus, in which to roast those priests who seek to curse the world with more new imaginary systems of religion. With turf I shall heat one which I name

Hell Usurpus, to roast the oppressors of the poor. These characters being so much worse than devils that they are not entitled to as good company. I shall now made a good clover pasture and chalybeate springs a heaven for good old horses, and in the same place with plenty of port and milk, shall be a heaven for good old dogs. I could make many more if I chose, and if I may barely give names, I could give every word in the English language as a name of a hell or heaven. Yet names are all you gave—fie! Mr. Campbell, are you really the great man you pretend to be?

Did you promise, learned sir, that if the reasoning which I have here overthrown, was not good logic, you would consent to go to school?

When Mr. Owen urged what reason would say to many scripture absurdities which he mentioned, you replied that you could laugh all the virtues out of the world! And do they really exist by the mere mercy of such wits as yourself? Is it possible?!! Could you not as easily frighten all the rules of logic. If your talents equalled your vanity you would do wonders on the right side of a question. Truth and virtue are of so sterling a nature, so certain of the respect of the good and the wise that the shafts of ridicule, the burlesque of wit, or the cariactures of even the affectedly pious, can never render them valueless in the estimation of rational beings. There are, 'tis true, some things called truths, and some things called by the names of virtues, which are too baseless to withstand ridicule; but the fact that they cannot, should destroy all confidence in them. You may make a man of straw and call it Mr. Owen's system—and what then? why, laugh at it. But mark well, when the petty disputant on water baptism, and voluntary belief as a means of salvation shall have sunk in oblivion, then will the now slandered name of ROBERT OWEN be uttered by thousands of happy intelligent beings whose happiness and intelligence owe their existence to the arrangements in society, the outlines of which were by him suggested, and whose benevolent mind and dauntless courage combined to give momentum to the circumstances which rendered their introduction so necessary then, and without which in a few years the wretchedness of man must have been complete.

As I can refute you, dear Sir, I will do it,
S. UNDERHILL

LETTER IV

June 4th, Anno Republico 54.

Mr. A. Campbell,

Sir:—I proceed now to show the inadequacy of your historical criteria for establishing the authenticity of antiquated records.

You say "that you will rest the whole merits of the controversy upon your ability to prove the three leading facts on which Christianity is based, and the consequent inability of your opponents to disprove them."

1st, "that Jesus was crucified as attested by the four Evangelists. 2nd, that his body was deposited in the tomb of Joseph of Aremethea. And 3dly that he rose from the dead, and appeared upon earth for forty days, having during that time frequent intercourse with his disciples, and at the end of that time he did actually ascend up to heaven."

To prove the authenticity of the Jewish and Christian legends by which you think you establish these three facts, as you call them, your criteria are as follows:

> 1st, "the facts relied upon were sensible facts."
>
> 2d, "They were facts of remarkable notoriety."
>
> 3d, "There now exists standing monuments in perpetual commemoration of these facts."

Lastly, "These commemorative attestations have continued from the very period in which the facts are said to have transpired to the present time."

I shall apply the argument called reductis ad absurdum (or reducing to an absurdity) to show the folly of relying on these criteria.

I refer you to the supernatural acts of the witches in New England, recorded by Cotton Mather, Doctor of Divinity and Fellow of the Royal Society, London, and written in America within 200 years, and, which but for the spread of science, would never have lost its credit among men. I now apply your criteria to them.

> 1st, the acts and facts related of these witches were sensible facts and acts.
>
> 2d, they were facts of remarkable notoriety.
>
> 3d, there now exists records of courts, and Cotton Mather's history as standing monuments in perpetual commemoration of these facts.

Lastly, these commemorative attestations have continued from the very period in which the facts transpired up to the present time. And yet you and I and all Christendom who have common school education consider them, as the intelligent will soon consider your arguments and your new fangled system of salvation, as the feverish dreams of bewildered fanatics.

Now the legends attributed to Moses are reported to be sensible facts. 2, of great notoriety. 3, there are monuments said to be in commemoration. 4, and they continue. But the facts are not more sensible, more notorious, not half so well attested as the Salem witchcraft. Then of the legends of Moses we may say—they are recorded by anonymous writers—not one man gives his name as a witness and the records carry conclusive evidence of being written many hundred years after the date of the events; and Esdras says the book of the law was burned and that he wrote it again by revelation. Then of the legends of Moses we have to witness, no proof that a monument was ever set up to commemorate them, only the declaration of the fanatic Esdras that he wrote them by revelation, and the council of Nice decreed this same Esdras' writings as Apocryphal or doubtful.

We find in the book of Kings and Chronicles an account of Hilkiah the priest presenting the book of Shaphan the scribe, in the reign of Josiah, who began to reign at eight years of age (a fit opportunity for priests to forge books) of which book no one in Israel knew any thing. Of course the King sent the priest and scribe and others to enquire of an old fortune teller called a prophetess, who only said that God would bring to pass the sayings of the book. Mr. Campbell, have you never observed that tho' the books of Moses enjoin the annual celebration of the passover, that from the holding it in Egypt, none are recorded to have been kept until the book was found in the reign of Josiah? Would David, would Solomon and others have neglected it had they knowledge of it? and yet Solomon built the house in which it was found! O mighty legends! O, consistent legends!! O, soul-saving legends!!! Woe to him that doubts them!!!!

Should twenty witnesses of unblemished character testify in the Supreme Court of the United States that they knew a virgin who was got pregnant by the Holy Ghost, and that the child turned water into wine, sent a legion of devils into 2,000 hogs, that he was killed and buried, and in 36 hours came out of the grave and eat and talked, came into a room where the doors were shut, &c., I am persuaded that if this testimony had a very important bearing on a cause before them, they would only be convinced that these men were deceived even if they esteemed them sincere; and how much more should we reject old legends presented as evidence. You would fain have us believe that sophistry has placed the history of the benevolent Jesus in a light which claims our assent with a force equal to self-evident fact.

You cannot deny that the original copies of the four tracts called gospels are lost. You know that each copy is destitute of a signature, and if our present copies had signatures it would be no more than the transcriber's assertion that the original had them.

We have then no one witness verbal or written, but only a report that there were witnesses who gave the Gospels as their testimony. Luke's Gospel, as it is called, professes to have been written from hearsay. Much disagreement abounds in these accounts. You have then the following criteria, only:—1st, There are reports that some persons who were present did testify to the sensible fact that a Jesus was crucified. 2d, There is a report that some witnesses recorded the above, and that he was buried. 3d, There are writings said to be copies of anonymous reports and some ceremonies, said to be commemorative of these events. 4th, The above named commemorative writings and ceremonies remain unto this time.

There, Mr. Campbell, your sophistry is unravelled; and he that runs can read that you are far from having even your four criteria, and that your facts are not half so well established as the Salem witchcraft. I have little doubt that there was such a person, as Jesus would appear, exempted from the charge of supernatural conception, acts of legerdemain, and having the impoliteness to come to life again after he was fairly dead. Even coming to life after apparent death is not uncommon, as any one may learn by reading the report of Dr. McNab to the Chamber of French Deputies, a few years since—by reading the life of Rev. Wm. Tenant, of New Jersey, and many others.

It is the unnatural details, both of Cotton Mather and the Gospellers, that my mind rejects. I do not dispute the sincerity of Cotton Mather, nor of the falsely called inspired penmen, but if I admit them to be sincere I must charge them with astonishing ignorance and credulity.

Were I to lay down historical criteria I think they would not be subjected to the same objections as those Mr. Campbell has borrowed from Mr. Leslie. Let me try.

1st. The facts relied upon were in accordance with the known laws of matter.

2d. They occurred in the presence of numerous and well qualified witnesses, who recorded the same and gave their names as a testimony.

3d. They set up monuments which they described, that were to perpetuate these remarkable facts.

4th. These commemorative attestations are proved to have existed from that day to this, &c.

Here are but slight alterations, yet they spoil all your fish and ram's-horn stories. Learned Sir, should you receive an anonymous paper stating that ten thousand men saw a whale swallow Jonah, would you say you had ten thousand witnesses—rather say not one. Where then are your many witnesses Mr. Campbell? Astonishing, Mr. C. that you should assert that no (historical relation or) fact that can abide these criteria of yours can be false.—Apollus Magnus, I am astonished! As you contend that the bible is a work written by inspired penmen, you will greatly oblige me by reconciling the 24th chapter of 2d Samuel, and the 21st chapter of 1st Chronicles, which both essay to record the story of David's numbering the people.

One says the Lord moved David—the other says Satan moved him—One makes Israel to contain eight hundred thousand men that drew the sword, and the men of Judah five hundred thousand, making in all 1,300,000. The other makes 1,570,000. One makes Nathan the prophet offer in God's name to David seven years' famine, and the other three years', &c. Doubtless all these things are true, but the natural man cannot understand them.

The truth is, to us it matters not, whether Moses or Jesus, Jonah or Paul, Ninevah or Sodom, the pot of manna or the 1000 wives of Solomon, ever existed, unless in their history we find some useful moral to reduce the practice, or some error to avoid. That men in ancient days were wiser or better than in the present day, we have no proof. That men in the present day are much wiser and better, we can urge much to prove.

They were ignorant of almost every science—composed of tyrants and slaves—mimicking the gods their distempered imaginations pictured to them, and if examples were here and there found, of a different nature, they were few and far between.

You may call these remarks by what name you please; you may attack them with ridicule as is common where you cannot reason. I utter only sober reflections, yet to you they may appear different. Taught from your infancy, as I was, to count every relation in the bible true, and every precept divine, you learn to view as ruthless, the hand that would remove the veil, and present their naked deformity.

You corroborate your divine testimony with the admission of Celsus and other early opposers of Christianity, that there were miracles in the acts of Jesus.

But my dear sir, you are not aware, that at the early or infant state of science, the most learned were believers in magic and legerdemain—In supernatural conceptions by gods and virgins—in wonderful feats under supernatural endowments—In genii, gods, and devils. But this proves nothing but their ignorance. The whole world at that time—all the learned, believed the earth was a plain, and doubtless would have considered him mad that should have avowed it a sphere.

The movements of the Roman armies were governed by the flight of birds, and with them as with you, ignorant traditions usurped the place of evidence. Had you met me as you were invited to, it would have saved you all your late boasting. Not because Mr. Owen did not establish to intelligent minds what he promised, but because I should have met you on the ground you wished, and where the people expected, and broke your own lance over your own steel-cap.*[2]

I find no security against imposition, but to test what I hear by what I know; and even then I may be induced to believe falsehoods; because twenty men might testify that the present king of England is dead; I would be unable to doubt it. At the same time, only two hours later, they might own that they forged the tale to impose on me. But no amount of testimony could induce me to believe that a Jonah lived three days in a whale's belly, and was then spouted out on dry land.

Mr. Campbell can believe testimony inconsistent with the known laws of matter, & therefore believes,	Dr. Underhill cannot believe testimony in opposition to the known laws of matter & therefore disbelieves,
That the sun stood still at the command of Joshua. That three men resisted the violence of fire.	The story of Joshua and the sun. Of Shadrach, Meshach and Abednego.

---

* The language of Mr. Campbell, in his reply to an invitation from Canton, Stark county, to meet me in public.

| That a God had carnal knowledge of a virgin. | The story of the miraculous conception. |

Thus you can see the ground we differ on. And let me add, reverend sir, that I see no way that I can consistently admit one religion supernatural, without admitting every religion supernatural, equally well attested. You cannot be ignorant of the miracle of Prince Hohenloe, and you ought to know that the Shakers have recorded numerous miracles of recent date, occurring on persons yet living, one of whom I have conversed with myself—yet who believes them. From "Dwight's Travels in Germany," we learn that even the professors of theology reject the authenticity of the old testament and that many of them place the new on similar ground with other histories. I close this letter, under a persuasion that when this country shall equal that in science, a similar result will follow. That this period may soon arrive, and that man may turn his attention from a degrading sucumbency to the teachers about other worlds, whilst he improves his condition in this, shall be my wish whilst I live.

Respectfully,
SAM'L. UNDERHILL

LETTER V

June 6th, 1830, Anno Republico 53.
Mr. A. Campbell,

Sir: In my last I commenced and finished my arguments on your historical criteria, but I had promised to review the story of the resurrection, and I proceed to do it. I have long since laid it down as an axiom that no occurrence, the cause of which is involved in mystery, ever did, or ever will prove, to a well instructed mind, any thing but its own existence. It is evidence of its own existence, but proves no other fact. I have for many years been familiar with various writers on the resurrection, from the apostle Paul, who ignorantly thought a seed did not grow unless it died; down to the Shakers, who prove, as they think, that the whole matter is to be understood spiritually, and to the metaphysical Drew, who, in attempting to make it consistent with sound philosophy, reduced it to philosophical nonsense. He affirmed that as the body had participated in good or evil actions, it justly merited a participation in the reward or punishment. But perceiving that the matter composing our bodies was never two days the same, it followed that it was neither the body that we were born with, nor the one we died with, not yet the one possessed at any intervening period that would rise, he abandons his previous reason for raising it, and contends that there is a germ, constituted of our identity, out of which the body that shall be, arises, &c.

I leave these very learned, unnatural (or metaphysical, the meaning is the same) writers, and like Mr. Owen, ask, what reason would say to the resurrection? Let the fact be established, or as it cannot be established, let it be admitted for argument's sake, that a being named Jesus died, was buried, and came to life again. I think the first questions that reason would dictate are,

Of what order, class, genus, and species of beings is this of whom we have this account?

Had christians settled this question, it would have saved me much labor. But the "Poor Fellows" have not had sufficient time, not quite two thousand years, I therefore excuse them.

That he was at least equal to man, all contend; many that he was something more; and not a few that he was of that order called Sui Generis, (or perfectly original,) and from before all other sensible existences was, is, and is to come.

We will view the resurrection as relating to each of these characters, and find the logical result.

Let us suppose a being called God, uncreated and eternal, should take it into his head to let his creatures kill and buy him—That after three theological days (i.e., 36 hours) he should come to life, &c. Now if this was a natural event, every god who dies will surely come to life in three theological days;—most certainly. If however it be a miracle, no inference can be drawn from it, only that it is not a predicate for any second occurrence.

It no more proves that man will rise, than it proves that elephants will rise. It is a God, we are men, our natures differ.

Suppose now that he was part God and part man, what follows? That all beings of the same species will be subject to the same laws. If one God-man being, comes to life, naturally, the third day, all such beings will come to life the third day, when they die. But if it be a miracle, no second similar occurrence can be predicated on it. Pursuing this unsophisticated course, let us consider him a man that lived, died, and came to life, on the third day. If a miracle, it predicates no second similar occurrence; if a natural event, then all men come to life on the third day. But all men do not come to life on the third day. Therefore it was not a natural occurrence. You perceive, Mr. Campbell, that you reason thus; Jesus came to life on the third day, therefore all men will come to life some time or other. But upon what ground you best know. It as certainly proves the when, as it proves that they will come to life. Failing in the when, I infer it fails in all.

Thus you see that could you establish the resurrection as a fact, it has no manner of relevancy to our happiness any more than other curious historical relations.

Can you see the blind infatuation of the heathen of every tribe, I pray you consider their condition a looking-glass for [your] own absurdities. Having experienced your situation I can sincerely pity you. I think the moral precepts of the new testament, though not unexceptionable, superior to every other system of morals. But the religious dogmas exceed in real absurdity many others. It is the only religion in which (to use the language of another) "the sacrifice, and the being sacrificed to are the same." Your system seems to say, there is but one God, and that one God died to appease the wrath of one God, and to atone for the transgressions of his law. Laying his own wrath upon himself, and encouraging men to sin by telling them, "if any man sin I am an advocate with myself, to obtain forgiveness for you." I turn from this view of the subject with disgust. A little while and your craft is at an end; a spirit of enquiry has gone abroad, which no effort of yours can put down, no sophistry blind; nor even your low and abusive witticisms successfully assail. I doubt not you are willing people should enquire, until they find the errors of all other systems but your own, but you wish them to believe the errors of other sects, proof positive of the truth of yours.

Had you been capable of that dignified love of truth, which marked Mr. Owen's manner, you would have come forward on the stage, at the debate, the cool dispassionate reasoner rather than the fiery pettifogger, which your very language indicates.

You manifested cunning rather than wisdom, vanity than honesty, and a love of Latin quotations rather than plain unsophisticated language. But I thank you for acknowledging that you would rest your whole argument on your historical criteria, thereby excusing me from reviewing your 12 hour speech, which, as few read, I feel no disposition to equal in copiousness.

If Mr. Owen had a darling plan for bettering the temporal condition of man, you were no less eager to furnish a new plan for saving the soul.

I shall, therefore, in my next, take some notice of your darling child, and before I purchase it, I shall examine its eyes by day light, and see if it is perfect in its organization.

I am not mad, most noble Campbell, but speak the words of truth and soberness.

I salute you with good will,
SAM'L UNDERHILL.

LETTER VI

June 7th, 1830, Anno Republico 54.

Mr. A. Campbell,

Sir:—It was a saying of a very good man, who flourished in the days of Luther, that an opinion could not make a fly stir.

As light has increasingly visited mankind, they have become more practical and less opinionative.

All christian teachers, notwithstanding their private feuds and open quarrels, have agreed in one thing, i.e. in requiring a renunciation of the reason of every true believer.

The doctrine of original sin, of total depravity, of vicarious atonement, of imputive righteousness, and of salvation by faith in, and reliance on, Jesus Christ, might very appropriately have prefixed to them that precious sentence of the Koran, which says "Blessed and happy is he who receives the divine word without examination."

I will not deny that your teaching brushes away many cobwebs, but if you reject many absurdities of old systems, you retain some of the worst, and by lessening the number, those retained exhibit by contrast their deformity with treble strength.

The world will forgive me, if in one thing, I compare you with a man whose shoe-strings you are not worthy to bear. I mean the venerable and venerated Elias Hicks. Some few have seen for many years that thousands of those, who by his ministry were released from the traditions of their fathers, would become too enlightened to settle down satisfied with the traditions of Elias Hicks. So also I think, that of the many who by your labors are stirred up to perceive the numerous absurdities of other systems, some few, I hope will discover the absurdity of yours. But Elias Hicks taught the sufficiency of right reason, and the fallibility of the bible, whilst you have the unblemished audacity to declare the bible, a full, clear, unerring guide, without explanation or commentary.

With the weapon of reason you have routed many absurdities set in array by Calvin, Huss, and Wesley. In the same breath, and with equal assurance, you set forth the dogmas of Peter, Paul, and other men, perhaps more ignorant than the former, and now casting aside the touchstone of reason, you command implicit faith. Whilst their confidence was divided with many, they relied less firmly on any, and had a chance to escape them all. Reducing dependence to one, and that one far beyond the sun, mental bondage is fairly begun, and reason is over the wall.

But I meant not to become poetical. It is, doubtless, the effect of my frenzy, and you will pardon. If I understand your system, and I think I do, it may be summed in a few words.

It is that mankind will eternally exist, and that, after this life will commence a state of happiness or interminable misery, the one in the world called heaven, and the other in the world called hell, both of which worlds you profess to be acquainted with. And that to secure a place in the better world, we can obtain a title in fee simple, be we as men, murderers, or liars, robbers or tyrants, in short be we the vilest of beings, simply by believing that a Jesus of whom some anonymous writers, who lived some eighteen hundred years ago, speak, is the son of God, and by thus believing, and wholly relying on him, we get all previous guilt in such a fix, that the moment we are, by a duly qualified person, soused under water, all the load of guilt will leave us, "and we can read our title clear to mansions in the skies."

Blame not me, in that it appears ridiculous, an angel's pen cannot make it appear otherwise.

Precisely at the moment I finished the brief delineation of your system, reason whispered, "and pray sir, what station do I hold in the above paragraph?" I replied none, sir.

"And wherefore?" asked reason dryly, "begging your pardon reverend friend said I, I was compelled to write down Mr. Campbell's system of religion, in which you sir, can have no place."

"What! no place in Mr. C's. system? I thought Mr. Campbell professed to reason—though I was always absent, except on some occasions when he was leveling other men's systems."

"Begging your pardon Sir, again, had you been present, your pew would have been behind the pulpit."

"And can you inform me, sir, why I am used to pull down and not to build up?"

"Because Mr. C., in pulling down, is only preparing a foundation to build on, in his own name, and should he continue to use you, his own more flimsy fabric would vanish as the morning mist before the sun."

"And pray of what builds he?" said reason.

"With you, as I said, he clears a way; and then of the sayings of men* whom you never know, who wrote many hundred years ago he builds up. These men being dead, he is enabled to inherit all the honors which he claims for them?"

Reason—"By what legerdemain does he enforce these old unreasonable stories?"

"You are aware that some stories like cheese, grow better with age. The reports, which, two thousand years ago, were rejected by all cool minded men of common intelligence, are by age ripened into holy doctrines, and inspired truths; and had not the invention of the printing press given a new era to man, I might expect the book of Tom Thumb to become an oracle in about one thousand years."

"I see it," said Reason.

Continued I, "well might you see it, when the lascivious songs of Solomon are connonical, and the stories or the rams-horns at Jericho; of Elijah calling fire from heaven on fifty men, twice told; of two she bears destroying forty children for calling a man bald head; of Samsons's having a spring of water break forth in the jaw-bone of an ass—of the three men in the hot furnace; of Jonah going a missionary voyage in the belly of a whale, are all counted now by thousands, otherwise rational beings, as divine truths, which it is sacrilege to render ridiculous.

When the mere persuasion of the mind that a certain being, said by anonymous writers to have been born, lived, and died, like other men, is the son of God, and able to save from sin, but above all to remit sin; that this persuasion, and an unmixed reliance on this belief is able to render inoffensive in the eyes of purity the most vicious life, is what reason might justly call the royal insurance office for losses sustained and to be sustained.

---

* Men who were inspired, and of course had no use for reason.

Blame not the catholic of ancient times for selling indulgences to sin, as you make your God to open a house for remitting the worst, and fix the conditions within the reach of all who will call "whilst the lamp of life holds out to burn."

Did I not know that man is governed by present motives, an aversion to pain, and a desire of pleasure, in the present tense, and did I not know that vice brings pain, and virtue peace, every day, I should apprehend from your system frequent repetitions of St. Bartholomew's eve, and horrors indescribable. But thanks to the enlightened sceptic, Jefferson and his associates, those days are shortened, and science, reason and common sense find an abiding place among men.

Your writing should be forever headed with that passage of scripture, which I have long considered the most vicious sentence which ever acquired the character of inspired, to-with:

"He that believeth and is baptised shall be saved, and He that believeth not shall be damned."

If God damns people for not believing, and we must be like our father in heaven, surely it requires no stretch of sophistry to infer that his disciples should damn unbelievers.

Thus the foundation is laid for the most bitter persecutions, as it is easily inferred, that, to believe wrong, is worse than not to believe at all.

Disgusted with the various systems of damnation, I shall extinguish my stone coal fire, and in proceeding to review the system of voluntary belief, I shall let you out of the Hell I made for you; and having so done, I wish you health and happiness.

SAM'L UNDERHILL.

LETTER VII

June, 1830, Anno Republico 54.

Mr. A. Campbell,

Sir—In common with many other sects you advocate the doctrine of free-will. To this you are probably driven by perceiving the absurdity that follows Calvin's system as a whole. If a God should (as Calvin contends on has,) make a race of beings, determining from all eternity, that he would make one happy, and ten thousands miserable, without reference to their actions, but whose good and evil actions were fore-fixed from all eternity; the necessary conclusion is, that, that God is, of all unfeeling tyrants, the worst.

Escaping scylla, you heedlessly dash on charibdis. My dear sir, of the two succeeding pictures, give the preference to which you like best.

Suppose a God to determine that his creatures should act in a particular manner, but that all should desire to act viciously; and that most of these should be compelled to do so—that after this life, which had been wholly directed by his will, he should take a few into a happy state; and as he had all along designed, put the remaining infinite millions into a lake of fire and brimstone.

Suppose, a benevolent, all-knowing, powerful, even Almighty, God, should make a hell and create a race of beings, and give them the power of acting independently of motives, (which constitutes free-will,) whilst he knew at the time, that the greater part of these beings, acutely sensible to pain, would wander into hell. Remember—he had the power, and could have created them subject to motives; and could have made motives to virtue always predominate, and yet, knowing all this, and having this power, he deliberately made the hell, and gave the liberty.

Suppose one of your neighbors should dig a pit, which contained water enough to drown a child, and then should place near it twelve children, having warned them of the danger, yet knowing most certainly, that eleven of them would wander to its brink, and then tumble into the pit. You dug the pit knowing this, when you might have avoided it—you placed the children there, perfectly conscious of the result. To this add the idea, that you had made all their propensities, and the comparison is perfect, and needs no comment. Such is the god of free will.

But the blackness of the picture is much lessened, when we learn that, to save the human race from this perdition, He put his own son to a cruel death. But its blackness is again redoubled, when we are told that all this labor results in the resuscitation of a very few, and that the plan is nearly abortive, whilst it damns, with double fury the unsaved.

Satisfied that unless you could overthrow Mr. Owen's thrice proven proposition, to wit: "that the belief in no case, is controlled by the will," that all was lost, you labored not to ascertain the truth, but like a pettifogger to maintain your side.

After being many days in travail with a case, it comes out on the murder of Col. Sharp of Kentucky, and the detection of Beauchamp the murderer. The bringing forward this case, implies that you, until then, had found none in point. The examination of this shall prove that this is an unsuccessful subterfuge.

You must have been deceived, or you hoped to deceive your hearers and readers. Fools must they have been, had you made them believe that the will to find the murderer of Col. Sharp was the antecedent of the jury's persuasion of Beauchamp's guilt. To understand this, suppose a whole country to will to find a secreted murderer. I presume it was the evidence, and not the people's will, by which the jury were actuated in pronouncing the guilt of Beauchamp.

It would be quite as rational to argue that the sun was the cause of the jury's belief in that case, as the will of the people. Had their been no sunshine then, there would have been no food; if no food, then no excitability in the people; if no excitability in the people, then no will to find the murderer of Col. Sharp; if no will, then no search; if no search, then no circumstances; if no circumstances, then no evidence presented to the jury; and if no evidence, then no belief. If I mistake not, there are numerous examples of this ridiculous kind of reasoning in your debate.

Woe to the world if its most enlightened teacher pays so little regard to truth. It is a dilemma indeed; to say that he did not see the fallacy of this argument would be a libel on his understanding; to say that he did, is a libel on his honesty. Choose which, reverend Sir, you please.

I call an action voluntary, when it follows a previous determination, and involuntary, when, like pulsation of the heart, it takes place without a previous determination. An action is free when it follows volition, and constrained when I will to go east and some persons bind me and compel me to go west. But in each case the determination is the result of an antecedent which we name a motive or motives.

"If an internal act, or willing of the mind be free, it must in like manner, be self-determined, or in other words the mind in adopting them must be self-determined." "Liberty, according to this hypothesis, consists in this, that every choice we make has been chosen by us, and every act of the mind, been preceded and produced by an act of the mind." "This is so true that in reality the ultimate act is not styled free from any quality of its own, but because the mind in adopting it was self determined, that is, because it was preceded by another act. The ultimate act resulted completely from the determination that was its precursor. It was itself necessary; and if we would look for freedom, it must be in the preceding act. But in that preceding act also, if the mind were free, it was self-determined, that is, the volition was chosen by a preceding volition, and by the same reasoning this also, by another antecedent to itself." "All the acts except the first were necessary, and follow each other as inevitably as the links of a chain do when the first link is drawn forward. But then, neither was the first act free, unless the mind in adopting it was self-determined, i.e., unless this act was chosen by a preceding act. Trace back the chain as far as you please, every act at which you arrive is necessary. That act, which gives the character of freedom to the whole, can never be discovered; and, if it could, in its own nature it includes a contradiction." You ridicule the Mormonites, and discard the Golden Bible; in this, you are perfectly inconsistent. The golden bible not only accords the doctrines of scripture, but of its truth we have living witnesses. True the natural man can perceive nothing interesting in it; but this is what we are taught to expect of the natural man. He that found it, and he that published it, unhesitatingly put their names to it. They prophecy, and have the Holy Ghost—at least they say so. But they testify against you, therefore you reject them. They call you a false teacher, you call them fanatics and imposters. Each teach faith in Jesus, and baptism for the remission of sins, as the way to happiness. Each sends unbelievers to hell. That the difference between you, in the eyes of common sense, is well expressed by Swift, on another subject.

> "Strange that such high contest should be
> 'Twixt tweedle dum and tweedle dee."

If one system is to be believed, because men are found who sincerely avow it; I cannot, by possibility, see how any system, having the same testimony can be rejected. Every system has had its prophecies, miracles, martyrs, and sincere devotees. And until we learn to discard all authority or belief not founded on analogy, every species of Mormonick fanaticism may be successfully propagated. How plain and simple is moral truth? How complex, dark, mysterious, and incomprehensible, are doctrines of religion? Man is the only religious creature in this world, and he is, beyond all others, wretched. Whether his wretchedness is the offspring of his religion, time and investigation will yet make fully known. I think it is. I think if the same energies and equal zeal were manifested in removing the evils of life that are now wasted in theological dreaming, the earth would become a paradise. It may seem strange to some, that any one should charge many of the grosser vices to a system that urges the terrors of fire and brimstone as a punishment to evil doers. But fear never produces virtue, and nothing but truth can secure the mind against temptation. Remote causes act faintly on the human mind. Present circumstances act irresistibly. All real vice; all real virtue produces happiness in this life, if it did not, it would not be virtue. To know then the necessary consequences of action, is to possess the pure basis of genuine morality. This is the only sure basis, and this acquired in early life will make us good and virtuous beings.

I remain, &c.
SAM'L UNDERHILL

LETTER VIII

June 10, 1830, Anno Republico 54.

If Mr. CAMPBELL, you will say that in your debate with Owen you did not profess to attempt a candid examination on the subject of discussion, but on the contrary, that you came forward to exert your skill to its utmost, to impress the audience with a belief that religion is true, whether such was or was not the fact, then you confess all that I have grounds to charge upon you. Lawyers feel bound to use every exertion to sustain the cause of their client however frail it may be—to garnish the sepulchres in which they have entombed the truth, and by every art of eloquence, to pervert the feelings of the jury when their cause is at war with truth and justice. The language of truth to such an audience would have been, "ere we come to this important inquiry, it behooves us to see that we come with willing minds; that we say not 'so far will we go and no farther,' we will make one step but not two, we will examine—but only so long as the result of our examination shall confirm our preconceived opinions. In our search after truth, we must equally discard presumption and fear. We must come with our eyes and our ears, our hearts and our understandings open; anxious, not to find ourselves right, but to discover what is right; asserting nothing which we cannot prove; believing nothing which we have not examined; and examine all things fearlessly, dispassionately, perseveringly." Contrast now, with the above remarks, your flaming eulogy on the christian religion in your first speech at the debate, and behold the spirit it indicates. Conscious that the people's minds were prejudiced in favor of your side of the subject, if you believe it unassailable, why depend on the suspicious resource of popular excitement[?] A great portion of your positions and references, stript of the festoons thickly interwoven, would on the face of them carry evidence of their futility. Your Latin quotations, what fine ornaments to a popular debate; merely because the judges could understand them, you justify yourself in being according to Paul's definition "a barbarian to the audience." On page 164 of the 1st volume of the debate is a fine specimen of your logical powers. After attempting to prove that experience is simple memory, (though memory be only a faculty, and experience things once recognized by the senses and yet remembered,) you have the following remarkable sentence: "Suppose that I should be some accident, some concussion of the brain, be deprived of the faculty of memory, what would my experience be worth after I had forgotten all I had ever heard, seen, read, or acted? And yet this experience is the mighty engine by which my friend expects to overturn every thing predicated on testimony."

Read this over Mr. C., and then suppose a man should depend on inspiration or testimony to establish the world in righteousness, and by some accident should get his brains knocked out, what would all his inspiration or testimony be worth[?] Fie, fie, Mr. Campbell, what must we think of you? I have learned from observation, that much more than half the world give to wordy harrangues more credit than to sound arguments.

Now a word on your conduct as editor of the discussion. On the fourth page in your preface (with which I find little fault, except in your calling Mr. Owen's twelve propositions "twelve apostle,") we find these words, "Every thing on my part has been done, to give the public the most faithful and credible report of this discussion." Had you avowed that you availed yourself of every means that you dare use to prejudice your readers against your opponent, facts would have borne you out in the assertion. Not that many gross abuses exists, for you dare not venture them—but wherefore Mr. C., your long notes, which of course Mr. Owen could not ever see. Some filling a space equal to a whole page, & in particular, why one on pages 163 and 164 of vol. 1st printed in the same type as the work, and so placed, that the reader often reads the latter half as a part of Mr. Owen's speech, until its incongruity undeceives him? Not a few have done this. Why I entreat you Mr. C., why is that strange poetical extract from the gloomy Young in the title page, if you wish the character of an impartial editor? It follows.

"What then is unbelief?—'Tis an exploit,
A strenuous enterprise. To gain it man
Must burst through every bar of common sense,
Of common shame—magnanimously wrong!
————Who most examine, most believe;
Parts, like half sentences, confound.
Read His whole volume, sceptic, then reply!"
—YOUNG

"O LORD OF HOSTS! BLESSED IS THE MAN THAT TRUSTETH IN THEE."
—DAVID

Suppose Mr. Owen had been editor, and that he had in the same place, put the following lines from another British poet.

"All tyrants have three magic words, God, Hell, and heaven;
How powerless the mightiest monarch's arm,
Vain his loud threat, and impotent his frown;
How ludicrous the priest's dogmatic roar,
The weight of his exterminating curse, how light;
And his effected charity to suit the pressure
    of the changing times.
What palpable deceit, but for thy aid
Religion! But for thee, prolific fiend, who
Peoplest earth with demons, Hell with
Men, and heaven with slaves."
—SHELLEY.

Would this have appeared pleasant, impartial, and consistent with the words cited in your preface? I think not. Did you feel sensible, after speaking twelve hours more than Mr. Owen, and about twice as much in each half hour, that something was yet wanting? If so, for once you and I are agreed.

At present Mr. C. I am done with you. I have no malice in what I say of your writings and conduct. If some shades are cast on your candor and honesty, remember you furnished the materials yourself. It is to undeceive the public that I write, and not to injure you. I shall expose myself to hard names, but for this I am prepared. You may tempt me to paraphrase still more on your religion, but I shall never forget that you have not made yourself, and with all your errors are entitled to commiseration.

Farewell,
SAM'L UNDERHILL.

NOTES

Chapter 1

[1] Roy Porter, *The Enlightenment* (New York: Palgrave, 2001): 33.

[2] The Enlightenment terms "natural law" and "environmentalism" had specific usages in the eighteenth and nineteenth centuries. "Natural law" was the notion that certain rules that are inherent to humanity and to nature govern such things as biology, politics, and religion. Reason and the observation of nature, it was believed, revealed these laws to humanity. "Environmentalism" was the belief that a person's intellectual growth and cultural development is the product of each individual's surrounding influences and social circumstances, rather than heredity. For additional information on the Enlightenment use and definitions of these concepts, see Gerald R. Cragg, *Reason and Authority in the Eighteenth Century* (Cambridge: Cambridge University Press, 1964).

[3] Eric Foner, *Tom Paine and Revolutionary America* (London: Oxford University Press, 1976), 256.

[4] The term "evangelical" is used in a broad sense throughout this study to refer to traditional Protestant Christians who espouse the need for personal conversion and stress the authority of the Bible as the inspired Word of God.

[5] Mark A. Noll, *A History of Christianity in the United States and Canada* (Grand Rapids, MI: William B. Eerdmans Publishing Company, 1992), 243.

[6] Albert Post, *Popular Freethought in America, 1825-1850* (New York: Columbia University Press, 1943), 231.

[7] To Campbell and his evangelical contemporaries, "unbelievers" were people who espoused heterodox views of God, the Bible, and Christianity. Advocates of antebellum orthodoxy often made interchangeable use of the words "skeptic," "infidel," "atheist," "materialist," "deist," and "freethinker" in their efforts to identify unbelievers. When used according to their formal definitions, however, each of the aforementioned terms identifies a variant nuance of unbelief. A "skeptic" is a person who questions the reliability of accepted religious beliefs and practices, while an "infidel" is an individual who altogether repudiates religious belief and practice. "Atheists" reject any notion of the existence of God or a supreme deity, while "materialists" contend that the physical world is the extent of reality and that nothing exists apart from the material universe (though some suggest that the material universe may include a deity). "Deists" believe that a creator deity exists, but they reject supernatural revelation as a legitimate source of knowledge about God. The only valid methods by which the deity can be recognized and understood, according to deists, is through human reason and observation of the natural world (i.e., the creation of the creator). Finally, a "freethinker" is a member of an organized group that opposes religious beliefs or claims to supernatural revelation. The "freethought" concept had its origin in the notion that certain individuals have been able to develop their beliefs and worldviews independently of religious influences. For a more detailed explanation of these terms, see Gordon Stein, ed., *The Encyclopedia of Unbelief* (Buffalo: Prometheus Books, 1985).

[8] Unitarianism denies the Trinitarian aspect of God, while Universalism suggests that all of mankind will ultimately be saved by a loving God who would not vanquish any soul to an eternal punishment in Hell. The Unitarians and

Universalists were independent denominations in America throughout the nineteenth century and much of the twentieth century. In 1961 the two groups merged to form the Unitarian Universalist Association of America. See Paul K. Conkin, *American Originals: Homemade Varieties of Christianity* (Chapel Hill and London: The University of North Carolina Press, 1997), 105-108.

[9] "Restoration Movement" is the name applied to the nineteenth-century American religious movement led by Alexander Campbell and Barton W. Stone (1772-1844). This movement stressed the primacy of the Bible as a guide to Christian faith and practice, and called for the unity of all Christians upon the ancient beliefs and practices found in the Bible. The modern descendents of the Restoration Movement include the Churches of Christ, Christian Churches and Churches of Christ, and Christian Church (Disciples of Christ).

[10] Alexander Campbell and Robert Owen, *The Evidences of Christianity: A Debate Between Robert Owen, of New Lanark, Scotland, and Alexander Campbell, President of Bethany College, Virginia, Containing an Examination of the "Social System," and all the Systems of Skepticism of Ancient and Modern Times* (1829; reprint, St. Louis: Christian Publishing Company, 1906), vi.

[11] Robert Richardson, *Memoirs of Alexander Campbell* (1868; reprint, Indianapolis: Religious Book Services, 1897), 1:312-317.

[12] For additional information on Campbell as a preacher, see Alger Morton Fitch, Jr., *Alexander Campbell: Preacher of Reform and Reformer of Preaching* (1970, reprint, Joplin, MO: College Press Publishing Company, 1988); and Archibald McLean, *Alexander Campbell as a Preacher: A Study* (New York: Fleming H. Revell Company, 1908).

[13] Richard D. Brown, *Modernization: The Transformation of American Life, 1600-1865* (1976, reprint, Prospect Heights, IL: Waveland Press, 1988), 104.

[14] Carl Bode, *The American Lyceum: Town Meeting of the Mind* (Carbondale and Edwardsville, IL: Southern Illinois University Press, 1956), 31.

[15] For an examination of some of Campbell's speeches see Alexander Campbell, *Popular Lectures and Addresses* (1863, reprint, Philadelphia: James Challen and Son, 1866).

[16] See Lewis O. Saum, *The Popular Mood of Pre-Civil War America* (Westport, CT: Greenwood Press, 1980), 124-127.

[17] Alexis de Tocqueville, *Democracy in America,* trans. George Lawrence, ed. J. P. Mayer (1966, reprint, New York: Harper Perennial, 1988), 243.

[18] See Harold Holzer, ed., *The Lincoln-Douglas Debates: The First Complete, Unexpurgated Text* (New York: Harper Collins Publishers, 1993).

[19] See Campbell's debates with Robert Owen (1829), Roman Catholic Bishop John B. Purcell (1837), and Presbyterian Minister Nathan L. Rice (1843).

[20] See J. J. Haley, *Debates that Made History: The Story of Alexander Campbell's Debates with Rev. John Walker, Rev. W. L. McCalla, Mr. Robert Owen, Bishop Purcell and Rev. Nathan L. Rice* (St. Louis: Christian Board of Publication, 1920); Bill J. Humble, *Campbell and Controversy: The Story of Alexander Campbell's Great Debates with Skepticism, Catholicism, and Presbyterianism* (1956; reprint, Joplin, MO: College Press Publishing Company, 1986); and Enos E. Dowling, comp., *The Campbell Debates by R. C. Foster* (Lincoln, IL: The Author, 1982).

[21] Thomas Campbell, *Declaration and Address* (1809; reprint, St. Louis: Mission Messenger, 1978), 106.

[22] Richardson, *Memoirs of Alexander Campbell*, 2:13-14.

[23] Alexander Campbell, *Debate on Christian Baptism, Between Mr. John Walker, A Minister of the Secession, and Alexander Campbell, Held at Mount-Pleasant, on the 19th and 20th June, 1820, in the Presence of a Very Numerous and Respectable Congregation* (1822; reprint, Hollywood, CA: Old Paths Book Club, n.d.), 141.

[24] Richardson, *Memoirs of Alexander Campbell*, 2:90.

[25] Alexander Campbell, "Religious Controversy," *Millennial Harbinger* (January 1830): 40-41.

[26] Ibid., 42.

[27] For additional information about the history of Christian apologetics see Avery Dulles, *A History of Apologetics* (Philadelphia: Westminster Press, 1971); J. K. S. Reid, *Christian Apologetics* (Grand Rapids, MI: William B. Eerdmans Publishing Company, 1970); Bernard L. Ramm, *Varieties of Christian Apologetics* (1961, rev. ed., Grand Rapids, MI: Baker Book House, 1965); and William A. Dyrness, *Christian Apologetics in a World Community* (Downers Grove, IL: Intervarsity Press, 1983).

[28] Campbell, "An End to the Controversy," *Millennial Harbinger* (March 1857): 169. For additional information about Campbell's views on religious controversy see Campbell, "Religious Controversy," *Millennial Harbinger* (March 1835): 126-129.

[29] Richardson, *Memoirs of Alexander Campbell*, 1:283-310. See also Gary Holloway, "Alexander Campbell as a Publisher," *Restoration Quarterly* 37 (1995): 28-35.

[30] Richardson, *Memoirs of Alexander Campbell*, 2:49-51.

[31] Campbell, "Impartiality of the Editor of the Harbinger," *Millennial Harbinger* (January 1846): 4-5.

[32] Campbell, "Queries Touching the Fugitive Slave Law, &c.," *Millennial Harbinger* (April 1851): 226.

[33] Robert Frederick West, *Alexander Campbell and Natural Religion* (New Haven: Yale University Press, 1948), 5.

[34] Campbell, publisher's preface to *Popular Lectures and Addresses*, v.

Chapter 2

[1] Richardson, *Memoirs of Alexander Campbell*, 1:100-102.

[2] Lester G. McAllister, *Thomas Campbell: Man of the Book* (St. Louis: Bethany Press, 1954), 29.

[3] For an expanded explanation of Baconianism, Scottish Common Sense Realism, and their influence on nineteenth-century American religious thought, see Theodore Dwight Bozeman, *Protestants in an Age of Science: The Baconian Ideal and Antebellum American Religious Thought* (Chapel Hill: University of North Carolina Press, 1977).

[4] Campbell and Owen, *Evidences of Christianity*, 262.

[5] Ibid.

[6] Bozeman, *Protestants in an Age of Science*, 23-31.

[7] Leroy Garrett, *The Stone-Campbell Movement: The Story of the American Restoration Movement*, rev. ed. (Joplin, MO: College Press Publishing Company, 1994), 23-24. For additional information regarding Campbell's use of Baconianism, Lockean Empiricism, and Common Sense Realism, see Michael W. Casey,

Saddlebags, City Streets, and Cyberspace: A History of Preaching in the Churches of Christ (Abilene, TX: Abilene Christian University Press, 1995).

[8] Campbell, "Religious Anecdotes of Dying Professors," *Millennial Harbinger* (August 1833): 427; Campbell "John Locke," *Millennial Harbinger* (March 1845): 143.

[9] Richardson, *Memoirs of Alexander Campbell*, 1:33.

[10] Locke, *An Essay Concerning Human Understanding*, 40-41.

[11] Campbell, "Replication—No. I," *Christian Baptist* 4 (September 1826): 271.

[12] Campbell and Owen, *Evidences of Christianity*, 50.

[13] Campbell, "Deism and the Social System—No. V," *Christian Baptist* 5 (October 1827): 375.

[14] Garrett, *Stone-Campbell Movement*, 27.

[15] Campbell and Owen, *Evidences of Christianity*, 146.

[16] Campbell, "The Social System and Deism. No. II," *Christian Baptist* 4 (June 1827): 344.

[17] Alexander Campbell, *The Christian System in Reference to the Union of Christians, and a Restoration of Primitive Christianity, as Plead in the Current Reformation* (1840; reprint, Joplin, MO: College Press Publishing Company, 1989), 37.

[18] Ibid., 93.

[19] Campbell, *Popular Lectures and Addresses*, 118.

[20] Ibid., 119-120.

[21] Ibid., 117.

[22] Ibid., 120-121.

[23] Garrett, *Stone-Campbell Movement*, 30.

[24] Albert E. Avey, *Handbook in the History of Philosophy*, 2nd ed. (New York: Barnes and Noble, 1963), 162.

[25] Campbell, *The Christian System*, 3.

[26] Campbell, "The Bible," *Christian Baptist* 3 (March 1826): 225.

[27] Campbell, "On the Rules of Interpretation—No. III," *Millennial Harbinger* (March 1832): 108.

[28] Campbell, *The Christian System*, 4.

[29] Campbell, "On the Laws of Interpretation—No. I," *Millennial Harbinger* (April 1831): 188.

[30] In 1827, Campbell changed the name of Buffalo to Bethany. During much of Campbell's life Bethany was in Virginia. With the onset of the Civil War, however, the western area of Virginia sided with the Union and became the State of West Virginia.

[31] Richardson, *Memoirs of Alexander Campbell*, 1:460-461.

[32] Ibid., 1:373.

[33] Ibid., 1:369.

[34] Ibid., 1:372-373.

[35] Ibid., 1:396-399. See also Campbell, "Anecdotes, Incidents and Facts—No. I," *Millennial Harbinger* (May 1848): 279-283.

[36] Campbell, "Anecdotes, Incidents and Facts—No. II," *Millennial Harbinger* (June 1848): 344-345.

[37] Campbell, "Preface," *Millennial Harbinger* (January 1846): 1.

[38] Henry Webb, *In Search of Christian Unity: A History of the Restoration Movement* (Abilene, TX: Abilene Christian University Press, 1990), 243. It should be noted that membership numbers for this period are little more than educated guesses since accurate attendance figures are unavailable.

[39] West, *Alexander Campbell and Natural Religion*, viii.

[40] Ibid., 222.

Chapter 3

[1] Post, *Popular Freethought in America*, 77.

[2] Ibid., 76.

[3] D., "To the Editor of the Christian Baptist," *Christian Baptist* 4 (September 1826): 270.

[4] Ibid.

[5] These articles, five written by Campbell and one written by his father, were reprinted in 1859 as a pamphlet entitled, *Letters to a Skeptic, Reprinted from the Christian Baptist*.

[6] Campbell, "Replication—No. I," *Christian Baptist* 4 (September 1826): 271.

[7] Campbell, "To Mr. D.—A Sceptic—Replication—No. II," *Christian Baptist* 4 (October 1826): 273-275.

[8] Campbell, "Replication—No. I," *Christian Baptist* 4 (September 1826): 271.

[9] Ibid., 272.

[10] Ibid.

[11] Campbell, "To Mr. D.—A Sceptic—Replication—No. III," *Christian Baptist* 4 (November 1826): 282.

[12] Campbell, "Replication—No. I," *Christian Baptist* 4 (September 1826): 272.

[13] Robert Owen is discussed more thoroughly in chapter four.

[14] Arthur E. Bestor, Jr., "Patent-Office Models of the Good Society: Some Relationships between Social Reform and Westward Expansion," *American Historical Review* 58 (April 1953): 505-526.

[15] Yaacov Oved, *Two Hundred Years of American Communes* (New Brunswick, NJ: Transaction Books, 1988), 70-71.

[16] Ibid., 72.

[17] Interestingly, Adams' diary entry described Owen as a "speculative, scheming, mischievous man" at the time of their 1817 meeting in London. Following an additional meeting in Washington, D.C., in 1844, Adams went on to note that Owen was "as crafty [and] crazy as ever." Quoted in Earl Irvin West, "Early Cincinnati's 'Unprecedented Spectacle,'" *Ohio History* 79 (Winter 1970): 8.

[18] Oved, *Two Hundred Years of American Communes*, 110-111.

[19] Ibid., 111-113.

[20] Robert Owen, "A Declaration of Mental Independence," in Oakley C. Johnson, ed., *Robert Owen in the United States* (New York: Humanities Press, 1970), 70. Owen's "A Declaration of Mental Independence" was originally published in the *New Harmony Gazette* 1 (July 12, 1826): 329-332.

[21] Ibid., 69.

[22] Campbell, "Mr. Robert Owen and the Social System. No. I," *Christian Baptist* 4 (April 1827): 327-328. See Campbell, "Deism and the Social System—No.

IV," *Christian Baptist* 5 (September 1827): 364, for an additional statement of Campbell's opposition to the deism of Owen's society rather than with the communal system itself. Commenting upon an attempt to develop a Christian co-operative community in Canton, Ohio, Campbell wrote, "As far as I understand the genius and spirit of their system of co-operation and their views of christianity, I can cheerfully bid them God speed."

[23] Campbell, "The Social System and Deism. No. II," *Christian Baptist* 4 (June 1827): 343. A condensed version of Campbell's challenge, accompanied by editorial comments, was printed in the *New Harmony Gazette* 2 (July 11, 1827): 319.

[24] Ibid., 344-345.

[25] Campbell, "Deism and the Social System—No. III," *Christian Baptist* 5 (August 1827): 357.

[26] W. R., *New Harmony Gazette* 2 (August 1, 1827): 342. Also printed as "From the New Harmony Gazette of August 1," *Christian Baptist* 5 (September 1827): 372.

[27] Campbell, Untitled Article, *Christian Baptist* 5 (September 1827): 372-373.

[28] Campbell, "Deism and the Social System—No. IV," *Christian Baptist* 5 (September 1827): 364-366.

[29] Campbell, "To Mr. D.—A Sceptic—Replication—No. III," *Christian Baptist* 4 (November 1826): 282.

[30] A Lover of Just Reasoning, "Deism and the Social System—No. V," *Christian Baptist* 5 (October 1827): 373.

[31] Campbell, "Deism and the Social System—No. V," *Christian Baptist* 5 (October 1827): 374-375.

[32] Ibid., 375. See also, H., "The Christian Baptist," *New Harmony Gazette* 2 (August 27, 1827): 364.

[33] A Lover of Just Reasoning, "Deism and the Social System—No. V," *Christian Baptist* 5 (October 1827): 373-374.

[34] Campbell, "Deism and the Social System—No. V," *Christian Baptist* 5 (October 1827): 376.

[35] Campbell, "A Problem for the Editor of the Harmony Gazette and his Doubting Brethren," *Christian Baptist* 5 (October 1827): 376-377.

[36] *New Harmony Gazette* 3 (October 24, 1827): 22.

[37] "The Christian Baptist, Again," *New Harmony Gazette* 3 (October 10, 1827): 4.

[38] Dr. Samuel Underhill is discussed more thoroughly in chapter six.

[39] A., "Mr. Alexander Campbell," *Christian Baptist* 5 (April 1828): 433-434.

[40] Campbell, "Mr. A.—," *Christian Baptist* 5 (April 1828): 434.

[41] *New Harmony Gazette* 3 (April 30, 1828): 215.

[42] Owen, "Address," *New Harmony Gazette* 2 (May 9, 1827): 254-255.

[43] Owen, "Robert Owen to the Ten Social Colonies of Equality and Common Property," *New Harmony Gazette* 2 (May 30, 1827): 278-279.

[44] George B. Lockwood, *The New Harmony Movement* (New York: D. Appleton and Company, 1905), 173.

[45] Arthur Bestor, *Backwood Utopias: The Sectarian Origins and the Owenite Phase of Communitarian Socialism in America: 1663-1829* (1950; reprint, Philadelphia: University of Pennsylvania Press, 1970), 201.

[46] Owen, "Address Delivered by Robert Owen at a Public Meeting of the Inhabitants of New-Harmony, on Sunday, April 13, 1828," *New Harmony Gazette* 3 (April 23, 1828): 204.

[47] Bestor, *Backwood Utopias*, 176.

[48] Owen, "Mr. Owen to the Clergy of New-Orleans," *New Harmony Gazette* 3 (March 26, 1826): 169. Also printed in the *Christian Baptist* 5 (May 1828): 443.

[49] Campbell, "Mr. Robert Owen's Challenge," *Christian Baptist* 5 (May 1828): 443-444.

[50] Owen, "Mr. Alexander Campbell," *New Harmony Gazette* 3 (May 14, 1828): 228. Also printed in the *Christian Baptist* 5 (July 1828): 455-456.

[51] Campbell, "To Robert Owen, Esq.," *Christian Baptist* 5 (July 1828): 456. Also printed in the *New Harmony Gazette* 3 (August 6, 1828): 324.

Chapter 4

[1] Richardson, *Memoirs of Alexander Campbell*, 2:242.

[2] Robert Owen to James M. Dorsey, July 14, 1828. The Indiana Historical Society, Indianapolis, Indiana.

[3] Ibid., 242-243. Campbell used an abridgement of this story as part of his argument against Owen during their debate. See Campbell and Owen, *Evidences of Christianity*, 389-390.

[4] Robert Owen, *The Life of Robert Owen* (1857; reprint, New York: Augustus M. Kelley Publishers, 1967), 1-3.

[5] Carol A. Kolmerten, *Women in Utopia: The Ideology of Gender in the American Owenite Communities* (1990; reprint, Syracuse, NY: Syracuse University Press, 1998), 13-14.

[6] Robert Owen, *A New View of Society*, reprinted in *The Life of Robert Owen* (1813; reprint, New York: Augustus M. Kelley Publishers, 1967), 292.

[7] Owen, *The Life of Robert Owen*, 12-13.

[8] Ibid., 27-28.

[9] Ibid., 42-43.

[10] Ibid., 50-55.

[11] Ibid., 56-57.

[12] Ibid., 59-60.

[13] Ibid., 61.

[14] Ibid., 61-63.

[15] Owen, *A New View of Society*, 284-285.

[16] Ibid., 266.

[17] Ibid., 270.

[18] Ibid., 283.

[19] Ibid., 285.

[20] Ibid., 296.

[21] Ibid., 300.

[22] Robert Owen, "A New Religion," *Niles' Register*, May 24, 1823 (reprinted from the *Limerick* [Ireland] *Chronicle*, January 27, 1823).

[23] Owen, *The Life of Robert Owen*, 4.

[24] Ibid., 16.

[25] Owen, "A New Religion," *Niles' Register*, May 24, 1823.

[26] Owen, *The Life of Robert Owen*, 16.

[27] In an 1825 speech, Owen referred to his concept of "true religion" as "rational religion." Furthermore, he described religion as being consistent and in unison with the facts of nature, *New Harmony Gazette*, 2 (May 9, 1827): 249. See also, Frank Podmore, *Robert Owen: A Biography*, vol. 2 (1907; reprint, New York: Haskell House Publishers, 1971), 497.

[28] Owen, *The Life of Robert Owen*, 102.

[29] Ibid., 103.

[30] Owen, *A New View of Society*, 298-299.

[31] Owen, *The Life of Robert Owen*, 105.

[32] Robert Owen, *Report to the Committee of the Association for the Relief of the Manufacturing and Labouring Poor*, reprinted in *The Life of Robert Owen*, vol. 1A (1817; reprint, New York: Augustus M. Kelley Publishers, 1967), 56.

[33] Robert Owen, *Report to the County of Lanark*, reprinted in *The Life of Robert Owen*, vol. 1A (1820; reprint, New York: Augustus M. Kelley Publishers, 1967), 287. Owen's size specifications for his co-operative communities fluctuate in various writings. Generally he seems to suggest 1,000 to 1,200 as the ideal population for his villages.

[34] Ibid., 303.

[35] G. D. H. Cole, introduction to *A New View of Society and Other Writings*, by Robert Owen (London: J. M. Dent and Sons; New York: E. P. Dutton and Company, 1927), xiii.

[36] Robert and Caroline Owen had eight children but their first-born son died in infancy.

[37] Robert Dale Owen, *Threading My Way: An Autobiography* (1874; reprint, New York: Augustus M. Kelley Publishers, 1967), 239-241.

[38] Robert Owen, "Memorial of Robert Owen to the Mexican Republic, and to the Government of Coahuila and Texas," *Free Enquirer* 1 (February 11, 1829): 122-123. Also reprinted in Wilbert H. Timmons, "Robert Owen's Texas Project," *Southwestern Historical Quarterly* 52 (January 1949): 292.

[39] Frank Podmore, *Robert Owen: A Biography* (1907; reprint, New York: Haskell House Publishers, 1971), 1:340-341. Podmore speculates that the likelihood that Owen actually received such a promise from the Mexican government "seems scarcely probable."

[40] Richardson, *Memoirs of Alexander Campbell*, 2:263.

[41] Campbell, "A Debate on the Evidences of Christianity," *Christian Baptist* 6 (August 1828): 469.

[42] *Daily Cincinnati Gazette*, April 9, 1829 and April 11, 1829.

[43] Campbell and Wilson appear to have had earlier reservations about one another. In an interesting letter published in the *Daily Cincinnati Gazette*, March 16, 1829, Campbell accused Dr. Wilson of attempting to sabotage the debate by publishing an article stating that Campbell and Owen were meeting in Cincinnati "to form a religion wholly true and consistent, out of all the religions of the world." Apparently Wilson obtained a copy of a letter Owen wrote to the *London Times*, in which Owen made such a claim. Campbell read the newspaper article in the debate and denied that he had ever agreed to such a plan. See Campbell and Owen, *Evidences of Christianity*, 31-32 and 36-38. R. C. Foster suggested that the primary reason for Wilson's dislike for Campbell derived from Campbell's overwhelming

debate victories over Wilson's fellow Presbyterians, John Walker (1820) and W. L. Maccalla (1823). See Dowling, *The Campbell Debates by R. C. Foster*, 36.

[44] Frances Trollope, *Domestic Manners of the Americans*, ed. Pamela Neville-Sington (1832; reprint, New York: Penguin Books, 1997), 113.

[45] *Cincinnati Chronicle and Literary Gazette*, April 25, 1829.

[46] Campbell, "Debate on the Evidences of Christianity," *Christian* Baptist 6 (June 1829): 552.

[47] Campbell chose Judge Burnet, Col. Samuel W. Davies, and Major Daniel Gano as his moderators. Owen selected the Rev. Timothy Flint, Col. Francis Carr, and Henry Starr. The Rev. Oliver M. Spencer was then procured as the seventh moderator.

[48] Campbell and Owen, *Evidences of Christianity*, 31.

[49] Trollope, *Domestic Manners of the Americans*, 112.

[50] Timothy Flint, "Public Challenged Dispute between Robert Owen, late of New-Lanark, Scotland, and last of New-Harmony, Indiana, Philosopher and Cosmopolite, and Rev. Alexander Campbell, of the Sect commonly called Free-Will Baptists, of Bethany West Virginia, near Wheeling: The Former Denying the Truth of all Religions in General; and the Latter Affirming the Truth of the Christian Religion on Logical Principles," *Western Monthly Review* 3 (April 1829): 641.

[51] Ibid.

[52] Campbell and Owen, *Evidences of Christianity*, 14-15.

[53] Ibid., 24.

[54] Ibid., 106.

[55] Ibid., 106-107.

[56] Nathan J. Mitchell, *Reminiscences and Incidents in the Life and Travels of a Pioneer Preacher of the "Ancient" Gospel; with a few Characteristic Discourses* (Cincinnati: Chase and Hall, 1877), 66.

[57] Humble, *Campbell and Controversy*, 95.

[58] Campbell and Owen, *Evidences of Christianity*, 31.

[59] Ibid., 40.

[60] Ibid., 41.

[61] For a more thorough coverage of the historical development of the ontological argument for God's existence, see Jonathan Barnes, *The Ontological Argument* (New York: St. Martin's Press, 1972), Graham Robert Oppy, *Ontological Arguments and Belief in God* (Cambridge and New York: Cambridge University Press, 1995), and Alvin Plantinga, *The Ontological Argument: From St. Anselm to Contemporary Philosophers* (Garden City, NY: Anchor Books, 1965).

[62] Campbell and Owen, *Evidences of Christianity*, 50-52.

[63] Ibid., 52.

[64] Ibid., 78.

[65] Ibid., 189.

[66] Ibid., 107.

[67] Ibid., 109-110. From very early in the debate, Campbell admitted that Owen's laws contain "a great many facts" (Campbell and Owen, *Evidences of Christianity*, 34). Of Owen's twelve laws (See Appendix A), the one law that Campbell refused to accept was the sixth law (Campbell and Owen, *Evidences of Christianity*, 244-246). This is also the law which Owen referred to as the central proposition of his system (Campbell and Owen, *Evidences of Christianity*, 204-208).

[68] Campbell and Owen, *Evidences of Christianity*, 115-117.

[69] Ibid., 107.

[70] Ibid., 224.

[71] Ibid., 250.

[72] Ibid., 256.

[73] Ibid., 119.

[74] Ibid., 99.

[75] Ibid., 105-106.

[76] Ibid., 71.

[77] Ibid., 108.

[78] Ibid., 134.

[79] Ibid., 122.

[80] Ibid., 167. Campbell's suggestion that David Dale initiated a series of reform programs designed to benefit the New Lanark employees is substantiated by Ian L. Donnachie and George Hewitt, *Historic New Lanark: The Dale and Owen Industrial Community Since 1785* (Edinburgh: Edinburgh University Press, 1993), 33-34 and 56-58.

[81] Campbell and Owen, *Evidences of Christianity*, 169-170.

[82] Ibid., 200.

[83] Ibid., 242.

[84] Ibid., 259.

[85] Haley, *Debates that Made History*, 89.

[86] Ibid., 259-404.

[87] Ibid., 404-405.

[88] Ibid., 405-414.

[89] Ibid., 424.

[90] Ibid., 429.

[91] Ibid., 464.

[92] "Religious Controversy," *Ohio Repository*, May 8, 1829 (reprinted from the *Ohio State Journal*, n.d.).

[93] "Mr. Campbell and Mr. Owen," *Western Intelligencer*, May 15, 1829 (reprinted from the *Cincinnati Pandect*, n.d.).

[94] "Messrs. Campbell and Owen," *The Cincinnati Chronicle and Literary Gazette*, April 25, 1829. Campbell reprinted this article in his *Christian Baptist* 6 (June 1829): 553-554.

[95] "Proposal to the Editor of the Washington City Chronicle," *Free Enquirer* 1 (June 10, 1829): 261 (reprinted from the *Washington City Chronicle*, n.d.).

[96] Flint, "Public Challenged Dispute," *Western Monthly Review, 647.* Owen responded to this article by referring to it as a "fanciful report of the recent discussion." See "Reply to the Reviewer by Mr. Owen," *Free Enquirer* 1 (June 3, 1829): 252.

[97] Robert Owen, *Robert Owen's Opening Speech, and his Reply to the Rev. Alex. Campbell, in the Recent Public Discussion in Cincinnati* (Cincinnati: Published for Robert Owen, 1829).

[98] Campbell, "An End of the Controversy," *Millennial Harbinger* (March 1857): 170. Campbell's wife, Selina, reported that Owen was "courteous and affable" in his post-debate visit to Bethany. See Selina Huntington Campbell, *Home Life and Reminiscences of Alexander Campbell* (St. Louis: John Burns, 1882), 306.

[99] Frederick Engels, *Socialism: Utopian and Scientific*, trans. Edward Aveling (1892; reprint, Moscow: Progress Publishers, 1970), 47.

[100] John F. C. Harrison, *Quest for the New Moral World: Robert Owen and the Owenites in Britain and America* (New York: Charles Scribner's Sons, 1969), 250. Campbell also commented on Owen's acceptance of spiritualism. See Campbell, "Necromancy—Alias, Spirit Rappings—Again," *Millennial Harbinger* (August 1853): 469-470.

[101] Lockwood, *The New Harmony Movement*, 308.

[102] Campbell, "Letter from Europe—No. 1," *Millennial Harbinger* (July 1847): 420.

[103] Campbell, "The Neotrophian Magazine," *Millennial Harbinger* (March 1859): 173.

[104] Haley, *Debates that Made History*, 178.

[105] Campbell, "Difficulties of a Sceptic," *Millennial Harbinger* (September 1840): 428-429.

[106] Campbell, "Memorabilia for June," *Millennial Harbinger* (June 1852): 350.

[107] Campbell and Owen, *Evidences of Christianity*, 461.

[108] Ibid., 201-202.

Chapter 5

[1] Campbell, "Obituary," *Millennial Harbinger* (September 1841): 432.

[2] A. C. Quisenberry, *The Life and Times of Hon. Humphrey Marshall* (Winchester, KY: The Sun Publishing Company, 1892), 11-16.

[3] Ibid., 114.

[4] Ibid., 18.

[5] Ibid., 113.

[6] Mary Willis Woodson and Martha Moore, *Through the Portals of Glen Willis* (N.p.: Franklin County Trust for Historic Preservation, 1989), 35.

[7] Quisenberry, *Humphrey Marshall*, 18-19. Noting that Marshall's infidel pamphlets "have perished from the face of the earth," Quisenberry suggests that his relatives collected and destroyed them. Of the many pamphlets published by Marshall, only a single pamphlet, a copy of *The Letter of a Private Student*, is known to remain extant. It is preserved in the archival collection of the University of Chicago.

[8] Humphrey Marshall, *The Letter of a Private Student, or an Examination of the "Evidences of Christianity" as Exhibited and Argued at Cincinnati April, 1829, by Rev. Alexander Campbell in a Debate with Mr. Robert Owen* (Frankfort, KY: J. H. Holeman, 1830), 50.

[9] Ibid., 56.

[10] Ibid., iii.

[11] Ibid., 6.

[12] Ibid., 11.

[13] Ibid., 12-13.

[14] Ibid., 33.

[15] Ibid., 22.

[16] Ibid., 23.

[17] Ibid., 33.

[18] Ibid., 16.

[19] Ibid.

[20] Acts 9:1-19; 22:1-21; 26:9-18.

[21] Marshall, *The Letter of a Private Student*, 17.

[22] Ibid., 22.

[23] Ibid., 53.

[24] Ibid., 55.

[25] Ibid., 49-50.

[26] Ibid., 53.

[27] Campbell, "Letters to Humphrey Marshal, Esq.—No. 1," *Millennial Harbinger* (November 1830): 513-514.

[28] Ibid., 514-515.

[29] Ibid., 516.

[30] Ibid., 517.

[31] Campbell, "Letters to Humphrey Marshal, Esq.—Letter II," *Millennial Harbinger* (December 1830): 529-530.

[32] Ibid., 530-531.

[33] Ibid., 531.

[34] Campbell, "Letters to Humphrey Marshal, Esq.—Letter III," *Millennial Harbinger* (January 1831): 16-17.

[35] Ibid., 17-18.

[36] Ibid., 18.

[37] Campbell, "Letters to Humphrey Marshal, Esq.—Letter IV," *Millennial Harbinger* (February 1831): 70.

[38] I Corinthians 15:13.

[39] Marshall, *The Letter of a Private Student*, 17.

[40] Campbell, "Letters to Humphrey Marshal, Esq.—Letter IV," *Millennial Harbinger* (February 1831): 70-73.

[41] Ibid., 73.

[42] Campbell, "Letters to Humphrey Marshal, Esq.—Letter V," *Millennial Harbinger* (April 1831): 150-153.

[43] Ibid.

[44] Campbell, "Letters to Humphrey Marshal, Esq.—Letter VI," *Millennial Harbinger* (June 1831): 258-261.

[45] Humphrey Marshall, "To the Rev. A. Campbell, Bethany, Virginia," *Millennial Harbinger* (August 1831): 370.

[46] Campbell, "Letters to Humphrey Marshal, Esq.—Letter VII," *Millennial Harbinger* (August 1831): 371-373.

[47] Campbell, "Humphrey Marshall, Esq.," *Millennial Harbinger* (November 1831): 523.

[48] Quisenberry, *Humphrey Marshall*, 104-105.

[49] Ibid., 136-137.

Chapter 6

[1] Samuel Underhill to Robert Owen, May 4, 1828. Robert Owen Collection (Item 126). Co-operative Union Ltd., Manchester, England.

[2] Underhill did not actually challenge Campbell to a debate. Rather, a reader of the *Christian Baptist* requested Campbell's assistance in confronting Underhill, "an emissary of infidelity." Campbell declined the offer to meet an "obscure" figure like Underhill, but said he would be happy to debate Underhill's "great master, Mr. Robert Owen." See chapter 3.

[3] Robert Owen to Samuel Underhill, June 20, 1828. Robert Owen Collection (Item 126). Co-operative Union, Ltd., Manchester, England.

[4] For additional information on the Underhill family, see Josephine C. Frost, ed., *Underhill Genealogy: Descendants of Capt. John Underhill*, 4 vols. (Brooklyn: Myron C. Taylor, 1932), and Edwin B. Deats, comp., and Harry Macy, Jr., ed., *Underhill Genealogy*, 2 vols. (Baltimore: Gateway Press, 1980).

[5] Samuel Underhill, "Reminiscences of Childhood," *Cleveland Liberalist* (November 12, 1836): 65-66.

[6] Underhill, "Reminiscences of Youth," *Cleveland Liberalist* (November 19, 1836): 77.

[7] Underhill, "Reminiscences of Childhood," *Cleveland Liberalist* (November 12, 1836): 66.

[8] Samuel Underhill, *A Lecture on Mysterious Religious Emotions, Delivered at Bethlehem, Ohio, by Dr. Samuel Underhill* (Steubenville, OH: Printed for the Author, 1829), 4.

[9] Underhill, "Reminiscences of Youth," *Cleveland Liberalist* (November 19, 1836): 77-78.

[10] Ibid., 78.

[11] Frost, *Underhill Genealogy*, 324.

[12] Elias Hicks opposed the ideas of Christ's substitutionary atonement, religious creeds and hierarchies, and Scriptural authority. Man's only governing authority, he taught, should be the Inner Light, which he equated to man's natural reasoning ability. For more information on Hicks, see Elias Hicks, *Journal of the Life and Religious Labours of Elias Hicks* (New York: I. T. Hopper, 1832), and Bliss Forbush, *Elias Hicks, Quaker Liberal* (New York: Columbia University Press, 1956).

[13] In his private journal, Underhill wrote that he had journeyed from "Hicksiteism [*sic*] to what is called infidelity." He also noted that "Hicksiteism or Gibbonism [a name given to the followers of Dr. William Gibbons, himself a disciple of Elias Hicks] is the high road to skepticism." See Samuel Underhill, "The Chronicles, Notes, and Maxims of Dr. Samuel Underhill," n.d., Stark County Historical Society, Canton, Ohio.

[14] Samuel Underhill to Alexander Campbell, April 8, 1830. See Underhill, "Chronicles, Notes, and Maxims of Dr. Samuel Underhill," April 8, 1830; and Underhill *Cleveland Liberalist* (June 30, 1828): 306-307.

[15] Underhill to Owen, May 4, 1828. See also Underhill, *A Lecture on Mysterious Religious Emotions*, 20-21.

[16] Post, *Popular Freethought in America*, 141. See also Underhill, *A Lecture on Mysterious Religious Emotions*, 18-19.

[17] Bestor, *Backwoods Utopias*, 97-100.

[18] Underhill to Owen, May 4, 1828.

[19] Samuel Underhill, "Forestville Community," *New Harmony Gazette* 3 (November 7, 1827): 34.

[20] For a complete history of the Kendal Community, see Richard J. Cherok, "No Harmony in Kendal: The Rise and Fall of an Owenite Community, 1825-1829," *Ohio History* 108 (Winter-Spring 1999): 26-38.

[21] *History of Green County, New York, with Biographical Sketches of its Prominent Men* (1884, reprint, Cornwallville, NY: Hope Farm Press, 1969), 242; "Kendall Community," *New Harmony Gazette* 3 (February 13, 1828), 141.

[22] For a more detailed account of the journey the Forestville residents made to Kendal, see "Death Recalls Local History," *Massillon Evening Independent*, April 18, 1910.

[23] "Constitution of the Friendly Association for Mutual Interests at Kendal, Ohio," March 17, 1826, Rotch-Wales Collection, Massillon Public Library, Massillon, Ohio. The record book of the Kendal Community, including the constitution, minutes and final balance sheet, were published by Wendall P. Fox in "The Kendal Community," *Ohio Archaeological and Historical Publications*, 20 (April-July 1911), 176-219.

[24] "Reports of Meetings," March 22, 1828. Rotch-Wales Collection, Massillon Public Library, Massillon, Ohio.

[25] "Kendal Community, Ohio," *New Harmony Gazette* 3 (February 13, 1828), 141. Although the author of this letter is not named, its content clearly indicates that it was written by Underhill.

[26] See chapter three.

[27] "Reports of Meetings," October 6, 1828.

[28] "Reports of Meetings," January 3, 1829.

[29] Campbell published a portion of Underhill's *A Lecture on Mysterious Religious Emotions* in his *Millennial Harbinger*, and noted its author's claim that the study of anatomy would cure people of religious superstition. This contention, Campbell wrote, is among the most "ludicrous and phantastic [*sic*] ebullitions" ever produced within "scepticism." See Campbell, "Sceptical Enthusiasm—Anatomy a Cure for Religion!," *Millennial Harbinger* (February 1830): 72.

[30] Underhill mentions numerous speaking engagements in his "Chronicles, Notes, and Maxims of Dr. Samuel Underhill." His published speeches include *A Lecture on Mysterious Religious Emotions* (1829, reprinted in 1832; also printed as a newspaper article, *Delaware Free Press*, April-May 1830); a temperance speech for the Temperance Convention of Northern Ohio (*Ohio Observer*, October 20, 1834); and two addresses in honor of Thomas Paine, one delivered at Brecksville, Ohio (1836) and the other at Shalersville, Ohio (1837).

[31] Underhill, "Chronicles, Notes, and Maxims of Dr. Samuel Underhill," July 20, 1829.

[32] Ibid., January 21, 1830.

[33] Ibid., April 8, 1830.

[34] Samuel Underhill to Alexander Campbell, April 8, 1830. "Chronicles, Notes, and Maxims of Dr. Samuel Underhill." A revised copy of this letter also appeared in the *Cleveland Liberalist* (June 30, 1838): 306-307.

[35] Alexander Campbell to Samuel Underhill, April 20, 1830. "Chronicles, Notes, and Maxims of Dr. Samuel Underhill." Along with Campbell's letter, Underhill wrote, "The following letter from Alexander Campbell is in answer to one which I sent to him in compliance with an invitation from him to oppose his arguments against Mr. Owen. It is a very singular one indeed; and will meet what it well

merits as coming from so celebrated a champion[,] a critical review. S. Underhill."
See also the *Cleveland Liberalist* (June 30, 1838): 307.

[36] While no extant copies of the pamphlet have survived, Underhill reprinted
the tract in a serial format in his skeptical newspaper, the *Cleveland Liberalist*,
between June 30 and August 22, 1838. The rough drafts of five of the eight essays
Underhill composed for this tract are recorded in his "Chronicles, Notes, and
Maxims of Dr. Samuel Underhill." Campbell's reply to Underhill's first correspondence is also recorded therein. A reproduction of the tract's content can be seen in
Appendix B.

[37] Samuel Underhill to Josiah Warren, May 7, 1830. "Chronicles, Notes, and
Maxims of Dr. Samuel Underhill."

[38] Underhill, "Answer to Campbell's Letter, Letter II," *Cleveland Liberalist*
(July 7, 1838): 318-319.

[39] This charge was edited out of Underhill's 1838 publication of his tract
in the *Cleveland Liberalist*, but it appeared in the rough draft of the essay in his
"Chronicles, Notes, and Maxims of Dr. Samuel Underhill." Campbell responded to
the allegation by calling it the greatest "of all the barefaced falsehoods ever penned
against me." See Campbell, "The Liberals; or, Sceptical Persecutions," *Millennial
Harbinger* (October 1831): 433-435. Some years later, in the initial issue of his
Cleveland Liberalist, Underhill retracted this statement and admitted that he had
"misrepresented" Campbell by relying on a report he had received from someone he
thought reliable. See Underhill, "The Discussion with Mr. Campbell in Cleveland,"
Cleveland Liberalist (September 10, 1836): 2.

[40] Campbell, "A Problem for the Editor of the Harmony Gazette and his
Doubting Brethren," *Christian Baptist* 5 (October 1827): 376-377; Campbell,
Evidences of Christianity, 120.

[41] See chapter four.

[42] Campbell, *Evidences of Christianity*, 121-122.

[43] Ibid., 168-169.

[44] Underhill, "Campbell Refuted: Letter III," *Cleveland Liberalist* (July 14,
1838): 321-322.

[45] Ibid.

[46] Underhill, "Campbell Refuted: Letter IV," *Cleveland Liberalist* (July 21,
1838): 329-330; Campbell, *Evidences of Christianity*, 190.

[47] Campbell, *Evidences of Christianity*, 174-175.

[48] Underhill, "Campbell Refuted: Letter IV," *Cleveland Liberalist* (July 21,
1838): 329-330.

[49] Campbell, *Evidences of Christianity*, 175.

[50] Ibid., 296-298.

[51] Underhill, "Campbell Refuted: Letter IV," *Cleveland Liberalist* (July 21,
1838): 329-330.

[52] Underhill, "Campbell Refuted: Letter V," *Cleveland Liberalist* (August 4,
1838): 345-346.

[53] Underhill, "Campbell Refuted: Letter VI," *Cleveland Liberalist* (August 11,
1838): 356-357.

[54] Underhill, "Campbell Refuted: Letter VII," *Cleveland Liberalist* (August 18,
1838): 365-366.

[55] Underhill, "Campbell Refuted: Letter VIII," *Cleveland Liberalist* (August
22, 1838): 375.

[56] Campbell, "The Liberals; or, Sceptical Persecutions," *Millennial Harbinger* (October 1831): 434-435.

[57] Underhill, Untitled Article, *Cleveland Liberalist* (May 20, 1837): 282. See also Samuel Underhill, "Willoughby University, No. 1," *Cleveland Liberalist* (January 7, 1837): 132; and "Willoughby University, No. 2," *Cleveland Liberalist* (January 21, 1837): 149.

[58] Gertrude Van Rensselaer Wickham, *The Pioneer Families of Cleveland, 1796-1840* (Cleveland: Evangelical Publishing House, 1914), 2:534-535.

[59] Ibid.; James Harrison Kennedy and Wilson M. Day, *The Bench and Bar of Cleveland* (Cleveland: The Cleveland Printing and Publishing Company, 1889), 62-63; Post, *Popular Freethought in America*, 214.

[60] Both Campbell and Post recognize the proliferation of unbelief in northeast Ohio. See Campbell, "Notes on a Tour to the North-East—No. 1," *Millennial Harbinger* (July 1836): 331; Richardson, *Memoirs of Alexander Campbell*, 2:409-411; Post, *Popular Freethought in America*, 116; and George Darsie, *A Historic Sketch of the Church of Disciples, at Ravenna, Ohio* (Ravenna, OH: Republican-Democrat Print, 1876), 10-11.

[61] Alexander Campbell to Samuel Underhill. *Cleveland Liberalist* (September 24, 1836): 13. Underhill's letter to Campbell no longer exists, but it is mentioned in this epistle.

[62] Campbell, "Notes on a Tour to the North-East—No. I," *Millennial Harbinger* (July 1836): 330-333.

[63] Campbell, "Notes on a Tour to the North-East—No. II," *Millennial Harbinger* (August 1836): 337-338.

[64] Ibid., 338.

[65] Ibid., 340.

[66] Campbell, "Notes on a Tour to the North-East—No. III," *Millennial Harbinger* (September 1836): 411.

[67] Campbell, "Notes on a Tour to the North-East—No. II," *Millennial Harbinger* (August 1836): 340.

[68] Campbell, "Notes on a Tour to the North-East—No. III," *Millennial Harbinger* (September 1836): 411.

[69] Ibid.

[70] Ibid., 411-412.

[71] Ibid., 412-414.

[72] Ibid., 414.

[73] Ibid., 414-415.

[74] Ibid., 416-417.

[75] Underhill, "The Discussion, Continued," *Cleveland Liberalist* (November 5, 1836): 64.

[76] Campbell, "Notes on a Tour to the North-East—No. III," *Millennial Harbinger* (September 1836): 413.

[77] Ibid., 417.

[78] Ibid., 418.

[79] *Cleveland Daily Herald*, June 10, 1836.

[80] Underhill, "The Discussion with Mr. Campbell in Cleveland," *Cleveland Liberalist* (September 10, 1836): 2.

[81] Ibid. Underhill later contradicted his statement to have only recorded the propositions of the debate when responded to a letter from Campbell by telling him he wrote down "the words from your own mouth at the moment they were uttered." See Samuel Underhill, "To Alexander Campbell[,] Editor of the Millennial Harbinger," *Cleveland Liberalist* (February 25, 1837): 188.

[82] Campbell, "Cleaveland Liberalist," *Millennial Harbinger* (January 1837): 35.

[83] Underhill, "Anonymous Letter," *Cleveland Liberalist* (November 12, 1836): 71-72.

[84] A. S. Hayden, *Early History of the Disciples on the Western Reserve, Ohio* (Cincinnati: Chase and Hall, 1875), 418-419.

[85] Richardson, *Memoirs of Alexander Campbell*, 2:411.

[86] Campbell, "Notes on a Tour to the North-East—No. II," *Millennial Harbinger* (August 1836): 341.

[87] Post, *Popular Freethought in America*, 63.

[88] For additional information on mesmerism, see Frank Podmore, *Mesmerism and Christian Science: A Short History of Mental Healing* (Philadelphia: G. W. Jacobs, 1909), and William Gregory, *Animal Magnetism: Or, Mesmerism and Its Phenomena* (London: Nichols and Company, 1909).

[89] *Cleveland Herald and Gazette*, August 13, 1838.

[90] Elroy McKendree Avery, *A History of Cleveland and its Environs: The Heart of New Connecticut* (Chicago and New York: The Lewis Publishing Company, 1918), 1:498. See also the *Cleveland Herald and Gazette*, January 21-23, 1839.

[91] See *Cleveland Herald and Gazette*, August 12, 1839; January 23, 1843; and February 2, 1843.

[92] Samuel Underhill, *Underhill on Mesmerism* (1868, reprint, Nevada, MO: Weltmer Book Company, 1902), 187.

[93] Ibid., 172.

[94] Ibid., 188-189.

[95] Kennedy and Day, *The Bench and Bar of Cleveland*, 63. Underhill's renunciation of his "atheistic belief" must not be construed as a conversion to evangelical Christianity. While it is likely that he accept some of the tenets of Christianity that he had rejected in his earlier years, his dedication to Spiritualism would at best make him a fringe member of the antebellum Christian community.

Chapter 7

[1] Campbell and Owen, *Evidences of Christianity*, 14.

[2] Walter T. Durham, "Charles Cassedy, Early Nineteenth Century Tennessee Writer," parts 1 and 2, *Tennessee Historical Quarterly* 36 (Fall/Winter 1977): 306-309.

[3] Durham, "Charles Cassedy," 310-311.

[4] Ibid.

[5] Ibid., 324-325.

[6] Charles Cassedy to James K. Polk, September 3, 1832. Herbert Weaver and Paul H. Bergeron, eds., *Correspondence of James K. Polk* (Nashville: Vanderbilt University Press, 1969): 1:499-501.

[7] Ibid., 1:507.

[8] Durham, "Charles Cassedy," 494.

[9] Charles Cassedy, "To Alexander Campbell, of Bethany, Virginia," *Millennial Harbinger* (January 1833): 35.

[10] Ibid.

[11] Ibid., 36-38.

[12] Ibid., 37-43.

[13] Campbell, "To Charles Cassedy, Esq., No. I," *Millennial Harbinger* (February 1833): 72-74.

[14] Ibid., 75.

[15] Campbell, "To Charles Cassedy, Esq., No. II," *Millennial Harbinger* (March 1833): 123-126.

[16] Campbell, "To Charles Cassedy, Esq., No. III," *Millennial Harbinger* (April 1833): 174-175.

[17] See Genesis 5:21-24 and Hebrews 11:5.

[18] Campbell, "To Charles Cassedy, Esq., No. III," *Millennial Harbinger* (April 1833): 175-179.

[19] Campbell, "To Charles Cassedy, Esq., No. IV," *Millennial Harbinger* (May 1833): 193-197.

[20] Cassedy, "Letter 2, from Charles Cassedy, Esq.," *Millennial Harbinger* (July 1833): 294-295.

[21] Cassedy, "Letter from Charles Cassedy, Esq., No. III," *Millennial Harbinger* (September 1833): 464-467.

[22] Campbell, "Reply to Charles Cassedy, Esq.—No. III," *Millennial Harbinger* (September 1833): 467-470.

[23] Cassedy, "Thomas Paine and Madam Bonneville," *Millennial Harbinger* (October 1836): 471-474.

[24] Ibid.

[25] Cassedy, "Atheism," parts 1 and 2, *Millennial Harbinger* (November/December 1836): 499-504.

[26] Ibid., 529-535.

[27] Ibid.

[28] Durham, "Charles Cassedy," 502.

[29] For additional information regarding Cassedy's writings on these and other subjects, see Durham, "Charles Cassedy," 500-506.

[30] Campbell, "Prospectus," *Millennial Harbinger* (January 1830): 1.

[31] Campbell, "Education," *Millennial Harbinger* (May 1838): 204.

[32] Cassedy, "Education," parts 1 and 2, *Millennial Harbinger* (February/March 1839): 120-124. Cassedy's letter to Trousdale was also printed in the Gallatin (Tennessee) *Union*, December 30, 1838.

[33] Cassedy, "Education," *Millennial Harbinger*, 87-88.

[34] Ibid., 88.

[35] Ibid., 122-123.

[36] *Sumner County, TN Poor House Records, 1849-1850*. Transcribed by Joyce Stark Blocker, 2001. Available [Online]: <http://www.rootsweb.com/~tnsumner/ph4950.htm> [May 13, 2001].

[37] Durham, "Charles Cassedy," 509-510.

[38] Ibid., 511. The poem that Cassedy recited that evening was something of an autobiographical allegory that he called "Bibo's Song." A copy of the poem is recorded by Durham, "Charles Cassedy," 305-306.

[39] Durham, "Charles Cassedy," 511.

Chapter 8

[1] Conkin, *American Originals*, 57.

[2] Post, *Popular Freethought in America*, 195.

[3] See George Wilson Pierson, *Tocqueville in America* (Baltimore and London: Johns Hopkins University Press, 1938), 156; and Thomas Low Nichols, *Forty Years of American Life, 1821-1861* (New York: Stackpole Sons Publishers, 1937), 48.

[4] Francis J. Grund, *The Americans in their Moral, Social, and Political Relations* (1837, reprint, New York and London: Johnson Reprint Corporation, 1968), 158-159.

[5] Campbell, "Life and Death," *Millennial Harbinger* (December 1844): 574.

[6] Campbell, "Universalism and Atheism. As Expected," *Millennial Harbinger* (March 1830): 144. Abner Kneeland, Russel Canfield, and Orson S. Murray were also well known for their trek from Universalism to Deism. See Post, *Popular Freethought in America*, 195.

[7] Campbell, "The Claims of the Messiah," *Millennial Harbinger* (January 1863): 12.

[8] Campbell, "Universalism," *Christian Baptist* 3 (December 1825): 203.

[9] See Campbell, "Reply to Letter of Robert B. Semple," *Millennial Harbinger* (August 1830): 358, and "Queries, From Baltimore and Richmond, Touching Universalism," *Millennial Harbinger* (July 1832): 314-316.

[10] J. C. Waldo, "Alexander Campbell," *The Sentinel, and Star in the West* (May 22, 1830): 262.

[11] Campbell, "An Evil Report Corrected," *Millennial Harbinger* (September 1831): 426.

[12] Russell E. Miller, *The Larger Hope: The First Century of the Universalist Church in America, 1770-1870* (Boston: Unitarian Universalist Association, 1979), 207-208.

[13] Jonathan Kidwell, "The Sentinel's Remarks on the Above Paragraph," *The Sentinel, and Star in the West* (October 15, 1831): 405.

[14] Campbell, "Remarks by the Editor of the Millennial Harbinger," *Millennial Harbinger* (December 1831): 533-534.

[15] Kidwell, "Alexander Campbell," *The Sentinel, and Star in the West* (January 7, 1832): 58-59.

[16] Kidwell, "Mr. Campbell, Again," *The Sentinel, and Star in the West* (January 14, 1832): 65.

[17] Campbell, "Logic and Candor of Universalism—Examined, No. 1," *Millennial Harbinger* (February 1832): 81-83. Reprinted in *The Sentinel, and Star in the West* (March 31, 1832): 153-154.

[18] Kidwell, "Analysis of Mr. Campbell's Remarks," *The Sentinel, and Star in the West* (March 31, 1832): 154-158.

[19] Kidwell never published Campbell's "Logic and Candor of Universalism—Examined, No. II" in the *Sentinel*, though his associate editor acknowledged receipt

of the article. See "Mr. Alexander Campbell," *The Sentinel, and Star in the West* (June 16, 1832): 243.

[20] Campbell, "Logic and Candor of Universalism—Examined, No. II," *Millennial Harbinger* (May 1832): 204-206.

[21] Ibid.

[22] See Adam Clarke, *The Holy Bible Containing the Old and New Testaments. The Text Carefully Printed from the Most Correct copies of the Present Authorized Translation, Including the Marginal Readings and Parallel Tests with a Commentary and Critical Notes Designed as a Help to a Better Understanding of the Sacred Writings* (New York: Carlton and Lanahan, 1832), 6:1059.

[23] Campbell, "Logic and Candor of Universalism—Examined, No. III," *Millennial Harbinger* (June 1832): 241-244. Reprinted in *The Sentinel, and Star in the West* (July 28, 1832): 289-290.

[24] Ibid.

[25] Kidwell, "Alexander Campbell," 59.

[26] Campbell, "Logic and Candor of Universalism—Examined, No. III," 242-243.

[27] Kidwell, "Mr. Campbell—Again," *The Sentinel, and Star in the West* (July 28, 1832): 289-294.

[28] Campbell, "Universalism," *Millennial Harbinger* (September 1832): 480.

[29] Miller, *The Larger Hope*, 208-212. For additional information on the founding of Philomath and the Western Union Seminary, see *Atlas of Union County, Indiana: To Which are Added Various General Maps, History, Statistics, Illustrations, Etc., Etc., Etc.* (Chicago: J. H. Beers and Company, 1884), 48 and 57. Erasmus Manford, a prominent Universalist minister and newspaperman in the Midwest, was decidedly opposed to the unorthodox teachings and antics of Kidwell. In referring to Kidwell's Universalist community of Philomath, he sneeringly called it "the city of refuge for outcasts of the Universalist denomination." See John E. Parsons, *A Tour Through Indiana in 1840: The Diary of John Parsons of Petersburg, Virginia*, ed. Kate Milner Rabb (New York: Robert M. McBride and Company, 1920), 110.

[30] Kidwell, "Alexander Campbell's Last Gasp," *The Sentinel and Star in the West* (October 13, 1832): 378.

[31] A letter writer to Campbell's *Millennial Harbinger* said that Kidwell told a group in Owingsville, Kentucky, that Campbell refused to meet him in a debate on Universalism because he was "too much inclined that way" himself. See S. K. Milton, Untitled Article, *Millennial Harbinger* (January 1835): 42.

[32] Kidwell left the editorial board of *The Sentinel, and Star in the West* in 1836 and began publishing his *Philomath Encyclopedia* in mid-1836. He continued to publish the *Philomath Encyclopedia* until 1846.

[33] Miller, *The Larger Hope*, 207. See also Jonathan Kidwell, *Philomath Encyclopedia* (January-June 1837). Kidwell reprinted his articles on the Campbell-Owen debate in the February-April editions of the *Philomath Encyclopedia*.

[34] Campbell, "Materialism Campbellism," *Millennial Harbinger* (July 1837): 307.

[35] Miller, *The Larger Hope*, 211-212.

[36] Spencer, "Everlasting Punishment," *Millennial Harbinger* (October 1835): 449-452; Alexander Campbell and Dolphus Skinner, *A Discussion of the Doctrines of Endless Misery* (Utica, NY: C. C. P. Grosh, 1840), 7-11.

[37] Campbell, "Answer to Mr. Spencer," *Millennial Harbinger* (October 1835): 452-455; Campbell and Skinner, *A Discussion of the Doctrines of Endless Misery*, 12-15.

[38] George W. Montgomery, "Everlasting Punishment," *Millennial Harbinger* (February 1836): 70-74; Campbell and Skinner, *A Discussion of the Doctrines of Endless Misery*, 16-21.

[39] Campbell, "Editor's Reply to Mr. Montgomery," *Millennial Harbinger* (February 1836): 74-78; Campbell and Skinner, *A Discussion of the Doctrines of Endless Misery*, 22-27.

[40] Ibid.

[41] Campbell, "Discussion of Universalism: Mr. Campbell to Mr. Skinner—No. 1," *Millennial Harbinger* (April 1837): 176-177; Campbell and Skinner, *A Discussion of the Doctrines of Endless Misery*, 48-49.

[42] Campbell and Skinner, *A Discussion of the Doctrines of Endless Misery*, 28-29. The correspondences of Campbell and Skinner were recorded in each editor's respective magazine before they were collectively published as a book in 1840. For the sake of time and space, only the book will be cited for reference to their written debate.

[43] Ibid., 30-31.

[44] Ibid., 32-33.

[45] "Rev. Dolphus Skinner," *Universalist* (October 23, 1869).

[46] Ibid.

[47] Miller, *The Larger Hope*, 381-382.

[48] Ibid., 388.

[49] Campbell and Skinner, *A Discussion of the Doctrines of Endless Misery*, 45-46.

[50] Ibid., 182-183.

[51] Ibid., 278.

[52] Ibid., 280.

[53] Ibid., 286.

[54] Richardson, *Memoirs of Alexander Campbell*, 2:433-434.

[55] Ibid., 431.

[56] W. K. Pendleton, "Universalism: Query About the Discussion with Dr. Skinner," *Millennial Harbinger* (April 1867): 168.

[57] Campbell, "Debate on Universalism," *Millennial Harbinger* (September 1840): 432.

[58] Richardson, *Memoirs of Alexander Campbell*, 2:245-248.

[59] H. Leo Boles, *Biographical Sketches of Gospel Preachers: Including the Pioneer Preachers of the Restoration Movement and Many Other Preachers Through Decades Down to the Present Generation who have Passed to their Reward* (Nashville: Gospel Advocate Company, 1932), 186.

[60] Ibid., 186-187.

[61] Enos E. Dowling, *An Analysis and Index of the Christian Magazine, 1848-1853* (Lincoln, IL: Lincoln Bible Institute Press, 1958), 2-4.

[62] In a letter to the *Millennial Harbinger* dated October 27, 1838. Ferguson verified his affiliation with the Disciples by providing details about his recent evangelistic work. See Jesse B. Ferguson, "News from the Churches," *Millennial Harbinger* (April 1839): 192.

[63] Dowling, *Analysis and Index*, 8.

[64] Boles, *Biographical Sketches*, 187.

[65] Dowling, *Analysis and Index*, 4.

[66] Boles, *Biographical Sketches*, 188-189. The *Christian Magazine* originated as the *Christian Review* in 1844. Under the capable leadership of Tolbert Fanning (1810-1874) the paper prospered in its initial four years. Because of his preoccupation with various other activities, however, Fanning handed the editorial duties of the magazine over to Ferguson, a regular contributor to the paper. Upon assuming the tabloid's editorial chair at the start of 1848, Ferguson renamed the paper the *Christian Magazine*.

[67] Ferguson had suggested a similar idea in an October 1845 article, entitled "Another State of Probation," that he published in the *Christian Review*. Interestingly, however, his earlier article raised little, if any, opposition. See Dowling, *Analysis and Index*, 217.

[68] Jesse B. Ferguson, "The Spirits in Prison," *Christian Magazine* (April 1852): 113-115.

[69] Campbell, "A New Discovery," *Millennial Harbinger* (June 1852): 313-329.

[70] Campbell, "Mission to Hades—No. 1," *Millennial Harbinger* (March 1853): 160-161.

[71] Campbell, "A New Discovery," *Millennial Harbinger* (June 1852): 313-329.

[72] Ibid., 328.

[73] Ferguson, "The Rewards and Punishments of the Life to Come," *Christian Magazine* (June 1852): 187.

[74] Campbell, "The Christian Magazine—No. 1," *Millennial Harbinger* (July 1852): 390-398.

[75] Ferguson, "The attack of the Millennial Harbinger on the Christian Magazine, and its Editor" *Christian Magazine* (August 1852): 341-346.

[76] Campbell, "The Spirits in Prison," *Millennial Harbinger* (August 1852): 440-441.

[77] Dowling, *Analysis and Index*, 201-202.

[78] On three separate occasions the members of Ferguson's Nashville church voted to retain him as their minister. When Ferguson resigned his position in 1853 because of the turmoil surrounding him, the elders of the congregation refused to accept his resignation and convinced him to continue his ministerial activities with the congregation. See Jesse B. Ferguson, *Correspondence Between the Christian Church at Nashville and the Rev. Jesse B. Ferguson: Together with a Letter from the Citizens of Nashville, Etc.* (Nashville: Union and American Office, 1853), and Campbell, "The Fall of Mr. J. B. Ferguson," *Millennial Harbinger* (November 1855): 636-640.

[79] Clapp's church was generally referred to as the "Stranger's Church" because of the large number of visitors drawn to the congregation. With the expiration of the church's charter in 1853 they renamed themselves the "First Congregational Unitarian Church." Two years later, however, they took the more ecumenical name, "Church of the Messiah."

[80] Miller, *The Larger Hope*, 813-821.

[81] Campbell, "Incidents on a Tour to the South, No. V," *Millennial Harbinger* (May 1839): 197-198.

[82] Campbell, "Reported Challenge," *Millennial Harbinger* (July 1851): 416-417.

[83] Campbell, "Mission to Hades—No. 1," *Millennial Harbinger* (March 1853): 162.

[84] Campbell, "Elder Jesse B. Ferguson," *Millennial Harbinger* (September 1833): 514-515.

[85] Campbell, "Millennium—No. II," *Millennial Harbinger* (April 1830): 147.

[86] Richardson, *Memoirs of Alexander Campbell*, 2:609.

[87] Campbell, "The Claims of the Messiah," *Millennial Harbinger* (January 1863): 11-13.

[88] See Jesse B. Ferguson, *Relation of Pastor and People: Statement of Belief on Unitarianism, Universalism and Spiritualism* (Nashville: Union and American Steam Press, 1854).

[89] Thomas Low Nichols, ed. *Supramundane Facts in the Life of Rev. Jesse Babcock Ferguson, A.M., LL.D., Including Twenty Years' Observation of Preternatural Phenomena* (London: F. Pitman, 1865), 50.

[90] Campbell, "Our Visit to Nashville," *Millennial Harbinger* (February 1855): 96-107.

[91] Ibid.

[92] See Campbell, "Spirit Rappings," *Millennial Harbinger* (May 1853): 249-259; "Spiritualism and Demonology," *Millennial Harbinger* (May 1855): 241-242; "Modern Spiritualism Compared with Christianity," *Millennial Harbinger* (November 1855): 656-657; and "Modern Spiritualisms," *Millennial Harbinger* (February 1860): 61-78.

[93] Campbell, "Modern Spiritualisms," *Millennial Harbinger* (February 1860): 65.

[94] Campbell, "Our Visit to Nashville," *Millennial Harbinger* (February 1855): 96-107.

[95] Boles, *Biographical Sketches*, 190.

[96] James Challen, "The Church in Nashville, Tennessee—Letter from Bro. Challen," *Millennial Harbinger* (April 1860): 215.

[97] Boles, *Biographical Sketches*, 190-191.

Chapter 9

Richardson, *Memoirs of Alexander Campbell*, 2:643-648.

[2] Campbell, "A. Campbell to his Readers," *Millennial Harbinger* (January 1864): 43.

[3] Campbell and Owen, *Evidences of Christianity*, vi-viii.

[4] Alexander Campbell to Samuel Underhill. *Cleveland Liberalist* (September 24, 1836): 13.

[5] Campbell, "Dialogue with a Jew," *Millennial Harbinger* (December 1830): 561-567.

[6] C. Shultz, "Copy of a Letter to the Editor of this Work," and Campbell, "Reply to Mr. Shultz," *Millennial Harbinger* (February 1830): 91-92. Campbell received no further response from Shultz, nor did he receive Shultz's "objections" to the divine nature of the Bible.

[7] Campbell, "Sidney Rigdon," *Millennial Harbinger* (February 1831): 100.

[8] Campbell, "Delusions," *Millennial Harbinger* (February 1831): 85-96

[9] Post, *Popular Freethought in America*, 93.

[10] Campbell, "Letters from Europe—#9," *Millennial Harbinger* (October 1947): 555-557.

[11] R. E., "Transcendentalism," *Millennial Harbinger* (November 1841): 490.

[12] A. W. C., "The Boston Investigator," *Millennial Harbinger* (August 1861): 470.

[13] Roderick S. French, *The Encyclopedia of Unbelief*, ed. Gordon Stein (Buffalo: Prometheus Books, 1985): s.v. "Boston Investigator."

[14] Campbell, "Notes on a Tour to the North-East—No. 1," *Millennial Harbinger* (July 1836): 331.

[15] Campbell, "Conclusion of Volume II," *Millennial Harbinger* (December 1831): 566-568.

[16] Campbell, "Mr. A.—," *Christian Baptist* 5 (April 1828): 434.

[17] In 1844, Campbell republished this book under the title, *Infidelity Refuted by Infidels: or, the Gospel Proved by the Testimony of Unbelieving Jews and Pagans.*

[18] Alexander Campbell, *The Christian Preacher's Companion: or, The Gospel Facts Sustained by the Testimony of Unbelieving Jews and Pagans* (1836, reprint, Shreveport, LA: Lambert Book House, n.d.), 5.

[19] See Origen Bacheler, *Discussion on the Existence of God, and the Authenticity of the Bible* (New York: Author, 1832). See also, Campbell, "There is a Creator," *Millennial Harbinger* (April 1831): 145-150.

[20] Campbell, "Dr. W. W. Sleigh vs. A. Campbell," *Millennial Harbinger* (October 1838): 462.

[21] See Origen Bacheler, *Mormonism Exposed, Internally and Externally* (New York: n.p., 1838).

[22] Alexander Campbell to Samuel Underhill. *Cleveland Liberalist* (September 24, 1836): 13.

[23] Ibid.

[24] Campbell and Owen, *Evidences of Christianity*, 6.

[25] Alexander Campbell to Samuel Underhill. *Cleveland Liberalist* (September 24, 1836): 13

[26] Campbell, "Notes on a Tour to New York—No. 6," *Millennial Harbinger* (February 1834): 80.

[27] Post, *Popular Freethought in America*, 32.

[28] West, *Alexander Campbell and Natural Religion*, 57.

[29] Post, *Popular Freethought in America*, 234.

[30] Post contends that "Christian apologists . . . carried on a continuous campaign against freethinkers." See Ibid., 199.

[31] Martin E. Marty, *The Infidel: Freethought and American Religion* (Cleveland and New York: The World Publishing Company, 1961), 123-124.

Appendix A

[1] Campbell and Owen, *Evidences of Christianity*, 22-24.

Appendix B

[1] Campbell, "Sceptical Enthusiasm—Anatomy A Cure for Religion!," *Millennial Harbinger* (February 1830): 71-74.

[2] See Underhill, "Campbell Refuted," *Cleveland Liberalist* (June 30, 1838-August 22, 1838).

[3] Samuel Underhill to Josiah Warren, May 7, 1830. "Chronicles, Notes, and Maxims of Dr. Samuel Underhill."

[4] See Campbell, "The Liberals; or, Sceptical Persecutions," *Millennial Harbinger* (October 1831): 434-435.

[5] The sentence enclosed in brackets was not included in Underhill's 1838 *Cleveland Liberalist* version of the tract. It was, however, included in Underhill's rough draft of the tract (see Underhill, "Chronicles, Notes, and Maxims of Dr. Samuel Underhill" in the Stark County, Ohio, Historical Society), from which this sentence was taken. This sentence is included here because Campbell quotes the tract, in a slightly altered form, as saying, "Since I learned the fact of your selling a blind Negro child in the night, and refusing to make restitution, I have conceived you capable of any species of twistification." See Ibid.

SELECTED BIBLIOGRAPHY

Source Materials

1. Manuscripts and Collections

Campbell, Alexander. Papers. Bethany College Archives, Bethany, West Virginia.

Cassedy, Charles. Letter to John D. Coffee, Esq., 25 February 1834. Dyas Collection. Tennessee Historical Society. Nashville, Tennessee.

Owen, Robert. Letter to James M. Dorsey, 14 July 1828. The Indiana Historical Society. Indianapolis, Indiana.

Owen, Robert. Papers. Co-operative Union Ltd., Manchester, England. The University of Illinois at Urbana-Champaign has a microfilmed copy of these papers.

Richardson, Robert Carter. Letter to A. C. Quisenberry, 4 February 1889. Richardson Papers. The Filson Club. Louisville, Kentucky.

Rotch-Wales Collection. Massillon Public Library. Massillon, Ohio.

Underhill, Samuel. "The Chronicles, Notes, and Maxims of Dr. Samuel Underhill." N.d. Stark County Historical Society. Canton, Ohio.

2. Published Materials

Bacheler, Origen. *Discussion on the Existence of God, and the Authenticity of the Bible.* New York: Author, 1832.

Campbell, Alexander. *The Christian Preacher's Companion, or the Gospel Facts Sustained by the Testimony of Unbelieving Jews and Pagans.* 1836. Reprint, Shreveport, LA: Lambert Book House, n.d.

------. *The Christian System in Reference to the Union of Christians, and a Restoration of Primitive Christianity, as Plead in the Current Reformation.* 1840. Reprint, Joplin, MO: College Press Publishing Company, 1989.

------. *Letters to a Skeptic, Reprinted from the Christian Baptist.* Cincinnati: H. S. Bosworth, 1859.

------. *Popular Lectures and Addresses.* 1863. Reprint, Philadelphia: James Challen and Son, 1866.

Campbell, Alexander, and Dolphus Skinner. *A Discussion of the Doctrines of Endless Misery and Universal Salvation: In an Epistolary Correspondence Between Alexander Campbell and Dolphus Skinner.* Utica, NY: C. C. P. Grosh, 1840.

Campbell, Alexander, and Robert Owen. *The Evidences of Christianity: A Debate Between Robert Owen, of New Lanark, Scotland, and Alexander Campbell, President of Bethany College, Virginia, Containing an Examination of the "Social System," and all the Systems of Skepticism of Ancient and Modern Times.* 1829. Reprint, St. Louis: Christian Publishing Company, 1906.

Clapp, Theodore. *Autobiographical Sketches and Recollections, during a Thirty-Five Years' Residence in New Orleans.* Boston: Phillips, Sampson and Company, 1857.

Ferguson, Jesse Babcock. *Address and Correspondence, Delivered December 30, 1855, in the "Christian Church," Nashville, Tennessee.* Nashville: Smith, Morgan and Company, 1856.

------. *Correspondence between the Christian Church at Nashville and New Orleans and the Rev. Jesse B. Ferguson: Together with a Letter from the Citizens of Nashville, Etc.* Nashville: Union and American Office, 1853.

------. *Divine Illumination. Discourses on the Ministry of Angels; The Idea of Endless Wrong an Abomination: Self-Knowledge the Knowledge of Spiritual Communion:*

Immortality is Life in God: Melchisedeck, or Divinity in Man: God will Teach His Creatures. Nashville: J. F. Morgan, 1855.

------. *The Efficacy of Prayer; A Discourse.* Nashville: J.T.S. Fall, 1851.

------. *History of the Relation of the Pastor to the "Christian Church" of Nashville: Being a Discourse.* Nashville: McKennie and Brown, 1855.

------. *Moral Freedom; the Emblem of God in Divinity and Life. A Discourse Delivered in Voluntarily Surrendering the House of Worship Built for His use, to its Doctrinal Claimants when their Claim could not be Legally Sustained, and when not Authoritatively Demanded.* Nashville: W. F. Bang and Company, 1856.

------. *Relation of Pastor and People, Statement of Belief on Unitarianism, Universalism and Spiritualism.* Nashville: Union and American Steam Press, 1854.

------. *Spirit Communion: A Record of Communications from the Spirit-Sphere with Incontestible Evidence of Personal Identity, Presented to the Public with Explanatory Observations, by J. B. Ferguson.* Nashville: Union and American Steam Press, 1854.

------. *Spirit Communion: An Immovable Fact in the Internal Consciousness and External History of Man. Being an Address, Delivered in the Regular Course of Public Ministration in Nashville, April 15, 1855, by Rev. J. B. Ferguson. Together with a Discourse on Christian Sympathy Angelic, Delivered in the First Congregational Church in New Orleans, La., by Theodore Clapp.* Nashville: McKennie and Brown, 1855.

History and True Position of the Church of Christ in Nashville, With an Examination of the Speculative Theology Recently Introduced from Neologists, Universalists, etc. Nashville: Cameron and Fall, 1854.

Marshall, Humphrey. *The Letter of a Private Student, or an Examination of the "Evidences of Christianity" as Exhibited and Argued at Cincinnati April, 1829, by Rev. Alexander Campbell in a Debate with Mr. Robert Owen.* Frankfort, KY: J. H. Holeman, 1830.

Mitchell, Nathan J. *Reminiscences and Incidents in the Life and Travels of a Pioneer Preacher of the "Ancient" Gospel; with a few Characteristic Discourses.* Cincinnati: Chase and Hall, 1877.

Owen, Robert. *The Book of the New Moral World: Containing the Rational System of Society, Founded on Demonstrable Facts, Developing the Constitution and Laws of Human Nature and of Society.* London: Home Colonization Society, 1842-1844.

------. *A Development of the Principles and Plans on Which to Establish Self-Supporting Home Colonies.* 1841. Reprint, New York: AMS Press, 1975.

------. *The Life of Robert Owen.* 2 vols. 1857. Reprint, New York: Augustus M. Kelley Publishers, 1967.

------. "A New Religion." *Niles' Register.* 24 May 1823.

------. *A New View of Society and Other Writings.* Edited by Ernest Rhys. London: J. M. Dent and Sons; New York: E. P. Dutton and Company, 1927.

------. *Report to the Committee of the Association for the Relief of the Manufacturing and Labouring Poor; March, 1817, and Subsequent Public Proceedings in London, in July, August, and September, 1817.* 1817. Reprinted in *The Life of Robert Owen*, Volume 1A. New York: Augustus M. Kelley Publishers, 1967.

------. *Report to the County of Lanark, of a Plan for relieving Public Distress and Removing Discontent, by giving permanent, productive Employment to the Poor and Working Classes, under Arrangements which will essentially improve their Character, and ameliorate their Condition, diminish the Expenses of Production and Consumption, and create Markets co-extensive with production.* 1820.

Reprinted in *The Life of Robert Owen*, Volume 1A. New York: Augustus M. Kelley Publishers, 1967.

------. *Robert Owen's New Harmony Addresses: A Compilation*. Edited by D. K. Ennis. Evansville, IN: Scholars Portable Publications, 1977.

------. *Robert Owen's Opening Speech, and his Reply to the Rev. Alex. Campbell, in the Recent Public Discussion in Cincinnati, to Prove that the Principles of all Religions are Erroneous, and that their Practice is injurious to the Human Race. Also, Mr. Owen's memorial to the Republic of Mexico, and a Narrative of the Proceedings thereon, Which led to the promise of the Mexican Government, to place a District, one hundred and fifty miles broad, along the whole line of frontier bordering on the U. States, under Mr. Owen's jurisdiction, for the Purpose of Establishing a New Political and Moral System of Government, Founded on the Laws of Nature, as Explained in the Above Debate with Mr. Campbell.* Cincinnati: Published for R. Owen, 1829.

------. *Two Discourses on a New System of Society: As Delivered in the Hall of Representatives of the United States . . . on the 25th of February, and 7th of March, 1825.* Pittsburgh: Eighbaum and Johnston, 1825.

Owen, Robert Dale. *Threading My Way: An Autobiography.* 1874. Reprint, New York: Augustus M. Kelley Publishers, 1967.

Parsons, John E. *A Tour Through Indiana in 1840: The Diary of John Parsons of Petersburg, Virginia.* Edited by Kate Milner Rabb. New York: Robert M. McBride and Company, 1920.

Richardson, Robert. *Memoirs of Alexander Campbell.* 1868. Reprint, Indianapolis: Religious Book Service, 1897.

Sumner County, TN Poor House Records, 1849-1850. Transcribed by Joyce Stark Blocker, 2001. Available [Online]: <http://www.rootsweb.com/~tnsumner/ph4950.htm> [13 May 2001].

Tocqueville, Alexis de. *Democracy in America.* Translated by George Lawrence. Edited by J. P. Mayer. 1966. Reprint, New York: Harper Perennial, 1988.

Trollope, Frances Milton. *Domestic Manners of the Americans.* Edited by Pamela Neville-Sington. 1832. Reprint, New York: Penguin Books, 1997.

Underhill, Samuel. *A Lecture on Mysterious Religious Emotions, Delivered at Bethlehem, Ohio, by Dr. Samuel Underhill.* Steubenville, OH: Printed for the Author, 1829.

------. *Oration Delivered at Brecksville, Jan. 29, 1836.* Cleveland: Printed for the Author, 1836.

------. *Underhill on Mesmerism.* 1868. Reprint, Nevada, MO: Weltmer Book Company, 1902.

Weaver, Herbert, and Paul H. Bergeron, eds. *Correspondence of James K. Polk.* 8 vols. Nashville: Vanderbilt University Press, 1969.

3. Periodicals and Newspapers

Christian Baptist (Bethany, VA), 1823-1830. Edited by Alexander Campbell.

Christian Magazine (Nashville, TN), 1848-1853. Edited by Jesse Babcock Ferguson.

Cincinnati Chronicle and Literary Gazette (Cincinnati, OH).

Cleveland Herald and Gazette (Cleveland, OH).

Cleveland Liberalist (Cleveland, OH). 1836-1838. Edited by Samuel Underhill.

Daily Cincinnati Gazette (Cincinnati, OH).

Evangelical Magazine and Gospel Advocate (Utica, NY), 1830-1850. Edited by Dolphus Skinner.

Massillon Evening Independent (Massillon, OH).

Millennial Harbinger (Bethany, VA), 1830-1870. Edited by Alexander Campbell.

New Harmony Gazette (New Harmony, IN), 1825-1835. Relocated to New York and became the *Free Enquirer* in October 1828. Various editors.
Ohio Repository (Canton, OH).
Philomath Encyclopedia (Philomath, IN), 1836-1846. Edited by Jonathan Kidwell.
The Sentinel, and Star in the West (Cincinnati, OH), 1829-1838. Edited by Jonathan Kidwell, Samuel Tizzard, and J. C. Waldo.
Western Intelligencer (Hudson, OH).
The Western Monthly Review (Cincinnati, OH), 1827-1830. Edited by Timothy Flint.

Secondary Materials

1. Articles

Bestor, Arthur E., Jr. "Patent-Office Models of the Good Society: Some Relationships Between Social Reform and Westward Expansion." *American Historical Review* 58 (April 1953): 505-526.
Buescher, John. "Jesse Babcock Ferguson." *Dictionary of Unitarian and Universalist Biography*. Available (Online): <http://www.uua.org/uuhs/duub/articles/ jesseferguson.html> (4 June 2002).
Cherok, Richard J. "No Harmony in Kendal: The Rise and Fall of an Owenite Community, 1825-1829." *Ohio History* 108 (Winter-Spring 1999): 26-38.
Durham, Walter T. "Charles Cassedy, Early Nineteenth Century Tennessee Writer." Parts 1 and 2. *Tennessee Historical Quarterly* 36 (Fall/Winter 1977): 305-329; 493-511.
Fetherling, Doug. "Printing and Culture in Early Wheeling." *The Upper Ohio Valley Historical Review* 11 (Autumn-Winter 1981): 2-9.
Holifield, E. Brooks. "Theology as Entertainment: Oral Debate in American Religion." *Church History* 67 (September 1998): 499-520.
Holloway, Gary. "Alexander Campbell as a Publisher." *Restoration Quarterly* 37 (1995): 28-35.
Morrison, John L. "A Rational Voice Crying in an Emotional Wilderness." *West Virginia History* 34 (January 1973): 125-140.
Robinson, Elmo A. "Universalism in Indiana." *Indiana Magazine of History* 13 (1917): 1-19.
Timmons, Wilbert H. "Robert Owen's Texas Project." *Southwestern Historical Quarterly* 52 (January 1949): 286-293.
West, Earl Irvin. "Early Cincinnati's 'Unprecedented Spectacle.'" *Ohio History* 79 (Winter 1970): 4-17.

2. General Studies

Bestor, Arthur E., Jr. *Backwoods Utopias: The Sectarian and Owenite Phases of Communitarian Socialism in America: 1663-1829.* 1950. Reprint, Philadelphia: University of Pennsylvania Press, 1970.
Boles, H. Leo. *Biographical Sketches of Gospel Preachers: Including the Pioneer Preachers of the Restoration Movement and Many Other Preachers Through the Decades Down to the Present Generation who have Passed to their Reward.* Nashville: Gospel Advocate Company, 1932.
Bozeman, Theodore Dwight. *Protestants in an Age of Science: The Baconian Ideal and Antebellum American Religious Thought.* Chapel Hill: University of North Carolina Press, 1977.
Cole, G. D. H. *The Life of Robert Owen.* Hamden, CT: Archon Books, 1966.
Deats, Edwin B., comp., and Harry Macy, Jr., ed. *Underhill Genealogy.* 2 vols. Baltimore: Gateway Press 1980.

Donnachie, Ian L., and George Hewitt. *Historic New Lanark: The Dale and Owen Industrial Community Since 1785.* Edinburgh: Edinburgh University Press, 1993.

Dowling, Enos E., *An Analysis and Index of the Christian Magazine, 1848-1853.* Lincoln, IL: Lincoln Bible Institute Press, 1958.

------. comp. *The Campbell Debates by R. C. Foster.* Lincoln, IL: The Author, 1982.

Duffy, John, ed. *Parson Clapp of the Strangers' Church of New Orleans.* Baton Rouge: Louisiana State University Press, 1957.

Durham, Walter T. *James Winchester, Tennessee Pioneer.* Gallatin, TN: Sumner County Library Board, 1979.

------. *Old Sumner: A History of Sumner County, Tennessee, from 1805-1861.* Gallatin, TN: Sumner County Public Library Board, 1972.

Garrett, Leroy. *The Stone-Campbell Movement: The Story of the American Restoration Movement.* 1981. Revised, Joplin, MO: College Press Publishing Company, 1994.

Haley, Jesse James. *Debates that Made History: The Story of Alexander Campbell's Debates with Rev. John Walker, Rev. W. L. McCalla, Mr. Robert Owen, Bishop Purcell and Rev. Nathan L. Rice.* St. Louis: Christian Board of Publication, 1920.

Harrison, J. F. C. *Quest for the New Moral World: Robert Owen and the Owenites in Britain and America.* New York: Charles Scribner's Sons, 1969.

Hatch, Nathan O. *The Democratization of American Christianity.* New Haven and London: Yale University Press, 1989.

Hayden, A. S. *Early History of the Disciples in the Western Reserve, Ohio: With Biographical Sketches of the Principal Agents in their Religious Movement.* Cincinnati: Chase and Hall, 1875.

Humble, Bill J. *Campbell and Controversy: The Story of Alexander Campbell's Great Debates with Skepticism, Catholicism, and Presbyterianism.* 1952. Reprint, Joplin, MO: College Press Publishing Company, 1986.

Lockwood, George Browning. *The New Harmony Communities. The New Harmony Movement.* New York: D. Appleton, 1905.

Marty, Martin E. *The Infidel: Freethought and American Religion.* Cleveland: World Publishing Company, 1961.

Miller, Russell E. *The Larger Hope: The First Century of the Universalist Church in America, 1770-1870.* Boston: Unitarian Universalist Association, 1978.

Nichols, Thomas Low. ed. *Supramundane Facts in the Life of Rev. Jesse Babcock Ferguson, A.M., LL.D., Including Twenty Years' Observation of Preternatural Phenomena.* London: F. Pitman, 1865.

Oved, Yaacov. *Two Hundred Years of American Communes.* New Brunswick, NJ: Transaction, 1988.

Post, Albert. *Popular Freethought in America, 1825-1850.* New York: Columbia University Press, 1943.

Quisenberry, A. C. *The Life and Times of Hon. Humphrey Marshall.* Winchester, KY: Sun Publishing Company, 1892.

Stein, Gordon, ed. *The Encyclopedia of Unbelief.* 2 vols. Buffalo: Prometheus Books, 1985.

Webb, Henry E. *In Search of Christian Unity: A History of the Restoration Movement.* 1990. Reprint, Abilene, TX: Abilene Christian University Press, 2003.

West, Robert Frederick. *Alexander Campbell and Natural Religion.* New Haven: Yale University Press, 1948.

Woodson, Mary Willis and Martha Moore. *Through the Portals of Glen Willis.* N.p.: Franklin County Trust for Historic Preservation, 1989.